W9-CEV-487

Lewis B. Mayhew

Foreword by Clark Kerr

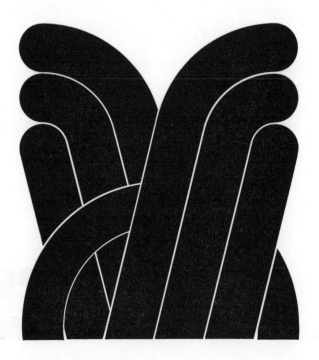

THE CARNEGIE COMMISSION ON HIGHER EDUCATION

Jossey-Bass Publishers

San Francisco · Washington · London · 1973

THE CARNEGIE COMMISSION ON HIGHER EDUCATION
A Critical Analysis of the Reports and Recommendations
        by Lewis B. Mayhew

Copyright © 1973 by: Jossey-Bass, Inc., Publishers
                     615 Montgomery Street
                     San Francisco, California 94111
                              &
                     Jossey-Bass Limited
                     3 Henrietta Street
                     London WC2E 8LU

Library of Congress Catalogue Card Number LC 73-7152

International Standard Book Number ISBN 0-87589-198-5

Manufactured in the United States of America

JACKET DESIGN BY WILLI BAUM

FIRST EDITION

Code 7339

Foreword

When the Carnegie Commission on Higher Education was established in 1967, it was charged with examining American colleges and universities and suggesting guidelines for planning for the 1970s and the remainder of the twentieth century. This task could not be undertaken by our commissioners alone. Although all of us have had long-standing interests in higher education, our combined experience and wisdom is far from complete. We had much to learn about certain types of institutions and about many important issues. To fill the gaps in our experience and to investigate some of the more complex questions that confronted us, we engaged the assistance of more than sixty authorities and observers in the United States and abroad. The reports of their investigations and findings, together with the reports the commission itself has made, constitute a modest library on current American higher education that is reviewed in this volume by Lewis Mayhew. Professor Mayhew undertook this task with my encouragement. He and I discussed the possibility of including his reactions in a volume within the series of Carnegie Commission documents. We concluded, however, that for him to be completely candid, he should report his observations apart from the commission series.

Professor Mayhew is in a particularly favored position to survey this output of commission publications. He reads as widely in this extensive area of scholarship and policy formation as any other person, and he has an enviable reputation for his fair and thoughtful reviews. When, on occasion, I have wondered whether anyone would read all of what we have published, I have consoled myself by thinking that Lew Mayhew might do so—and now he has.

CLARK KERR
Chairman
Carnegie Commission on Higher Education

Preface

In 1971 a television commercial added a new phrase to the language as it portrayed a somewhat uncomfortable man having completed an uncommonly large meal. His remark was: "I can't believe I ate the whole thing!" That comment sums up my feelings after having read and tried to digest all the printed studies, reports, and policy statements of the Carnegie Commission on Higher Education. That effort was made with several purposes in mind. Each of the chapters in this book is designed to epitomize one of the publications of the commission in sufficient detail that the substance can be used safely by a reader who has never examined the original report. But an epitome is insufficient for many readers, hence an attempt has been made to critique the reports in the light of generally available knowledge about higher education and to suggest implications for individuals, institutions, or the entire profession. These efforts can be made as quickly as the reports are released. The more dangerous undertaking was to try to gauge the real or potential impact of the work of the commission on the nature, structure, functioning, and significance of American higher education. This is an attempt to compress in one volume more than fifty documents ranging from relatively few pages to almost a thousand pages.

The book was attempted for several reasons. I have long been a bibliographer for higher education, and as the Carnegie Commission began its work it became apparent that its efforts would stand as one of the major publishing ventures in higher education during the 1970s and possibly beyond. Hence there was a logical compulsion to do for the work of the Carnegie Commission what each year had been attempted for all monographic literature on higher education. But this same compulsion led to an attempt to do more than simply review and critique. It led to the attempt to present in condensed form the actual substance of the work of the commission. This urge came out of an admiration for the quality of many of the reports and recommendations and an awareness that many professionals and laymen who should read and ponder those documents would probably not attempt to work through over four feet of books. And such an attempt is made in part for the same reason that people climb mountains—the reports were simply there.

Several limitations should be mentioned. Although all reports in print have been included, as well as a dozen or more yet to be printed, a few documents yet to be produced are not included.[1]

[1] The following documents are planned but are not included: Margaret Gordon (Ed.), *Higher Education and the Labor Market;* Ann Heiss, *An Inventory of Academic Innovation and Reform;* Alain Touraine, *The Academic System in American Society;* Edward Gross and Paul Grambsch, *University Goals and Academic Power, American Universities, 1940–1972;* Thomas Juster (Ed.), *Education, Income and Human Behavior;* Charles Bidwell, *The University College;* Richard Freeman, *Black Elite: Discrimination in Education;* Saul Feldman, *Escape from the Doll's House: Women in Graduate and Professional School Education;* Alexander Mood, *Speculations on Management Efficiency in Higher Education;* Michio Nagai, *Some Dilemmas in Higher Education Today;* Earl Cheit, *Follow-Up Study on "New Depression in Higher Education";* Martin Trow, *Outcomes of Nationwide Survey of Students and Faculty;* Stephen Steinberg, *The Academic Melting Pot: Protestant, Catholic and Jew in American Higher Education;* Roy Radner, *Resource Use in Higher Education;* Harland Bloland, *The Dissenting Academy and Academic Associations;* Seymour Martin Lipset and David Riesman, *Harvard Trends;* Seymour Martin Lipset, *The Politics of American Academics;* Earl Cheit, *The Productive Professions in Higher Education;* Martin Trow, *Essays on Higher Education;* Virginia Smith, *A Profile of Proprietary Schools;* Laura Howe, *Women in Higher Education;* Verne Stadtman, *The Public Service Function of American Higher Education;* Robert Berls, *Comparative Effectiveness of Different Types of Higher Educational Institutions;* June O'Neill, *Sources of Funds to Colleges and Universities;* Joseph Ben-

It might have been well to await the final reports of all the commission projects as well as the summary statements of the chairman of the commission, Clark Kerr; to do so would have involved waiting a full year or more. Meanwhile higher education was in the process of change, and critical decisions were being made daily that could be affected by commission findings. The resolve to proceed with publication before the completion of the studies was strengthened by the belief that the principal themes and the principal empirical bases were already available and that future reports would be variations on those themes. A second limitation is that no systematic or theoretically consistent effort to assess impact has been made. Rather, judgments as to potential impact are based on my own impressions gathered by traveling around the country, visiting institutions, and participating in various higher education conferences. During the summer of 1972, however, I did conduct a seminar as part of the Danforth Workshop on Liberal Arts Education, entitled "The Carnegie Commission on Higher Education: Professional and Institutional Implications." Many of my ideas as to potential significance came from the ideas of the seventeen representatives from as many different institutions expressed in that seminar. Lastly, it should be indicated that there is some disjointedness from chapter to chapter. This is a product of the kind of effort the book represents. The commission sponsored many different projects, each subject to the idiosyncrasies of the individual writer or group of writers. This book suffers from the weaknesses or gains from the strengths and insights of the various contributors.

As this project comes to an end, I must acknowledge the many kinds of assistance and encouragement I have received. Clark Kerr, Verne Stadtman, Virginia Smith, and members of the Carnegie Commission on Higher Education encouraged me to initiate the project and made available all reports as well as critical commentary when available. Catherine Phinney, who has typed most of my recent manuscripts, performed extraordinarily in typing this often complicated report under serious constraints of time. She probably now knows much more about higher education than she wants to

---

David, *Comparative Effectiveness of Higher Education; Outcomes of the Villa Serbelloni Conference.*

know. My wife, Dorothy, has provided the tranquil environment in which one can work the long hours such an undertaking requires and at the same time has provided warmth, companionship, and affection when the day's writing ends. It is to her that this book is lovingly dedicated.

September 1973   Lewis B. Mayhew
Stanford, California

Contents

The Carnegie Commission on Higher Education

A Critical Analysis of the Reports and Recommendations

I

Context and Themes

The Carnegie Commission on Higher Education represents the most comprehensive organized attempt ever made to portray the condition of higher education, to analyze its components, and to indicate probable and desirable directions for future development. The conditions making such an attempt desirable and the difficulties encountered in such an attempt are well revealed by a number of developments. The first and most significant of these is sheer growth of the American higher educational enterprise. Indeed, growth alone is almost sufficient to explain most of the major malfunctions that began to appear in the mid-1960s. Growth in numbers of institutions is paralleled by expansion in enrollment; both accelerated abruptly during the post–World War II period.

Similar growth has taken place in income and expenditures for higher education. Growth in expenditures has been more rapid recently than even the expansion in enrollment. These increases in en-

1

rollment and expenditure have been accompanied by increases in the complexity of the system of higher education as the full magnitude of potential expansion came to be realized. The federal government expanded agencies and bureaucracies concerned with higher education. In three areas of the country (the South, New England, and the Far West), states created regional compacts to coordinate some higher educational activities. Within most states, as a result of master planning, agencies to coordinate statewide systems of higher education came into existence, and the number of multicampus universities increased radically. Similar increases in complexity took place on individual campuses, and structural complexity was compounded as colleges undertook in a large and expensive way activities that prior to World War II had been of only modest significance. The research effort in particular began to compete favorably with the historic educational mission of collegiate institutions. The magnitude of the increase in complexity of higher education is further indicated by the growth of an entirely new scholarly subspecialty, the professional study of higher education, that reflected an effort to understand a profession that had assumed gargantuan proportions. One of the missions and major accomplishments of Carnegie Commission on Higher Education has been to study and elucidate the complexities of higher education and to help both professionals and laymen understand an enormously complex, costly, and influential social institution.

As might be surmised from this rapid growth, higher education has become highly influential in the society. Education is a major device through which people can move upward in socioeconomic levels. After World War II and the successful combining of federal financial resources with university expertise to produce the atomic bomb, the proximity fuse, and radar, the university came to be regarded as the fountainhead of the expanding research necessary to the growth of a technological society. Government, business, industry, the military, and labor looked to the colleges for specialized knowledge. The knowledge industry was to become the principal industry of the economy, and among the components of that industry (publishing, research institutes, and the like) colleges and universities were paramount. The influence of higher education is revealed by the conclusion of the White House Conference on Education, convened by President Lyndon Johnson, that education had become the major instrument for the achievement of national policy, and by the observation of one university president that higher education or the university had become the pivotal institution in society.

Although student protest on college campuses concerning a variety of social ills is not a new phenomenon, the student protest activities of the late 1960s appear to have been quantitatively and qualitatively so different as to constitute a major parameter of higher education which the Carnegie Commission had to consider. Given technique, force, and direction by student involvement in the civil rights movement and student concern over engagement in an undeclared war in Vietnam, the protest movement that erupted in 1964 at the University of California, Berkeley, spread rapidly across the country. Although it affected different colleges and regions differently, it became so pronounced and so well publicized that it conditioned thinking about education for half a decade. The protest movement proved that prevailing systems of academic governance were inadequate; it underscored the fact that colleges had expanded so rapidly that they had become unresponsive to emerging educational needs; it contributed to a general backlash that called into question the legitimacy of institutions of higher education. While a definitive history of the protest movement and its consequences has yet to be written, several consequences of great significance are already apparent. Protest activity did produce financial reprisals against institutions. It did produce cleavages between the intellectual community and the rest of society. In some states it did promote the election of conservative political leaders. It did lower the regard in which higher education had been held a scant decade earlier, and it may have produced a fundamental realignment of the political forces in the nation. Some have argued that the student protest movement brought about the downfall of the political hegemony of President Johnson and may have produced a revitalized Republican Party in opposition to a Democratic Party whose national leadership seemed to favor the goals, objectives, and occasionally the techniques of dissenting students. Certainly the protest movement brought about profound changes in the way institutions related to students: the movement toward codification of regulations and processes on campus, for example, and the larger involvement of the courts in campus affairs. The student protest movement may also have accelerated needed educational reforms and hastened the passage of legislation lowering the voting age to eighteen. The significance of this legislation is only now being examined. It could conceivably eliminate out-of-state tuitions important to the well-being of publicly supported institutions and could reorient radically the posture of local government in college communities.

Historically, institutions of higher education have been supported either privately through gifts and student tuition or through state appropriations. The federal government has always maintained some involvement in higher education as witness the passage of the two Morrill Acts, which provided federal lands for the support of higher education; the passage of the Smith-Hughes Act, which began support for vocational education; the Depression-born programs such as the National Youth Administration; and the post–World War II federal provision of funds for veterans' education. However, federal concern for higher education became critical by the 1970s. The establishment of the National Science Foundation in 1950 facilitated the growth of university-based research. The Federal Housing Act allowed institutions to expand residential facilities. The National Defense Education Act provided support for students and expansion of programs. The Higher Education Facilities Act of 1963 allowed institutions to double, triple, or quadruple their educational facilities. The magnitude of this federal involvement is illustrated through several data. In 1947–1948, institutions received about 527 million dollars in federal funds, an amount that was reduced to 427 million dollars by 1953–1954. But by 1964 institutions received 2.3 billion dollars and in 1967, 4.6 billion dollars.

Federal grants and loans in 1967 helped to finance campus construction and the purchase and rental of equipment: Grants and loans supported students at all levels in all disciplines; federal funds, usually as part of research grants, paid part of the salaries of thousands of faculty members; institutions received aid to offset the cost of educating federally supported students, to perform various public services, to improve academic programs and teaching, and to finance cooperative projects.[1]

By 1970, approximately one-third of the funds for higher education came from federal sources; the general recognition was that that proportion properly should increase. No planning or speculation about the future of higher education can be done without persistent consideration of federal posture, policies, and programs.

The attempts of the Carnegie Commission on Higher Education to describe, evaluate, and recommend policy must be regarded in the context of the work of a number of other commissions, both within and without the United States, that have sought solutions to similar problems. These efforts have been varyingly successful in affecting higher educational policy and particularly in gauging correctly the operative social forces that could facilitate or retard implementation of policy recommendations. The first of these commissions to examine higher education following World War II was the President's Commission on Higher Education, convened by President Harry S. Truman. In six slim volumes the commission sought to examine the state of higher education and to indicate likely and desirable directions for evolution. That commission caught the prevailing social mood, and several of its recommendations have been highly influential, not only with respect to the thinking and writing of educators but with respect to political and economic decisions concerning higher education. The commission suggested that many high school graduates not attending college could profitably do so if serious barriers were removed. It recommended that government and the private sector remove those barriers—of race, religion, economic status, and residence—so that at least 50 percent of high school graduates could receive higher education. This recommendation represented a major step that was to culminate in a generalized belief in the desirability of higher education. The rationale and even some of the language of the recommendations of the Truman Commission have been incorporated in virtually every state study or master plan for higher education

[1] R. A. Wolk, *Alternative Methods of Federal Funding for Higher Education* (Berkeley: Carnegie Commission on Higher Education, 1968), p. 5.

subsequently completed. These documents generally affirm that there should be institutions of higher education within commuting distance of most youth in most states. The commission envisioned and may have helped produce the junior college movement during the 1950s and 1960s. The junior college could overcome geography by being located close to where people lived; it could overcome economic obstacles by charging little or no tuition; and the junior college, operating as a color-blind public institution, could overcome the barriers of race and religion. But the Truman Commission did more than stress egalitarianism of access to higher education. It attempted, in a way few other commissions have, to understand the purposes of collegiate education and to anticipate curricular responses to those purposes. It codified conventional views into a statement of purpose and provided a framework for the expansion of the general education movement during the 1950s and 1960s. General education was not a new concept. The phrase was used in its contemporary sense in the 1820s. In 1918, Columbia College developed a prototype course in general education, and in the 1930s several institutions, including the University of Chicago, produced elaborate programs of general education. However, the post–World War II expansion of general education into the predominant curricular mode derived its primary ideological strength from the publication of *General Education in a Free Society* (the report of a select Harvard faculty committee that urged a program of general education) and from the statement of purposes and goals posited by the Truman Commission. In the years following the publication of these two documents, institutions across the country reviewed their curricula, clarified their objectives, and developed programs in general education. The language for those objectives came typically from either of these two sources or from *Design for General Education* (a document used as a framework for tests of general education development by the United States Armed Forces Institute). In some respects the Truman Commission may have been relatively more influential for its time than the Morrill Act of 1862. The Morrill Act of 1862 was interpreted with a great deal of egalitarian rhetoric urging collegiate education for the agricultural and industrial classes. However, the programs developed in the land grant colleges during the first several decades after passage of the legislation tended to resemble aristocratic curricula and to attract students from the upper middle and intellectual classes. Following the Truman Commission report however (although clearly affected by many other forces) there was an expansion of junior colleges, and serious attempts were made to increase the proportion of high school graduates attending college.

A second commission was much less successful in interpreting the tenor of the times and in proposing recommendations that would ultimately be implemented. The Commission on Financing Higher Education was sponsored by the Association of American Universities and directed by John D. Millett. That commission's report was essentially aristocratic and elitist, visualizing only relatively slow growth of higher education. It suggested that because of the intellectual nature of higher education not more than 25 percent of the individuals in the relevant age group were capable of college-level work. It did note that a large proportion of qualified students were not attending and urged better guidance to ensure entry of the intellectual elite into college. When the commission considered barriers to college attendance, it remarked that socioeconomic status and racial factors were involved but that the primary barrier was the lack of individual motivation. The commission went out of its way to suggest that economic factors had been very much exaggerated. Although the commission expected expansion of higher education and viewed it as an outstanding element of the culture, it saw no necessity for searching for radically new sources of income. The commission recognized that additional funds would be needed to develop appropriate vocational and professional programs and that institutions would be expected to provide additional services. However, the commission believed that student fees and private benefactions (when suitably increased)' would be sufficient for privately supported higher education, particularly if the states provided limited categorical financial assistance. Public institutions that receive the bulk of their financial support from state appropriations and a limited amount from student fees would be able to function effectively, largely by expanding those two sources. The commission rejected out of hand any increased reliance on federal governmental control as being without appreciable benefit. The commission report reflects complacency in the assumption that higher education was in relatively sound shape.

> There is no reason to believe that so great and respected an institution as higher education must succumb to some imagined tidal wave of environment. There are still elements of choice which confront the constituent units of higher education: boards, administrators, and the faculty. They may look for a panacea, a nostrum; if so, they will probably look in what appears to be the easy direction of more federal government assistance. Or they may seek to preserve diversity, to "find their freedom" for the future as they have in the past, by a wide variety of sources of support. The students and their families can provide part of the needed income, private benefactions another part, and even the federal government a part. There is no formula for the combination of these elements. Circumstances and situations will vary from time to time and place to place, but surely there is one absolute for higher education which would be free, even as there is for a society which would be free. That absolute is to cultivate and promote competing centers of power, to avoid any centralized or single power, and to learn how to live successfully amid the complexities of diversity. Historical tradition provides no sure forewarning of doom for our society. Rather the very optimism of man's nature suggests that blind force may be countered by rational choices. This is the challenge of higher education today: to make effective choices and in the process to vindicate and to perpetuate the best elements of a free society.[2]

This commission report was issued just two years before Ronald Thompson published *The Impending Tidal Wave in Higher Education*, which predicted quite accurately although somewhat parsimoniously the expansion that proved inevitable for higher education during the 1960s.

A third policy document emerged from the Conference on Education Beyond High School, convened by President Dwight D. Eisenhower. Its recommendations were relatively bland and provided little guidance for those seeking to prepare institutions for the

---

[2] J. D. Millett, *Financing Higher Education in the United States* (New York: Columbia University Press, 1952).

deluge of students. Indeed, relatively little subsequent literature cites the Eisenhower report. However, in one important regard the document was prophetic. It recognized the faltering financial condition of the professoriate and called for a doubling of faculty salaries between 1958 and 1970. It thus gave public expression to the positions of such organizations as the American Association of University Professors, which began the annual inventory of faculty salaries to force them up through competition. The efficacy of the issuance of the policy statement and the publicizing of faculty salaries derived from a market condition. As enrollments began to increase rapidly there were simply not enough fully qualified professors. The law of supply and demand operated, and across the nation the policy goal of doubling salaries in twelve years was almost completely realized.

Another national effort that may have been made at an inopportune time was the White House Conference on Education, called by President Lyndon B. Johnson. That quickly organized conclave of educators from all levels met in the euphoria of the first years of the Johnson administration, which seemed capable of completing the social revolution initiated by Franklin D. Roosevelt. Out of diverse meetings and varied speeches evolved the conviction that education had emerged as the primary instrument for solution of major domestic vexations. Few in attendance suggested that some of those vexations might prove too burdensome even for the growing power and talent of the educational enterprise. Virtually no one anticipated that the protests on campus would accelerate to such an extent as to discredit the legitimacy of education, and even fewer apprehended that United States involvement in Vietnam would escalate and eventually contaminate attempts to solve most domestic problems. The White House Conference on Education expressed ringing ideals but has had little effect on the conduct of higher education. Rather, higher education has been directed and redirected by impersonal and generally uncontrollable forces.

Other commissions include one convened by the Southern Regional Education Boards to discuss higher educational goals for the South; it released these in a widely disseminated and widely utilized document titled *Within Our Reach*. It observed that the South had lagged behind the rest of the nation for too long and that the time had come to enter the mainstream of national intellectual life. The report was promulgated at a time of major changes in the economy of the South and at a time when some of the older, more conservative political leadership in state government was giving way to younger, more enlightened leadership convinced that higher education was the solution to the problems of the South. The report also came when avenues for racial accommodation were beginning to open. The time was right and the recommendations were realistic; the southern states supported higher education in an unprecedented manner. A decade later the South had not yet assumed leadership in higher education, but some of these states (Virginia, Georgia, and Florida, for example)—following almost exactly the recommendations of *Within Our Reach*—had emerged as true frontiers of higher educational development. Another commission that until its demise seemed to have detected the spirit of the times was the Educational Policies Commission of the National Education Association. It caught the spirit of expansionism and egalitarianism and urged that the question was no longer whether to implement universal higher education but simply when to do so. That commission report was widely quoted in the ensuing several years as districts across the country bonded themselves, increased their tax rates, and produced the flowering of new junior colleges. When the peak was reached in about 1968 or 1969, a new junior college was being created once a week or more.

Other commission reports either were poorly timed or produced recommendations that would require a generation or more to be implemented. Former Harvard president James B. Conant undertook a comprehensive review of public education. He found much that was deficient, not only in the structure of public education but in the substance as well. He and his colleagues made a number of recommendations: changing credential requirements, freeing institutions from possible domination by state departments of education, aiding aspirant teachers financially, improving the substantive preparation of teachers in the liberal arts and sciences, and creating a new professional role for clinical professors who could bridge the gap between whatever colleges, universities, and schools of education did in their ivory towers and the real world of the school. The reports attracted some attention in the six months or so after they were published, but for the most part the key recommendations do not appear to have been widely instrumented. It is difficult to determine why, but several hypotheses can be advanced. The principal report, entitled *The Education of American Teachers,* was released in 1963, a time when expansion in construction and enrollment in public schools was approaching its zenith. Schools of education were so preoccupied with producing the individuals needed to staff the growing numbers of classrooms that they had little time for a searching analysis of the recommendations. Similarly, leadership in school districts had more than enough to do just to keep abreast of the escalating demands for space and services. A second hypothesis is that Conant's report went unheeded because its didactic tone had little basis in theory or in empirical data; it was relatively easy for unsympathetic professors and administrators in teacher preparation programs to reject the entire report without fear of successful contradiction.

A cluster of more politically sensitive commission reports advanced recommendations that were seriously opposed by one or the other major political party. The commissions on the causes and prevention of violence, on civil disorders, on obscenity and pornography, and on population control have all issued serious and compendious reports, but it is still too early to tell whether there has been an immediate effect or whether there is likely to be any long-term effect. Some anecdotal evidence, such as the response of President Nixon on receipt of the report, suggests that the Scranton Commission on Campus Disorders may have produced a degree of reconciliation between the federal government and the universities, and some of the principal recommendations of that commission are in the policy statement on campus disruption of the Carnegie Commission. The significance of the findings of the Commission on Obscenity and Pornography or the Commission on Population Control may not be felt until the reasoning and evidence they provide begin to affect court decisions and legislation. Certainly, the opposition of principal political leaders to major findings minimizes the immediate impact those commission reports might have had.

Other commissions are ostensibly probing the same subject as is the Carnegie Commission and for similar reasons. Somewhat consistent with the aims of the Carnegie Commission are many of the goals of the Assembly on University Goals and Governance. It urges greater access, greater mobility in and out of college, and far less emphasis on the attainment of degrees. But it speaks also directly to matters of substance: "Present modes of access to the academic profession are too restrictive; training for the professions is frequently narrow." "General education, which is in retreat, needs reformulation"; it should be concerned "with interpreting and understanding man's modern political and social predicament, seeing this in a context that takes account of his psychic and spiritual needs," as well as finding new ways of presenting materials from science and foreign languages. Noting the expansion of professional occupations, the assembly calls for reform in professional education, including the opening of professional courses to undergraduate students and the offering of interdisciplinary studies taught jointly by professional faculties and faculties of arts and sciences. While those professors inclined to do research should be encouraged, "certain types of large-scale sponsored research are more suited to outside research institutes than to universities," and "there is no reason for universities to serve as holding companies for large laboratories or research projects." With respect to service, it should be stressed that institutions of higher education have neither the resources nor the political capacity to solve directly the difficult problems of modern society, hence the major contribution of higher education should be an intellectual one, with individuals pointing out courses of action worth the consideration of those responsible for solving public problems. The overall posture of the assembly is reflected in the claim that colleges and universities are an incomparable resource. However, an academic system that was forged in the latter decades of the nineteenth century, that came to maturity in the 1920s and 1930s, and that was remarkably uncritical of itself in the 1950s and 1960s, when it grew to unprecedented dimensions, is now required to rethink its fundamental orientation."[3]

Much more iconoclastic is the so-called Newman report, titled *Report on Higher Education*. Its authors believe that simply expanding the system of higher education as it now exists is counterproductive. They favor diversity in types of institutions but believe that institutions are becoming more alike. They want colleges and

[3] *The Assembly on University Goals and Governance* (Cambridge, Mass.: American Academy of Arts and Sciences, 1971).

universities to be less concerned with prestige and more concerned with becoming effective centers of learning. Rather than demanding more financial support, institutions should, they feel, be forced to use present resources more effectively. Universities should free themselves from responsibilities unrelated to the purposes of an educational institution, responsibilities such as operating government laboratories, financing or subsidizing low-cost housing projects, and maintaining publishing companies. Individual institutions should concentrate resources on a few limited activities, for there are limits to which comprehensive, general-education colleges and universities can perform adequately. Rather than add professional instruction in existing institutions, the authors of the Newman report would create separate professional institutes for those who wish to begin true professional education during the first years of college. Similarly, it would not be necessary for all institutions to stress research. Indeed, the research needs of society could be met through relatively few research universities. "There should not be a single order of excellence in higher education. We need a variety of institutions each excellent at its own appointed mission."[4]

Although these three commissions—the Carnegie Commission on Higher Education, the Assembly on University Goals and Governance, and the (Newman) Task Force on Reform in Higher Education—manifest some similarities, they also have substantial differences in point of view. None of the three questions the values of education, and all three believe that increased diversity in educational experience should be provided. All three stress a reordering of priorities so that most existing institutions would refocus energy on education and deemphasize or reject research and direct public service. In effect, all three assume an expansion of higher education but ask that its claims be more modest. These three commissions do, however, differ. The Assembly on University Goals and Governance looks almost nostalgically to the past for a system of higher education that must have been more satisfying. But the Newman Task Force takes a caustic and critical look at the past and prevailing practices, finds most to be wanting, and seems to hope to elicit fundamental changes in the higher educational enterprise through the

[4] *Report on Higher Education* (Washington, D.C.: Government Printing Office, 1971).

sheer hyperbole of its criticism. Its report abounds with brilliant insight into the shortcomings of education, yet elaborates these so dramatically as to repel many central decision makers in higher education. Immediately after the Newman Task Force published the first of what will be a series of reports, the major educational organizations (such as the American Council on Education), based in Washington, D.C., took a unanimous stand in opposition to it. The Carnegie Commission however has adopted the posture that higher education is a very large, complicated enterprise that can be moved only slowly and with some consensus on the part of the various elements of leadership. Thus most of the Carnegie Commission reports and policy statements are only critical to a degree and generally reflect optimism that some changes can be made. It is as though members of the commission have agreed not to alienate purposely or to antagonize any major element in higher education in the hope of gaining support for the principal directions of change that the commission advocates. Though it is still too early to antici- pate ultimate impacts, the lack of sustained discussion of the As- sembly on University Goals and Governance suggests that those reports are not likely to be influential. The fact that a number of the recommendations urged by the Newman Task Force will cost additional funds at a time when funds are scarce and the fact that a number of recommendations are destructive of long-existing institu- tions such as accreditation and thus generate powerful resistance suggest that in the long run that task force will not be likely to achieve its purposes. Therefore if major new policies on higher edu- cation are to emerge from the efforts of such commissions, they will be likely to derive from the Carnegie Commission.

The Carnegie Commission on Higher Education is dissemi- nating its research and policy statements by means of some sixty-odd sponsored research project reports, twelve commission reports, and miscellaneous other documents. The sponsored research projects deal with academic policies; specific types of academic institutions and their particular problems and goals; functions of higher educa- tion; the financing of higher education on both the individual and the institutional level; the government of higher education—includ- ing the external political climate, government within an institution, and academic power; various approaches to the evaluation of higher education; general analyses from historical, geographical, and more strictly theoretical standpoints; special concerns of higher education; and resource data for the Carnegie study.

The research reports and policy statements of the Carnegie Commission make hundreds of recommendations of varying degrees of significance, complexity, and specificity. In aggregate the materials issued by the commission reveal a few themes that represent the central thrust of the thinking of the commission. These themes are all related to its overarching conviction of the centrality of higher education in society.

Directly derivative from that overarching faith is an implicit belief in the validity of traditional values and techniques of education. The documents imply that higher education develops intellectual skills, contributes to the socialization of the young, provides vocational preparation, screens individuals, conducts research, and provides a reasonably wide range of services. These goals are to be achieved, for the most part, through existing educational structures such as courses, set curricula, and the predominant modes of instruction: lecture, discussion, and laboratory work. Some changes in these elements are anticipated and urged, but for the most part no radical modification is suggested. The commission seems to accept a working definition of education as what colleges and universities are doing and to assume that the way to improve education is to improve somewhat the activities of colleges and universities. In aggregate, the documents imply acceptance of colleges, universities, educational bureaucracies, and increasingly complex systems; an almost deterministic evolution of the system of higher education is assumed. Rarely does the material question the validity of courses or the rational and analytical mode in which they are taught. The radical educational premises of the counterculture, with its emphasis on feeling, are not seriously considered or examined.

A basic assumption of the Carnegie Commission documents is the continued expansion of higher education but at a somewhat slower rate than has been true in the past. It is suggested that some people attending colleges and universities be discouraged from doing so, but in general it is assumed that the system of higher education is sufficiently commodious and that it will continue to attract larger and larger proportions of the population. The commission reports imply that people will spend a large proportion of their lives in some form of educational activity. They anticipate a time when it will be relatively easy for individuals to enter, leave, and reenter collegiate institutions during most of their lives and that such a pattern is rapidly becoming reality. They assume that as colleges, universities, and other higher educational organizations complete some limited but needed reforms, the steady increase in the growth of higher education will follow inexorably. The needs of society for skilled workers in both the productive and service sectors of the economy will ensure the continuance of the vocational preparation responsibilities of institutions, even though collegiate institutions may change the vocational programs they offer—for example, deemphasizing preparation of teachers but strengthening programs in the health fields. Similarly, as people gain discretionary control over the uses of their own time, they will need, want, and expect collegiate institutions to help them develop skills and tastes.

Running throughout the commission reports is a real but cautious egalitarianism. It is assumed, for example, that a major reason for intensive federal involvement in higher education is to ensure that minority and disadvantaged groups are provided equal access to higher education, unhindered by the traditional barriers of race, economic status, and geography. Institutions should be rewarded for efforts they make to extend access opportunities, and counseling and guidance should be liberally provided to encourage people with low educational expectations to modify and enlarge them. However, the commission espouses no extreme doctrinaire egalitarianism. It recognizes the need for elite institutions preoccupied with preparing high-level professional people, and it also recognizes that for many individuals (including some now in colleges and universities) the collegiate experience is inappropriate; the Commission points out many satisfying life styles not requiring formal post-secondary education. It implicitly accepts class structure in society and believes that class levels are based on merit: Every individual should have the opportunity to develop merit, but all will not or should not take advantage of the proferred opportunity.

The commission reflects a liberal rather than a radical posture regarding academic values and social change. It clearly respects academic freedom but seems to imply limitation to avoid license. It pleads for dissent as an essential in the marketplace of ideas but abhors violence, disruption, and exhortation to violence. It assumes an ordered quality of academic life, governed both by long-standing principles and values and by detailed statements of rules and processes within which individuals can function freely and comfortably. Though the documentation does not explicitly support such institutions as tenure, one can infer that the commission would generally support at least the intent of the 1915 and 1940 statements of principles of the American Association of University Professors. One can infer also that the commission would support academic freedom for both students and faculty members, attempts on the part of faculty members to develop codes of behavior, and judicious use by administrators of the powers needed to govern as long as due process was scrupulously observed. Clearly, a commission seeking consensus within the academic community cannot appropriately take positions on specific and controversial cases; but the tone of the full body of the policy statements strongly implies that the commission would have supported the decision at Stanford University to terminate the appointment of H. Bruce Franklin, found guilty by a faculty committee of transcending the boundaries of appropriate academic conduct.

In sharp contrast to the report (cited previously) of the Commission on Financing Higher Education, the Carnegie Commission not only does not fear federal financial involvement but insists that an expansion of that involvement is imperative. Federal resources and interests are such that only the federal government can solve such critical problems as the provision of adequate medical education or the assurance that students from economically deprived backgrounds can indeed attend institutions of their choice. The commission insists that in the public sector states continue to have the primary obligation to maintain colleges and universities but that state efforts should be reinforced by federal efforts in categorical ways. The commission does not discount the responsibility of the private sector to maintain diverse kinds of institutions, but again federal support is necessary, and the commission seems to assume that it will be forthcoming. At no place has the commission become bogged down over older issues such as the church state issue, which long prevented public support for private higher education. The assumption is that the doctrine of separation of church and state can be circumvented without violating Constitutional intent. As to the particular formula by which federal aid should be provided to institutions, the commission adopts a generally eclectic posture. It does tend, however, to favor channeling broad, noncategorical support through students rather than through unrestricted direct institutional grants. Institutional grants should be made only in specific areas related to major federal interests, such as the extension of opportunity to minorities and other disadvantaged students.

Overall, the commission favors diversity of higher education to meet the needs of a pluralistic society. It calls not only for maintaining and strengthening such traditional diverse institutions as the historically Negro college but for the invention of some new options and for their accommodation within the higher educational structure. However, there may be a slight undertone of favoritism for public institutions, an undertone that may derive from the same determinism that characterizes other commission postures. That is, the steady increase in proportional enrollment in the public sector and the steady decline in proportional enrollment in the private sector may be viewed as an inexorable tendency. Hence it would be wise to favor those institutions of most service to the entire society. In several research reports the plight of the private sector is examined, and palliatives are suggested. But the commission has not gone on record with strong recommendations to stabilize the proportional enrollments in public and private institutions. It may be that the commission simply does not believe stabilization is possible. Or it may not regard stabilization as particularly beneficial. Thus the inference (possibly strained) is that leadership of the Association of Land Grant Colleges and State Universities would feel more comfortable with the bulk of the commission recommendations than would the leadership of the Association of American Colleges. These comments may be unfair, for distinguished members of the commission serve privately supported institutions, and the commission itself has sponsored research reports on liberal arts colleges, on evangelical church-related colleges, and on Catholic colleges. But the impression persists that the stereotypic institutions of most concern to the commission are the large universities, state colleges, public junior colleges, and prestigious liberal arts colleges. It makes specific references to small experimental institutions such as Goddard or to the declining but still functioning private junior colleges.

A major preoccupation of the commission is with education for the health-related fields. The commission reaches the conclusions that "the United States today faces only one serious manpower shortage, and that is in health care personnel," and that "higher education as it trains the most skilled personnel has a great responsibility for the welfare of the nation."[5] A crisis in health education has required early policy pronouncements and will require new methods of funding and massive increases in staffing and enrollment. During the rest of the 1970s there should be a substantial reduction—on the order of a million people—preparing for teaching and educational careers; there should be a corresponding increase of about a million people preparing to enter the health services fields. The commission is apparently convinced that severe shortages in only one major field are likely to be critical during the 1970s and 1980s. Engineering, business, architecture, agriculture and the rest seem in reasonably good shape; only medicine, dentistry, nursing, and the emerging paramedical fields face acute shortages.

Although the commission generally avoids a number of highly controversial and divisive educational issues, it nonetheless supports a few ideas about which there is substantial difference of opinion. The commission gives its support to the doctor of arts as an appropriate teaching degree (one of the commission research studies approves and another rejects the validity of that degree as an effective substitute for the Ph.D.). The commission also supports at least the underlying principle of a three-year degree, although a number of institutions that have examined the concept have rejected it, and although a counterargument can be made that the social imperative is to keep young people in school longer rather than to have them leave earlier. As indicated previously, the commission opposes broadly distributed, relatively unrestricted grants to institutions even with the sharp opposition of leadership from the private sector. It also favors increased support and expansion of predominantly Negro institutions, although the literature on the subject is split, with some authors, such as Earl J. McGrath, urging

[5] Carnegie Commission on Higher Education, *Higher Education and the Nation's Health* (New York: McGraw-Hill, 1970), p. 2.

the commission point of view and with David Riesman, a member of the commission, recommending that at least the weaker predominantly Negro institutions be allowed to die. Of a somewhat different character is the commission support of the concept of the community junior college. Higher education leaders generally accept junior colleges as an important addition to the system. Hence the commission espousal is not particularly surprising. However there is some difference of opinion as to whether junior colleges will ultimately educate the vast majority of lower-division students or whether they will make their contributions in other ways such as through programs of adult education and technical and vocational education. Although the commission does not deal specifically with this issue, both the background research study and the policy statement allow room for inference that the commission would not be surprised to see junior colleges become the primary lower-division educational vehicle; the creation of almost 300 new institutions by 1980 is urged.

Additional insight into the intent and productivity of the Carnegie Commission can be obtained by examining some matters that either were ignored or were given relatively superficial treatment. The first of these concerns teaching and instruction. The commission assumes that teaching will go on but refrains from specific consideration of how teaching can be evaluated and improved. It seems to assume that there is so little agreement on the dynamics of teaching, the ways people prepare to become teachers, and reasonable assessment of teaching that to raise the subject in any policy statement would be unnecessarily divisive and could possibly open the commission to strong criticism. This stance is understandable. Yet evidence has mounted regarding the ineffectiveness of teaching, and institutions have begun to create centers for the improvement of teaching. Undergraduate deans or deans of instruction have been appointed to try to engineer improved instruction; even research-oriented universities have begun using student evaluation of teaching not only to help faculty members improve themselves but for such administrative purposes as promotion and tenure decisions as well. Now it may be that the widespread interest in teaching will prove to be as transitory as have critiques of college teaching in the past. In that event the commission decision will be validated. However, on the off chance that consensus might eventually be reached on the possibility of improving teaching, some future commission might give explicit attention to a process that is presumed to be at least close to the center of education.

A second gap concerns the substance of the curriculum, graduate, undergraduate, or professional. The commission does suggest that old labels such as general education and liberal arts education have become meaningless and that new nomenclature is desirable. But academic leadership is constantly concerned with other major issues. There is the matter of balance between common contextual and specialized studies for undergraduate students. There is the sensed lack of relationship between college studies and subsequent careers. There are questions as to whether professional curricula should be more applied or more theoretical. There are serious curricular questions in the preparation of teachers, and difficult questions involving such things as transfer problems requiring technical answers. There may have been good reason for the commission, concerned as it is with broad policy, to minimize discussion of the techniques of education. However, the curriculum is still the most costly part of enormously expensive higher education, and curricular issues can most quickly divide faculties from administration. It might therefore have been wise, even though dangerous, for the commission to at least elucidate the issues in such matters as general education and make some attempt to indicate trends.

Another technical matter on which the commission remained silent is the nature of counseling, advising, and guidance and how these important services can be provided. The commission recognizes the importance of counseling and urges its expansion, particularly for new kinds of students; yet it never addresses itself to the problem of deploying the necessary manpower to provide individual students with this intensive service. Quite obviously it would have been inappropriate for a policy commission to take sides on the directive–non-directive approach to counseling. It probably would also have been inappropriate to lend commission support to behavior modification, which is still undergoing serious testing. Yet the amount of support that should be provided for counseling and guidance services and ways of deploying professional resources might properly have received some commission attention.

Another gap is discussion of the nature of education. As indicated earlier, the commission comes perilously close to equating education with what colleges and universities do. Thus the commission has devoted little attention to the philosophy of education or even to suggesting how contrasting practices might be operated from differing philosophic positions; these differing philosophic positions can be of great significance in determining the structure and financing of higher education. A college premised on Rosseau's romanticism would appear radically different from one premised on John Dewey's pragmatism. A general education program rooted in instrumentalism would be substantially different from one based on rationalism or neo-humanism. It is probably appropriate that a commission seeking consensus not take a single philosophic position and assign it the status of orthodoxy. Yet a policy statement indicating, for example, the different practices of medical education produced by different beliefs regarding the fundamental nature of education might have been helpful and might have tempered the impression that although the commission does not speak philosophy, its many statements constitute a single, coherent, philosophic set of presuppositions.

Psychological techniques are also avoided although in a paradoxical way. A number of the reports and policy statements assume systematic psychological testing to be a device to ensure increased curricular flexibility for nontraditional learning. Yet the commission avoids discussing the validity of intelligence or aptitude testing and the appropriateness of those devices as criteria for college admissions. It avoids discussing the use of examinations to validate course experience; the use of examinations given periodically, such as aptitude and achievement examinations administered at the end of high school; and the administration of the graduate records or professional aptitude examination upon completion of the bachelor's degree. And the commission is also silent on such technical questions as how large-scale testing can be accomplished in a nontraditional educational setting. At least one research report on testing and evaluation and a policy statement on the implications of formal testing of instruments and programs would have been valuable.

The commission also seems to have neglected much of the student personnel movement, with the exception of a policy statement on student dissent and violence. By the late 1940s, the student personnel movement had emerged as one of the three major administrative divisions of colleges and universities and had assumed responsibility for virtually all student activity outside the classroom. A handbook on the administration of student personnel services published in the early 1950s by the American Council on Education included counseling, testing, guidance, health services, student activities, student discipline, residence halls, student social life, and athletics as responsibilities of student personnel workers and called for professionally trained staffs. In part, some of the student protest of the late 1960s may have been directed at the oppressive protectiveness of such an organizational structure. It seems a serious oversight not to deal with trends in the rendering of student personnel services since they lie at the heart of the relationship between institutions and their students. Perhaps the commission correctly sensed that student personnel services are in flux and that many once-operative positions will be replaced. There is some reason to believe that institution-supported prosecution and defense might be substituted for the disciplinary work of deans of students. Ombudsmen might replace other student personnel workers; students themselves might assume responsibility for the conduct of residence halls. Yet even though in flux, these issues deserve examination and elaboration.

The commission also does not discuss in any systematic way a group of topics involving the concepts and agencies that allow the American system of higher education to function; a number of these concepts and agencies have been severely criticized for malfunctioning, and there have been recommendations that they be eliminated. The first of these concepts is voluntary accreditation either by regional agencies or by specialized agencies. Accreditation is an expensive and sometimes influential device that grew out of fear of governmental study of standards. Some of the contributions of accreditation, such as ensuring minimal quality in educational programs, have been validated time and again, yet accreditation has been severely criticized as standing in the way of innovation, as being relatively ineffectual in dealing with large and wealthy institutions, and as consuming institutional time which could be better spent rendering direct educational services. A second topic neglected by the commission is the various regional and national professional scholarly associations that provide a reasonably effective communications network and allow higher education to speak out on many issues. Associations have typically grown without any particular pattern and with no logical relationship to one another, although the American Council on Education presumes to speak for most of higher education, and it does informally try to coordinate activities of a few other associations. A few attempts have been made to analyze professional associations and to suggest improvements, but as yet no influential group has backed any particular type of association or mode of operation. A third neglected topic is the relationship between colleges and universities and various certifying agencies of state governments. There are no guidelines for the evolution of effective ways of dealing with the necessary problem of certification. Though each of these three topics could become somewhat controversial, a thoughtful, middle-of-the-road approach could conceivably reduce emotion so that a consensus might evolve.

Related to curriculum is the matter of student values. During the 1960s scarcely an educational conference was held that did not give explicit attention to the question of whether an institution could appropriately inculcate certain values or should restrict itself to suggesting that students ponder alternatives. The problem of values lies at the heart of education, hence the Carnegie Commission might at least have been expected to allude to it. Yet, except in a few of the research reports, the commission is silent on the question. The subject is complex and does arouse intense emotions, but a subject so potentially divisive seems significant enough to warrant research and a policy statement, if only to establish that irreconcilable differences do exist.

The Carnegie Commission has made and is making an enormous contribution to the understanding of higher education. For limited sums its production of research has far surpassed any other organized research effort in higher education. Its policy statements, while rarely recommending extreme solutions, have dealt with some of the perplexing issues facing higher education and have presented reasoned direction for decision. The range of subjects is large, but with the exception of a few gaps the commission presents a reasonable portrait of higher education as it enters the last fourth of the twentieth century. Operating with a relatively small staff, the chairman and his professional associates have obtained wide dissemination and discussion of the commission findings.

The style of the research reports is, as can be expected, uneven. Some reports weave relevant data into coherent portraits, but others are disjointed, garbled, and without perceivable logic or structure. By and large the quality is good and compares favorably with that of other series such as those produced by the Center for Research in Education or the periodic reports emanating from some of the centers for the study of higher education. The quality of the policy statements is uniformly high, and the documents are presented in a consistent manner which ensures maximum utility. Perhaps one of the greatest strengths of the series is the length of the reports; they are, with a few exceptions, long enough to be adequate yet short enough to be utilitarian. One caveat that may have more to do with the subject of the deliberations than with the reports is that the volume of material is immense.

If there is such a thing as an establishment for higher education, the Carnegie Commission probably reflects its thinking. The commission values higher education and sees it as an important social institution that does creditable work. Colleges and universities, according to the commission, have successfully surmounted difficulties in the past and have the capability of doing so in the future. Quite likely, higher education as a total enterprise grew too rapidly during the 1960s, but it did so in response to imperious social demand. The enterprise is essentially rational, and the appeal of the commission is to this presumed rationality within the academy. The commission rejects extreme nihilistic criticism as it does revolutionary change; it favors the kind of evolution that it believes to be inevitable.

II

Policy
Statements

The Carnegie Commission has produced much research, theory, and discussion on higher education, and it may be that those elements will constitute its ultimate contribution. However, at the heart of the commission's deliberations stand the several policy recommendations designed to suggest and hopefully bring about needed changes and reforms. In aggregate the recommendations reveal the main thrust of commission thinking and provide evidence upon which assessment of its posture can be based.

The resultant profile of policy judgments is impressive, reasonably comprehensive, and somewhat predictable given the state of higher education and the leadership roles the commission members have occupied in that enterprise. The major themes stress the significance of higher education in the society, the need for expansion but at somewhat slow rates, the continued responsibility of the states and the private sector for the support of higher education, and a substantially increased federal presence in the directing and financing

26

of higher education. Overly simplified, the various policy postures can be quickly epitomized: Both high-quality, almost elite education and egalitarian, universal higher education are desirable and attainable social goals. These may be achieved through careful planning, which should result in many different forms of higher education needed by the different people living in a pluralistic society. If higher education is to be an effective intellectual force, it must be characterized by freedom for controversy and dissent. However, that freedom can quickly be destroyed if campuses become scenes of disruption and violence. Hence a clear distinction must be made between dissent and disruption, with the latter proscribed—hopefully through reformed campus mechanisms but through legal and police power if necessary.

The costs of higher education increased during the 1960s more rapidly than did other indices of the economy, and for justifiable reasons. Increased expenditures are still required but at slower rates. Higher education can accomplish this needed slowdown by recognizing that not everyone needs or desires a college experience; some should be encouraged to seek other means of personal development. Fewer students, coupled with reformed and economical methods of organization, management, and instruction should bring the cost of higher education within the financial limits of such a rich industrial nation. The federal government must obviously increase its support for higher education but in quite precise and well-defined ways. Direct, unencumbered grants to all institutions do not seem warranted, but direct grants for specific purposes, such as the improvement of predominantly black institutions or the support of medical education, do. In addition to support for research, substantial federal funds should be channeled directly to students to enable them to find and pay for the education best suited to their needs. Increased federal support should not be considered a replacement for state involvement; the states have historically been responsible for education, and this responsibility must continue. But state support, to be effective given the increased costs and complexity, will require new instruments for coordination, control, and planning of higher education. A coordinating council to mediate between individual institutions and state government seems the most desirable device.

Though college students generally seem reasonably satisfied with the education they receive, significant educational weaknesses and deficiencies still need to be corrected. The most promising approach to reform is through genuine diversity of educational opportunity and through realistic efforts to make education relevant in the best sense of the word. But reforms, to be effective, must not deviate too greatly from existing practice with the one major exception allowed by increased use of educational technology. The computers, videotape cassettes, and the like now available should create a fourth educational revolution equal in significance to the shift of responsibility from the home to the school, the shift to the written word as the principal medium, and the invention and use of printing. Full utilization of the technology evolves slowly but, it would seem, inexorably.

As universal access to higher education becomes a reality, the already significant two-year junior or community college will become even more important. This distinctively American institution, using state and federal resources but controlled by local boards, is the best way to ensure higher education for all, regardless of economic condition or previous disadvantage. Although social policy stresses integration of the races, the predominantly Negro institution must continue to provide service for the Negro community for at least several generations. These colleges, with the help of massive federal subsidy, should be encouraged to expand enrollments and diversify programs until they have moved from their historic isolation into the mainstream of education.

The most critical need for professional people during the remainder of the twentieth century is for more health workers, better prepared and more diversified than those of the past. Because health is a national concern, the federal government should provide massive financing to create new schools; expand and improve existing ones; support students; and encourage doctors, nurses, and dentists to practice in the poorly served regions of the country.

In the reviews that follow, these recommendations are elaborated and criticized. These recommendations will not radically change the nature of higher education. Rather, they seek to correct the course of higher education much as booster rockets correct the course of a space ship within a generally satisfactory vector.

Quality and Equality: New Levels of Responsibility
for Higher Education

From the beginnings of the republic, education has played a vital role in democratic society. Institutions of higher learning meet a number of needs: equal opportunity through education, support of the economy through basic research, technical experts for such a complex society, and improvement of the quality of life.

It is difficult to determine whether higher education has the resources to provide both high educational quality and equality of educational opportunity. Higher education is encountering pressures created by its accomplishments. More and more young people are attending college. Colleges and universities have had to increase their functions in response to the needs of society, yet they face steadily increasing costs, which have been met partly by federal funds but chiefly by funds from state and local governments and the private sector. These latter sources are beginning to reach their limits, but the demand for support increases. The Carnegie Commission believes that a much greater federal investment is essential to the evolution of new ideas, the development of intellectual skills, and the extension of equality of opportunity.

The well-being of higher education is a concern that the federal government shares with state and local governments and with private individuals and organizations. Although by 1967–1968 federal aid to institutions had reached a total of almost 4 billion dollars and was affecting 2100 colleges and universities, there were still regional and institutional disparities in federal aid. The Commission believes that there should be greater grants and loans to students, direct support to institutions for specific program needs, and extension of support for research, construction, and special programs. These measures are preferable to extending tax credit to parents of children in college or subsidizing the states.

The Commission sees several highly critical problems. The first is to remove financial barriers for all youth entering higher education. Aid should be scaled to the differing costs at different types of institutions; grants to students should be augmented by loan programs and work-study programs to provide financial flexibility; and aid can be better administered through national programs than through state, local, or regional ones.

Secondly, because the need for highly trained professional workers is so great, and because many qualified students do not enter appropriate programs, funds should be made available to enable institutions to search for potential talent and to provide them with funds to help support talented students. These funds would, of course, come from increased federally supported fellowship programs.

Although educational opportunity grants and work-study programs may remove financial barriers, assistance might also be provided through the creation of a national student loan bank that would lend money at low rates of interest to be repaid over extended periods. It is difficult to anticipate how many students would avail themselves of such loan provisions, but experience with the National Defense loan program suggests that the volume would be substantial.

Because tuition and fees rarely cover the full cost of education, expanding the pool of applicants for higher education without providing assistance to institutions would, in the long run, prove detrimental. The Carnegie Commission recommends that the federal government grant cost of education supplements to colleges and universities, based on the numbers and levels of students holding grants enrolled in the institution. These grants could be used discretionarily by institutions.

A third particularly critical problem facing higher education is that of providing adequate medical and health services. The Carnegie Commission recommends a massive program of federal aid for medical education to stimulate expansion of capacity of existing schools, create additional medical schools, expand programs for training medical care support personnel, and increase availability of health services in the medical school community. Federal support should take several forms. There should be directed payments to institutions based on enrollment. There should be construction funds at the 100 percent level for the creation of new student spaces. There should be grants to facilitate the creation of at least twenty new medical schools, and there should be community health service programs and programs for the training of medical support personnel. There should also be a radical increase in funds provided for research. Institutions that engage in major research should be provided about 10 percent of total research grants to use at their discretion.

Because higher education has emerged as so important and so expensive a part of national life, greater organization is needed to provide financial support, to provide guidelines for educational development, and to stimulate innovation. The Carnegie Commission has recommended the creation and funding of a national foundation for higher education.

In this first policy document released by the Carnegie Commission, the main theme to be elaborated in subsequent reports stands clear. The Commission is concerned with quality of educational opportunity, with the identification and training of professionals, and especially with providing needed medical and health workers. It recognizes that the support of higher education is pluralistic but believes that there should be massive increases in federal support. The Commission premise is that higher education is a national good for which the government should assume considerable responsibility. Certainly, within higher education few individuals would take issue with the posture of the Commission. (Those few are officers in the institutions that have deliberately rejected all federal support.) Within other segments of society such unanimity does not exist. National educational policy is created by the interaction of many interests. Groups shaping opinion within the higher education community, such as the Carnegie Commission, should suggest alternatives and consequences. This posing of alternatives is one of the lacks of the commission. The commission sees a problem of such magnitude that only the federal government has the resources to solve it, but it is conceivable that for a number of reasons federal response might not be appropriate to the task. Should not alternative ways of meeting educational needs be suggested?

New Students and New Places: Policies for the Future Growth and Development of American Higher Education

The 1960s were characterized by explosive growth in American Higher Education with enrollments leaping from 3.8 million in 1960 to 8.5 million in 1970. This rapid increase followed several

decades of steady but relatively slow expansion and was a result of
the high birth rates of the immediate post–World War II period.
Two sectors of higher education experienced atypically high rates
of increase—graduate schools and junior colleges. Students attended
five kinds of institutions: institutions granting doctoral degrees
in 1970 which enrolled 30 percent of all students; comprehensive
colleges, which accounted for 31 percent of all students; liberal arts
colleges (by far the most numerous), which enrolled 8 percent of all
students, two-year institutions, which accounted for 28 percent of
enrollments, and the large heterogeneous group of specialized and
multicampus institutions. Within increased enrollment trends are
several serious discrepancies. Racial minorities were seriously under-
represented in 1970, but there have been substantial increases in enrollment rates of minorities, especially blacks, since 1970. College
and university students tended to come from middle and upper income families, and this tendency still continues. Females attended
college at a much lower rate than did men, although a higher proportion of black females attended college than did the proportion
of Caucasian females. During the 1960s there were major regional
variations in rates of college attendance, with the Pacific and
mountain states, New England states, and central states sending
higher rates to college than did the Southwest or Southeast. Out of
state enrollments also differed. Generally, during the 1960s enrollment rates were higher than for any other country in the world.
However, when graduate enrollments were compared, the United
States proportions were like those of other developed nations.

The period of intense expansion seems over, but the nature
of future developments is not clear. Projections for future growth
can be developed on differing assumptions. One projection indicates a
reduced rate and an actual decrease during the 1980s because of the
decreasing size of the college age population, but only if the rates of
increase in attendance proceed as they did during the 1950s and
1960s. That straight line projection with the critical variable of decrease in birth rate can and very likely will be modified by a number
of policy decisions that can serve either to increase or to decrease
enrollment. Forces tending to increase enrollment are such things as
grants for students from low income families, direct involvement of
institutions in programs to improve the quality of education in

ghetto and rural schools, or a substantial increase in the number of open access institutions, especially junior colleges. Factors tending to reduce enrollment are such things as a three-year bachelor's program or an attenuated associate of arts program. Several policies that would strengthen private institutions are federal cost of education supplements to institutions, state aid to private institutions, and expanded federal aid to black colleges. A cluster of policies would serve to make the student bodies more heterogeneous. These include encouragement of stop-outs, increased emphasis on adult education, and a system of external degrees. Forces that would equalize educational opportunity among the states are expanded federal aid and substantially increased effort in states that have lagged in supporting higher education. Factors that reduce the size of institutions are the mandating of optimum size ranges for institutions and experimentation with new instructional devices such as cluster colleges and consortia. The quality of instruction could be improved by implementing a doctor of arts degree, by placing strict time limits on the completion of advanced degrees, and by establishing three-year professional degrees in such fields as medicine and dentistry.

The Carnegie Commission foresees the 1980s with a total student enrollment slightly smaller than that of the 1970s but one which more equitably accommodates various groups. It urges increased student aid, new comprehensive colleges, and new community colleges, all of which will tend to increase enrollments. But it also urges more precise reporting to potential students of changes in the demands of the labor force, which should curtail enrollment somewhat.

Future enrollments can, of course, be accommodated in extremely large institutions. But there are sound reasons to suggest optimum sizes for different types of institutions: small enough to be governable yet large enough to support an adequately rich educational program. Minimum size for institutional effectiveness would be 5000 for institutions granting doctorates, 5000 for comprehensive colleges, 1000 for liberal arts colleges, and 2000 for two-year institutions. At the other extreme, maximum enrollments from the standpoint of education and economics would suggest 20,000 for institutions granting doctorates, 10,000 for comprehensive colleges, 2500 for liberal arts colleges, and 5000 for two-year institutions. Particularly in the institutions granting doctorates and the comprehensive colleges, some of the virtues of the small liberal arts college might be achieved through experimentation with cluster colleges, which are economically viable only when their costs can be spread over the larger enrollments of the parent campus. A second major device—to achieve program richness, especially among smaller institutions—is consortia or other cooperative arrangements.

If enrollment projections are accurate and if institutions generally follow the size guidelines suggested by the Carnegie Commission, some estimation of the need for new institutions can be made. The greatest need seems to be for new urban institutions which are of reasonably open access. Concretely, by 1980 there will be a need for 60 to 70 new comprehensive colleges and 80 to 120 new community colleges, many of which would be located in the metropolitan areas. There is also need for new institutions in less populated areas if the goal of universal access is to be realized.

But these new campuses alone are insufficient. Patterns of participation must be more flexible. One such new pattern is modeled after the University of London and the more recently created Open University in England: television and correspondence courses permit people to bypass residency standards. Especially in populous cities, there is currently experimentation with programs of extended degrees or with the university without walls, a device to facilitate entry, departure, and reentry.

The Carnegie Commission, in short, makes several specific recommendations regarding prospective enrollments. Excessively large or uneconomically small campuses should be avoided. There should be considerable experimentation and expansion of the cluster college idea. Institutions should be encouraged to use resources more effectively through participation in consortia or other cooperative arrangements. There should be created 60 to 70 new comprehensive colleges in metropolitan areas and between 80 and 120 community colleges. However, there should be between twenty and thirty-five new comprehensive colleges in smaller metropolitan areas as well as state-wide expansion of external degree programs and open universities. Should these programs fail, there should be a corresponding increase in the number of comprehensive colleges and junior colleges created.

In general, this report is possibly a slightly expansionist pro-

jection into the future. The possible error in the projections lies in underestimating the numbers of sudents (low in ability, achievement, and socioeconomic status) who will seek to enroll in colleges and in over-emphasizing the willingness or ability of institutions to adapt programs to meet the needs of these new students. It can be argued that by 1972 college students of reasonably high ability, achievement, and socioeconomic status were attending colleges in saturation numbers and that the next big growth in enrollment will come from a new group of students never before affected by higher education. If such anticipated increases do materialize, institutions will have to change their curricula and teaching methods if a backlash of disillusionment is to be avoided. The report also may have over-emphasized the contributions of cluster colleges and consortia. Cluster colleges have worked quite satisfactorily in a few places, but large institutions such as the University of Minnesota or the University of Illinois might not be able to accommodate cluster colleges in the form developed at the University of California, Santa Cruz, or the University of the Pacific. Some regrouping of students may be possible, but many institutions are limited by physical plants designed at a different time and according to a different ideology. Similarly, consortia could enrich curricula but in practice have done so for only limited numbers of students and at a considerable increase in cost. A growing body of opinion already holds that although in a few regions such as the vicinity of Amherst consortia can work, they may be ineffective for groups of institutions scattered over a larger geographic area.

New Students and New Places *has several implications of consequence. The projected enrollments seem reasonable as does the likely distribution of those students among the various kinds of institutions. Careful institutional reading of those projections should result in less romantic planning and a more accurate realization of what the pools of prospective students actually are. Secondly, the indication of optimum sizes for institutions advances defensible goals for planners. Although those optimum sizes may be unrealistic for some institutions—that is, mammoth institutions such as the University of Minnesota or Michigan State University, or the small liberal arts colleges in states or regions with static or declining populations—for the large majority of public and private institutions present states of evolution could still allow impositions of limits or efforts to reach minimal limits.*

Dissent and Disruption: Proposals for Consideration by the Campus

Campus unrest is neither a single nor a simple phenomenon. One element is dissent, which is an individual or organized activity expressing grievances but carried on within the limits of the democratic processes of freedom of speech, assembly, and petition. Disruption, on the other hand, is activity that is not protected by the First Amendment and that interferes with the rights of others. Coercion is interference with the normal activities of other persons and groups that stops short of violence. Violence is willful behavior that inflicts or seriously threatens to inflict physical injury on individuals or damage to property, or both. Dissent is properly protected in a democracy, whereas disruption must be sternly condemned, suppressed, and punished. Dissent is essential to democratic life, generating as it does new ideas. Disruption, on the other hand, is contradictory to the values and purposes of an educational institution and to the processes of a democratic society. Dissent respects the rights of fellow citizens, whereas disruption is based on disregard of the rights of others. Most campus protest has taken the form of dissent, and the public reaction has been to reject dissent as well as disruption. A distinction must be drawn between dissent and disruption. Dissent should be protected as a democratic right and a major means of renewal for society, and repression should be rejected; disruption on the other hand should be met by full efforts to end it, by general law where necessary. However, there should be guards against excessive force in law enforcement.

Campus response to dissent or disruption must take into consideration the many problems underlying current dissatisfactions. Student dissatisfaction derives from conditions of minority and impoverished groups, the problems of war and peace, the problems resulting from the rapid growth of technology, and the problems of higher education both internally and in society. Both campus and society share some responsibility. Although students and faculty members are divided about means and ends, they stand predominantly against disruption and violence and for ordered change. Actions by society in response to coercion and violence should be undertaken only with reference to the specific individuals and groups involved and never against the campus or the system as a whole. Campuses must discourage disruption and protect dissent to better serve students and society. They should therefore develop bills of rights and responsibilities for all members of institutions, consultative processes and contingency planning for emergencies, and a fair and effective procedure to handle violations of campus rules.

College and university campuses historically have few explicit guidelines for the rights and responsibilities of members. Several gaps have appeared in traditional arrangements, such as provision for faculty responsibilities, provisions for safeguarding student rights, definition of appropriate political action on campus, and definition of disruption and violence. To close these gaps, bills of rights should probably contain a provision that all members of the campus community respect the rights of other individuals and of institutions; the statements should also guarantee members their basic rights as citizens. The enumeration of responsibilities and rights should be based upon the nature of the educational process and the requirements of the search for truth and its free presentation. These would include the right to expect the freedom to teach, to learn, and to conduct research and publish findings; a prohibition against institutional or individual censorship and intolerance of the opinions of others; and a prohibition against interference with the freedom of members on a campus to pursue normal academic and administrative activities. Institutions and their subdivisions also have rights and responsibilities, such as the obligation to provide an open forum for members of the campus and the right to prohibit individuals who are not members of the campus from using its name. Institutions have the obligation to remain silent on controversial and political issues except those which directly affect campus autonomy. Obviously a statement of rights should provide that all members of the campus have a right to fair and equitable procedures to determine the validity of charges of violation of campus regulations.

Campus governance historically has been devised for gradual change and has proved inadequate for dealing with emergency situations. Grievance procedures have been either too slow or non-existent. Rules governing protest activities have been unwise or imprecise. Too few campuses have adequately thought through the handling of emergencies and developed alternative procedures. There is a long-held myth that the campus is a sanctuary, a myth producing a reluctance to employ the police power of the state. Therefore, institutions should develop regular procedures for hearing grievances and suggestions. Rules governing time, place, and manner of peaceful assemblage should include provisions for monitoring such events and reporting violations of campus regulations. Presidents should be given specific authority to deal with emergency situations. Institutions should develop and codify alternative procedures to be used according to whether disruptions are violent or nonviolent. These could range from negotiation to the use of injunctions or even the closing of the campus. Guidelines should be made a matter of public record; there should be a stipulation as to who has the authority to close a campus and under what circumstances: The circumstances should always be clear danger of violence to persons or property. Policies should also specify what happens to faculty and administrative staff pay, student credit, hospitalization, and the like.

Campus response to alleged violations must be characterized by an impartial hearing leading to a fair decision and to acceptance of the hearing and the decision by members of the campus; in the past such mechanisms did not exist. Significant actions in violation of general law should be handled by the courts. Updating should be related to the nature of violations and the severity of penalties which could be imposed. Campus regulations should provide for informal handling of minor infringements of standard operating rules, for more serious violations of academic rights and responsibilities, and for violating the general law. These new procedures might well provide for ombudsmen, hearing officers, and campus attorneys. They might also provide for greater use of external persons serving in a judicial capacity.

Though extremists would reject the distinctions and recommendations made in this report, they should appear to most as eminently reasonable and fair. The elucidation of the values of dissent undergirds the commission's belief in civil and academic free-

dom, and the consistent proscription of disruption is based on the conviction of the commission that campuses must be ordered places to be effective. Although the conditions on any one campus may require modification in the substance of a bill of rights and campus regulations, the elements presented in this report constitute a model. But the report does more. It presents as appendices a range of statements, regulations, and procedures adopted by educational institutions and organizations. Within that rich vein of resource each institution should be able to find appropriate rhetoric.

More Effective Use of Resources: An Imperative for Higher Education

The Carnegie Commission on Higher Education proposes that the cost of higher education in 1980 can and should be pared ten billion dollars under what the cost will be if trends of the late 1960s continue. Half of this ten billion dollar savings can be accomplished by attenuating degree programs at all levels and the other half by reducing the increase in cost per student per year from 3.4 percent to 2.4 percent.

By the late 1960s only one-third of the institutions of higher education in the United States were not in some degree of financial trouble. Private colleges and universities began experiencing financial difficulties earlier, but by the fall of 1971 the financial status of public institutions began to deteriorate. The financial problems derived from a number of factors. The rapid expansion of educational activity during the 1960s led institutions to commitments that required continued expansion of income. When growth of income slowed, institutions were forced to use current operating funds to maintain costly new buildings, facilities, and tenured faculty. Expenditures on higher education rose from 1 percent to 2 percent of gross national product during the 1960s. Higher education began to encounter increased competition with other demands for public support. Compounding the problem was the continued acceleration of rate of inflation. Institutions that maintained medical schools felt a serious drain on total resources. Public institutions, by the end of the decade, experienced increasing gubernatorial and legislative reluctance to support large increases in appropriations and voter reluctance to approve bond issues for construction of needed facilities. Private institutions, forced to increase tuitions steadily, found that they had priced themselves out of previously stable markets. As the competition for students increased, private institutions put more and more money into student aid, thus intensifying budgetary imbalance. At the same time, endowment income declined in relative importance as a source of revenue for private colleges and universities. Although the financial crisis has not deepened to the extent that large numbers of institutions face immediate bankruptcy, the financial situation is serious. The crisis is already forcing institutions to curb increases in expenditures; the vitality and effectiveness of institutions are therefore in jeopardy.

Higher education is a labor-intensive service sector of the economy in which it is difficult to economize by radically increasing productivity. From school year 1953–1954 to school year 1966–1967, educational cost per student credit hour increased at an annual average of 3.51 percent, but the consumer price index increased annually by only 1.6 percent. Private institutions experienced greater cost increases than did public institutions because of increases in the ratio of graduate enrollments to total enrollments. The significantly lower rate of increase for public institutions was due to the sharp increase in the share of total enrollments absorbed by low-cost public two-year colleges. Costs in both public and private institutions increased as they absorbed more upper division students, as they entered graduate education on a large scale, and as they increased library and computer expenditures to accommodate this more advanced education. Now, presumably, economies to scale could slow cost increases, but they are muted as large institutions enter new fields, especially at the graduate level.

Institutional budgets reflect available income, and some institutions have attracted funds more easily than have others. Universities with outstandingly high ratings for graduate programs tend to cost more than less prestigious institutions. Minimum and maximum enrollment indexes also affect cost. Costs for extremely small institutions are excessively high and costs for large institutions increase with the complexity of the institution.

All institutions could strive to achieve optimum full-time enrollment for their campuses; economies to scale would result, and rich educational programs could still be offered. Very likely economies to scale will appear more frequently in individual programs than in institutions as a whole. Therefore institutions facing budget cutbacks should compile precise data for each sub-unit. But even total institutional expenditures can be examined more intelligently, and individual institutions should compare their fiscal profiles with those of comparable institutions to determine whether unnecessary expenditures are being made. The need for more refined program and fiscal analysis suggests that all large institutions should maintain offices of institutional research and that smaller institutions should seek better data through cooperation.

The most promising single avenue toward more effective use of resources is change of degree structures. A number of such changes are currently being examined. The last year of high school and the first year of college could be combined. The bachelor's degree could be made a three-year program by reducing requirements or operating on a year-round basis. More academic credit could be given by examination. Bachelor's and master's degree programs could be integrated. Master's degree programs could be revised and articulated more closely with work requirements. New two-year Master's degree programs could be developed to produce professional workers who do not require doctoral level research training. The four-year doctor of arts degree deleting dissertation requirements could be adopted as the standard degree for college teachers, and the length of time required to complete the work for the Ph.D., the M.D., and the D.D.S. degrees could be reduced by one or more years. Such changes not only can achieve economies but are desirable on educational grounds. Further, they are not utopian, for already in 1972 a number of institutions have inaugurated one or several of the suggested reforms. These extant examples range from relatively small institutions such as Ripon College or Stephens College that have adopted optional three-year bachelor's programs to similar adoptions by such complex institutions as Princeton and Yale. The trend toward acceleration of undergraduate education is certain to result in substantial economies for students and for high schools as well as for institutions of higher education. Perhaps the greatest economies for colleges will come from a slowdown in capital expansion. There will of course be some savings in operating costs if acceleration allows institutions to accommodate substantially larger numbers of students without making significant program expansions; but such savings will usually be less than the savings in capital costs. Acceleration seems particularly appropriate for professional education. It can be attained by shortening preprofessional requirements or eliminating such things as the internship year for medical students. Acceleration of Ph.D. programs will be much more difficult to accomplish, but recent reforms indicate that even doctoral level work can be made more efficient.

Modifying retention rates of students also has significant fiscal implications. The Carnegie Commission on Higher Education urges universal access to higher education, which is not the same as universal attendance in higher education. Colleges and universities have historically experienced a steady dropout rate of about 50% of each entering freshman class. Recent studies suggest that that rate may be slowly dropping, but the rate could be reduced still further if institutions would improve counseling programs. Adequately staffed, such programs could show students who should remain in college how they might do so and also help other students decide on alternatives to college. This decision-making with counseling could be facilitated if all entering students received the associate of arts degree at the end of two years and all beginning graduate students received the master's degree at the end of one or two years because attainment of a degree is a good time for decision-making. Better counseling is needed in high schools, not only to direct students to appropriate colleges, jobs, or occupational programs, but also to direct poorly motivated students away from college.

Faculty salaries are a major expense in higher education, accounting on the average for about one-third of expenditures. Achieving a significant increase in the student-faculty ratio is therefore desirable, provided it can be accomplished without sacrificing quality. Wide variations in student-faculty ratios do exist among institutions of similar quality. It has been assumed that small classes provide better learning situations, yet evidence is lacking. It may be that a judicious blend of very large classes and quite small seminars would be more economical and efficient than maintaining a large number of medium sized classes. Variety of course offerings should also be examined: The number of courses offered and the number of professors employed could be reduced. Faculty weekly teaching loads have declined significantly from about 16 weekly class hours in the 1930s to about 7 class hours in the late 1960s. A number of states and institutions are examining the ways faculty members use their time, in the hopes that more professional time could be devoted to instruction. Another concern is appropriate allocation of time to research, public service, and consulting activities. The combination of higher education and research has produced generally superior results, but because research is essentially a national concern, the bulk of research expense is borne by the federal government or major foundations. Faculty consulting activities, visible in larger research-oriented universities, are not really a substantial drain on faculty time. By far the biggest single source of supplemental income for college teachers is summer teaching rather than consulting or working on additional research projects. Thus, except for an occasional abuse which can be corrected by responsible supervision on the part of deans and department heads, consulting activities represent no appreciable drain on institutional resources. Institutions in financial difficulty may restrict sabbatical leaves and cut back on support personnel. These policies should always be subject to re-evaluation, but across-the-board cuts are not warranted.

Much of the cost increase during the 1960s resulted from sharply escalating faculty salaries. Increases during the 1970s are not likely to be at such a high rate. However, the full impact of unionization on faculty salaries has yet to be felt. Clearly there is a tendency for faculties to unionize, and institutions should seek professional help in anticipation of collective bargaining.

A critical problem for institutions is budgetary flexibility. In times of expansion, flexibility was brought about through the creation of new programs and positions. But in times of retrenchment that approach to flexibility is terminated. Under new conditions, flexibility can be obtained through curtailing or dropping programs for which demand has declined, and through paying closer attention to changes in the labor market. Cutting back some programs to release funds for others is difficult, but there are at least six different approaches. Selective cutbacks in programs no longer demanded can be quite useful provided institutions do not overreact to a superficial decline in demand. Some major research universities are attempting selective cutbacks through curtailment of graduate programs, a legitimate undertaking so long as the quality of the research university is not seriously jeopardized. The Carnegie Commission recommends that leading research universities refrain from cutbacks in graduate programs except on a carefully considered selective basis. However, it also recommends that institutions having recently developed an emphasis on research consider curtailment or elimination of doctoral programs. A second approach, the across-the-board cut, is an emergency measure to be taken occasionally by institutions to halt a deteriorating fiscal situation. Case-Western Reserve University and the University of Minnesota have used this device without serious harm. The third and fourth approaches involve consolidating existing programs to remove redundancy or readapting programs to deal with more contemporary problems. A fifth approach is to establish the general policy that every major sub-unit in a university should be expected to generate the resources of its own program. This has long been a policy at Harvard University, and if new safeguards to the prerogatives of central administration are maintained, it does represent a way to gain flexibility. A last device to gain flexibility is to ensure that central administration controls all vacant positions rather than to allow sub-units to perpetuate control of positions vacated through resignation, retirement, or death. Centralized control allows central administration to redeploy its resources to respond to new conditions. Cutbacks will always be painful, hence decisions about them should be made only after full consultation with the many constituencies affected. Cutbacks can also produce institutional atrophy, hence institutional budgets should always contain as much as 1 to 3 percent of the total budget to be used for self-renewal.

One major obstacle to effective use of resources is the fact that budgetary procedures are generally so structured as to discourage change and innovation. Under typical budget procedures, surplus funds at the end of the year revert to central administration or the state. Budgetary procedures could be modified so that individual departments, divisions, and schools that innovated to effect savings could realize some gain themselves. Private industry has long made use of financial incentives, and there is no reason colleges and universities could not do so.

Higher education, as it enters a period of declining growth, will encounter a number of new kinds of problems. There will be declining needs for faculty, and redeployment of faculty from under-utilized fields to new fields will be necessary. The somewhat different personnel policies required may include establishing position control for central administration, hiring more temporary and part-time faculty members in the late 1970s, and investigating such palliatives as early retirement.

Although collegiate institutions have done long-range planning for physical facilities, they have done relatively little with respect to long-range educational planning. Currently available techniques for generation of data and program budgeting now allow institutions to engage in better long-range capital planning and educational planning and to ensure that full costs for every aspect of institutional conduct be budgeted for and accounted for. An important element of better management is fuller utilization of existing facilities, hence the Carnegnie Commission on Higher Education recommends that all institutions examine the feasibility of year-round operation to make greater use of facilities.

Significant economies can be achieved through consortium agreements and other forms of institutional cooperation, particularly in graduate and specialized education. The consortium movement has expanded rapidly during the 1960s, and its further expansion is to be encouraged. Institutions may also contrive more effective management through better trained and more technically competent administration and management. Additionally, more control over escalating computer costs is desirable as is placing auxiliary enterprises on a self-sustaining basis. Particular attention should also be given to extremely expensive education such as medical or dental education. St. Louis University, in a drastic measure, eliminated a dental school in favor of retaining a medical school. Some new budgetary arrangements may be necessary so that medical and dental schools do not drain other university resources. Institutions can also be more effective in the management of income and endowment by at least examining less conservative investment policies.

The More Effective Use of Resources *is potentially one of the most useful of the policy statements of the Carnegie Commission on Higher Education. It forthrightly faces the financial problem and makes, for the most part, well founded recommendations to bring about economies. Many of the recommendations have long been suggested, such as slowing the proliferation of courses and programs, obtaining better data, and insuring better management. What the Commission has done is to codify and portray them in the context of the existing financial crisis. Only two of the major recommendations have serious flaws.*

First, cutting the bachelor's degree from four to three years will clearly bring about economies for students and their parents and for institutions through slowing physical plant expansion, but the national economy may not be equipped to absorb people finishing academic work at an accelerated rate. An historic trend in American society has extended the period of youth from relatively few years in the nineteenth century (from about age 11 to 16 for females and 12 to 18 for males) to the present range (from about age 9 to 23 for females and 11 to 30 for males). The recommendation that less time be spent in college opposes such historical tendencies, which may be sufficiently powerful to negate the recommendation.

Secondly, the commission stresses the doctor of arts degree; given the fact that there is an oversupply of Ph.D. candidates, a doctor of arts degree is likely to fare badly in competition and could become unsalable. The counterrecommendation that institutions make the Ph.D. degree more flexible is more viable.

The More Effective Use of Resources *has enormous implications for institutional practice and should be required reading for every administrator in higher education. Not all the suggestions are actual guides to action, but all are suggestive of devices to be used, and all are well illustrated.*

Institutional Aid: Federal Support to Colleges and Universities

Since 1952 the climate of opinion in higher education has shifted perceptibly from considerable skepticism about federal assistance to an assumption that increased federal aid is desirable, almost inevitable. Operating funds beyond the capacity of state or private sources are essential to improve or maintain quality of instruction and to accommodate further expansion in enrollment. The present categorical grants are insufficient because they give benefit to a few institutions, leaving the majority untouched. Hence general support funds are needed to offset this unevenness of impact. Unless federal funding is provided for some operating expenses, institutions will need to increase tuition, thus placing a burden on students and their parents and denying access to children of low socioeconomic levels. Difficulties arose from increased national needs and increased financial needs of individual institutions. The premise is that higher education is a national asset and therefore a national responsibility. In the past, federal funds have been used primarily to support the research and service functions of institutions. Now federal funds are needed to support the teaching function. Educational programs, especially in the health fields, are essentially national in character and thus justify federal support. Further, certain federal programs already in existence place financial burdens on institutions that should be offset by direct institutional grants. It is national policy to enhance the welfare of society, and institutions require additional funding to participate in this endeavor. Greater innovation is needed, yet innovation requires additional funding which must come primarily from the federal government. And federal funds are necessary if private colleges and universities are to be preserved as important components of our higher educational system.

Assuming the desirability of support for institutions, it is imperative that efficient and equitable techniques be developed, for seemingly simple formulas favor one type of institution over another. Finding equitable and efficient techniques will require careful manipulation of components of a grant system, and careful attention to controlling definitions. Generally the components are allocations tied to general inputs (such as enrollment measures); allocations tied to some general output measure such as degrees awarded; special increments for small colleges; allocations made for specific groups of students, such as returning service men, low income students, or highly able doctoral students; and allocations based on growth factors or increases in costs. A system of grants will also depend on the definition of the basic unit. A formula could be based on all students taking courses, only students matriculated in degree programs, or only full-time students. If an enrolled-student formula were used, public colleges and universities would gain an advantage, whereas a degree-program definition would penalize two-year institutions. Equitable and efficient solutions can be found only by examining the likely consequences of various combinations of components and definitions.

A number of proposed formulas for direct institutional assistance are aimed at assisting small colleges. However, most of the proposed solutions, such as $500 for each baccalaureate degree awarded if the number of degrees awarded is not over 200, do not reach the majority of small institutions experiencing financial difficulty. To examine this problem and other problems, several formulae are possible. The first would grant an institution a specified amount for each recipient of an educational opportunity grant enrolled in the institution. The second formula would be based on a percentage of the total amount of educational opportunity grant aid to students. The third formula would allocate a portion of funds to institutions participating in the equality of opportunity effort; the remaining portion would be based on other considerations. A fourth formula would be a dual choice arrangement allowing institutions, for example, to receive a sum for each full-time student enrolled or grants connected with educational opportunity grants. This formula would clearly penalize universities and assist public two-year colleges. A fifth formula involves three factors: enrollment levels, equality of opportunity efforts, and amounts of research funds previously obtained.

Historically, broad support for the operations of collegiate institutions has been provided either by the states or by private sources. Federal funds have been for categorical purposes or categories of students, and this policy is wise. If some across-the-board formula were developed with the federal government making direct grants to institutions, it is likely that the states and private sources would diminish their contributions, placing the federal government in the role that state governments have held in the past.

A major need is for a diverse and pluralistic system of higher education to be maintained, evolved, and allowed to flourish. However, many of the suggested programs of direct institutional grants could conceivably discourage innovation and diversity. First, definition of eligible institutions could make experimental colleges ineligible. Secondly, many recommendatons assume a higher cost for upper-division than for lower-division students, yet the validity of this assumption can be seriously questioned. Institutional grants, to be easily administered, must be based on quantifiable factors. Yet rigorous adherence to quantification can result in disregard for differences in quality. Further, across-the-board formulas have not accommodated classes of institutions having specific needs for extraordinary support, such as colleges originally created for Negroes that now seek to become integrated and comprehensive institutions.

Part of the concern of those urging federal institutional grants is based on the financial crisis of higher education, yet the crisis is not universally experienced. There are large numbers of institutions that do have resources to provide an extremely expensive education. Although other categories of institutions are in financial difficulty, major research universities, private liberal arts colleges, private junior colleges, and black colleges are experiencing the most stress. Even within those groups there are institutions not in a precarious financial position. Any system of formula-based institutional grants would be likely either to produce windfalls for a substantial number of institutions or to be insufficient to meet the needs of the most distressed institutions. Further, as was previously indicated, federal grants that do not specify that current sources of revenue must continue their support could reduce financial assistance to institutions simply by replacing other sources.

A related problem is that state support differs widely. For example, taxpayers in three states spend over $1\frac{1}{4}$ percent of per capita income on education, but taxpayers in four other states spend less than $\frac{1}{2}$ percent. Formula based institutional grants, unable to distinguish between states making different efforts, would raise a substantial question of social equity.

There is concern that private higher education be sustained as an influential force, and many of the proposed institutional grant programs are designed to assist private institutions. However, closer analysis suggests that in many respects private institutions are already more favored than are public ones. Faculty salaries were higher in private institutions, and though private institutions enrolled only 30 percent of all students in the fall of 1967, they collectively received almost 40 percent of current funding income. Unless an extremely complicated formula were developed (and such a formula would be virtually impossible to administer), direct institutional grants could further widen the gap between the financing of public institutions and private institutions. The private sector contends that it is at a loss competitively because of its necessary raises in tuition. Few institutional grant proposals could alleviate that problem even by preserving existing differentials. Such proposals could even intensify the gap.

Federal involvement in education must be justified chiefly as a means of achieving federal priorities. Across-the-board institutional grants substitute institutional interests and needs for federal imperatives. Rather than across-the-board aid, institutions should receive aid based on their efforts to extend grants, fellowships, and loans and based on their efforts to supply the professional workers needed by society.

Two last objections remain. Direct institutional grants do not seem likely to help prospective students most in need of assistance and could force a constitutional impasse that would jeopardize the effort to gain greater federal support.

The Carnegie Commission therefore opposes across-the-board institutional grants. Rather it favors a variegated system providing funds for specific purposes. The commission would have certain funds provided directly to institutions: cost of education supplements; funds for construction; funds for research; funds for a foundation for post-secondary education, which would assist institutions in improving their educational programs; funds for special programs, such as health; and some monies for institutional scholarship grants. Funds would also be made available directly to students: educational opportunity grants, funds for work-study programs, funds for doctoral fellowships, loan monies, funds to facilitate search for graduate talent, and funds to improve counseling.

This particular set of policy statements attracted an enormous amount of criticism from the private sector on the ground that opposing institutional grants was equivalent to signing death warrants for as many as half the private institutions in the country. Private institutions, even those reasonably well endowed, have been facing a steady deficit spending situation for three or four years, and no end is in sight save through the draconian measures taken by St.

Louis University when it eliminated its school of dentistry and school of engineering. The direct institutional grant, it is contended, is the only means of alleviating that deficit spending situation. The Carnegie Commission took a somewhat intransigent stand on the matter of institutional grants. No member of the Commission with the possible exception of Kenneth Tollett is associated with the kind of institution which has experienced the severe limitations on operating budgets as have such universities as Boston College, Boston University, the University of St. Louis, or the liberal arts colleges. The Commission may be right in raising objections to institutional grants, but different categories of institutions might have suggested different postures regarding grants. The Commission has based many of its policy statements on the premise that the states and the private sector should continue their historic roles in the support of higher education and that federal involvement should represent primarily an extrapolation of federal use of categorical grants and support for categories of students. Alternative mixes might well have been examined. Institutional aid implies a moral position that should be examined historically. The Commission indicates that too many institutions would experience windfall gains from institutional grants and that this eventually is somehow bad. It also implies that institutions are likely to continue traditional practices or even regressive practices if they are allowed access to across-the-board grants from the federal government. These moral considerations are no more relevant here, in an educational context, than they are in a welfare context.

It is difficult to gauge the implications of institutional aid for individual institutions. Clearly the analyses of some of the issues, such as how best to encourage the quality of educational opportunity, suggest worthwhile considerations. Intensive comparative study of those institutions in good health by those in distress would be advisable. And the report should indicate that institutional aid cannot be solved with clichés. Thus, the significance of the report may well be the contribution of one reasonably well thought out position to be examined during the early 1970s as the problem of financing of higher education is reexamined and as new patterns are evolved.

must be made. The United States seems adequately supplied with graduate universities, hence there is probably no need for the creation of other graduate institutions within the predominantly Negro institution orbit. However, ways must be provided for graduates of those institutions to be given adequate financial support to attend existing graduate institutions. Several other programmatic changes are desirable. The Carnegie Commission recommends that Negro colleges with strong resources enter deeply into Afro-American studies. All predominantly Negro institutions should engage much more heavily in adult education, and most of the institutions in this category should grow to optimal size. It recommends that by the year 2000, colleges founded for Negroes have enrollments in keeping with the guidelines suggested for all institutions of higher education of comparable types. Comprehensive colleges should have 5000 students, liberal arts colleges should have at least 1000 students, public community colleges should have at least 2000 students, and colleges with very low enrollments and with little prospect of meeting these goals should consider relocation or merging with institutions that have complementing programs and facilities.

Predominantly Negro institutions also face serious financial problems. It is in the private sector that financial problems are most acute. Within Negro institutions educational expenditures are comparatively lower than they are in predominantly white institutions. Student fees are of necessity quite low. However, partly because of the need for compensatory programs, expenditures on student aid and expenditures for student services are quite high. Faculty salaries in the private Negro institutions are substantially lower than in counterpart institutions. Salaries within the public sector, however, are beginning to reach parity with their predominantly white counterparts. Gifts and endowments have been a significant source of income for private Negro institutions but of relatively less significance for public institutions. For public institutions there was a time when support per student was lower than that provided white institutions, but in recent years a number of the states have increased support so that financing of Negro institutions is approaching parity with that of white institutions. A few states, notably North Carolina, have specifically allocated funds for special financial assistance to the predominantly Negro institutions. Recently increased federal aid programs have tended to assist Negro institutions although the amount of federal aid is proportionally less than for white institutions, especially in view of the special costs to Negro institutions of providing compensatory education.

To assist Negro institutions, the Carnegie Commission recommends educational opportunity grants of $1000 per year for undergraduate students and $2000 per year for graduate students and a work-study program sufficient to enable students to earn $1000 during an academic year. Supplemental grants should be made as needed. In addition, funds should be provided Negro institutions for construction and renovation of academic facilities, continued library support, cost of education supplement programs to provide discretionary funds, and funds to allow institutions themselves to grant scholarships to especially needy students. Because the problems of the predominantly Negro institution are unique, the Commission also recommends that a federal agency be created for the development of colleges founded for Negroes and that a special subdivision of the recommended national foundation for development of higher education be created for those institutions. Both the large philosophic foundations and the business community are encouraged to increase levels of support for Negro institutions. In addition, a great deal of attention should be given to the development of more highly trained professors and cadres of administrative officers.

Several goals for 1980 can be posited: doubling of enrollments, bringing salary levels to parity with those in white colleges, creation of more comprehensive curricula, and greater utilization of Afro-American cultural material. To this end, the federal government should provide massive financial support, and the state governments should provide financial support and encourage complementary programs between black and white institutions. Foundations can contribute greatly to research and development for Negro education. Black colleges should seek internal reform, and other colleges should participate as is feasible in cooperative programs. The colleges founded for blacks are a national asset. They should be encouraged and assisted along with other colleges to the extent that their problems are similar and to the extent that they have special problems as they move from isolation into the mainstream of higher education.

The question as to whether predominantly Negro institutions should be encouraged to survive or to die has divided scholars of the subject. People such as Earl J. McGrath argue that these institutions are too important a resource to be allowed to die, whereas David Riesman and others see many of them as academic disasters. The Carnegie Commission has clearly opted for the McGrath position and has made sensible and forthright recommendations for the refurbishment of the predominantly Negro institution. With respect to most of the recommendations there can be no serious fault found, but a more critical posture could have been taken with respect to the internal functioning of Negro institutions. David Riesman was right when he observed that many predominantly Negro institutions had mimicked white institutions and had adopted their worst features. Such institutions experiencing decline in enrollment have only to look at their curricular requirements to understand why students are staying away. When a small South Carolina institution attracting Negro youth from rural areas insists on maintaining a two-year foreign language requirement, a two-year mathematics requirement, a disciplinary course in history of western civilization, and other such requirements, it is no wonder that young black students contend the curriculum is irrelevant to their needs. If the predominantly Negro institutions are going to achieve the goals set for them by the Carnegie Commission, substantial reordering of the curriculum, styles of teaching, and styles of administration must somehow be accomplished.

Continuity and Discontinuity: Higher Education and the Schools

During the period from 1870 to 1970 there has been steady evolution of accommodation between schools and colleges. In 1874 the Michigan Supreme Court set the stage for dramatic enrollment growth when it established the principle of using taxation to support secondary education. From 1870 to 1910 both secondary and higher education offered academic education to a very small minority of students. From 1910 to 1940 the proportion of the appropriate age group attending high school skyrocketed, but there were not similar leaps in college enrollments. From 1940 to 1970, college enrollments began to experience the growth that secondary education had experienced earlier. From 1870 to 1910, educators searched for ways of moving students from secondary schools to colleges. A college was defined by the requirements it imposed for admission. The validity of secondary work came to be established by accreditation by voluntary groups and by examination of students, first by colleges themselves and then by external examining agencies such as the College Entrance Examination Board. While accreditation could help, it proved insufficient for the ordered movement of students from school to college, especially in the Northeast. Hence the growth of external examinations. The expansion of secondary schools from 1910 to 1940 came in response to changes in the society, including the emergence of progressivism and the expansion of industrialism. Progressivism had many elements that forced change, such as the drive for vocational education and the striving for social reform. Progressivism also was involved in the evolution of a new psychology that demolished the older faculty psychology and opened the way for cafeteria-like school curricula. And this new psychology led directly to the new science of psychological measurement which came to undergird the process of moving students from schools in college. New tests helped demonstrate the invalidity of certain curricula prescribed in secondary schools for successful college work. Freeing secondary schools from collegiate domination led to the evolution of comprehensive high schools offering wide varieties of programs. To help steer students through that variety and ultimately on to college or vocations, counseling developed as an important educational adjunct. At the end of World War II, college enrollments began to increase rapidly, and with this expansion came the creation of new devices to cope with large numbers of students moving on to college. The Educational Testing Service was founded in 1948, and The American College Testing Program was established in 1959. Progressive education as a vital movement disintegrated, and American society was startled by the threat imposed by the Russian launching of Sputnik in 1957. Programs to ferret out academically gifted students were developed, and community colleges were expanded in numbers to accommodate the pressure of applicant demand. As part of this confusing and evolving picture, high school curricula were strengthened; some individuals urged both high schools and colleges to give radically more attention to the educational problems of disadvantaged groups.

As higher education moves toward the year 2000, each state should create a system of higher education that will allow universal access, with community colleges serving as a primary vehicle for the achievement of that goal. States should ensure that there are enough such free access institutions. Free access institutions are relatively low in cost, have relatively low admission standards, and are in close proximity to where students live. During the 1960s, although there were some regional differences, the number of free access institutions grew; the growth was largely attributed to the growth of community colleges. At the same time that the concept of free access was evolving, there also developed highly selective institutions that could accept only one out of seven or eight applicants. Actually, there are relatively few highly selective institutions, but publicity given them created a general belief that all higher education was equally selective. Even during the 1960s this was not the case, and as supply increases with respect to demand in higher education, the selectivity of many institutions will decrease. Many institutions experiencing enrollment decline will search for new clientele. Should they find new clientele, institutions may very well require teachers prepared in different sorts of ways. The proposed doctor of arts degree is an innovation that hopefully will produce these new kinds of teachers. In soliciting new kinds of students, institutions should reexamine their admissions policies and not rely solely on rank in class and measured academic aptitude.

The entire admissions process is indeed in need of serious reexamination. High schools are changing their curricula as are colleges, and the principle of credit by examination seems once again in the ascendancy. Schools should be encouraged to experiment and should be expected only to require that students acquire competence in the basic skills of reading, writing, and arithmetic. If schools do so diversify their curricula, then colleges must review their admissions requirements and not require particular courses of study at the secondary level except for reading, writing, and arithmetic. However, because mathematics has come to play such an important

role in American life, high schools should be encouraged to require
four years of mathematics for all or most students. As curricula
change, so must tests. It is generally recognized that existing testing
procedures penalize members of some minority groups, and it is also
charged that existing tests have restricted curricular innovation.
Further, it is becoming apparent that some of the traits measured
by existing tests of academic aptitude are not germane to many vocations. Testing agencies should therefore be encouraged to reexamine the philosophy of testing in order to conform better to emerging conditions. It is also essential that because of greater variety in
both secondary schools and colleges, counseling and guidance services must be drastically improved. Counselors have tended to know
very little about college guidance and even less about career guidance. There is relatively little systematic knowledge to help people
guide others or guide themselves. Among possible reforms are the
use of college students to do guidance work in secondary schools and
the use of larger cadres of better prepared professionals. The college admissions officer, especially, is emerging as a highly significant
figure; greater attention should be paid both to preparing admissions officers and to selecting them. Within the broad testing program, experimentation with a number of reforms should be encouraged. Given the power of the computer, it is now possible for
colleges to cooperate so that students prepare only one application
form and pay only one application fee. Stumbling blocks to such experimentation include inertia, tradition, lack of research base, and
so forth. Examples now available of successful experimentation with
the admissions process are convincing models. Similarly, experimentation with criteria for awarding financial aid is necessary and
will require resolving such new and vexatious matters as the significance of awarding majority to eighteen-year-olds. But modifying
these procedures will not prove efficacious unless improvement in
the schools is accomplished. Though it is difficult to determine how
good American schools are, there is enough disquieting evidence to
suggest considerable reform. Reform in teaching is needed in the big
city schools where there is presently a demonstrably high failure
rate. Schools of education should give special attention to training
teachers for the inner city. However, wealthy suburban areas are

also afflicted with serious educational problems, and teachers must be prepared to deal with the turned-off feelings of many students. A key issue of many schools today is the old problem of freedom versus strength. Faculties are divided over the matter; the way the issue is resolved will determine how well schools will be able to develop pluralistic approaches to common ends. Schools can be assisted as they struggle with such matters if universities lend their research potentials to solving problems of pedagogy and curriculum. Research productivity with respect to education has in the past been notably infertile, but the current imperative and new mechanisms could change that situation. Subsumed under the issues of freedom versus prescription are other matters such as the content of general education. Perhaps new content should be introduced into general education programs to make them current with the needs of contemporary American life. Perhaps some general education functions can be better assumed by other institutions than the school—notably the communications industry. Also, schools need to give greater attention to vocational preparation and vocational counseling. Very likely also the time has come when high school curricula in the humanities and social studies can be reformed much as the fields of mathematics and science were reformed in the 1960s. And this reform will require reform in the production of educational materials as well. There should be a national study of the relationships between teachers, school systems, state bureaucracies, university professors, and the educational materials industry in order to improve educational materials. There should also be experimentation with new methods and resources such as schools without walls, independent studies, students teaching students, cluster colleges, and the variety of educational technology now available. Though schools should be encouraged to experiment, they must constantly be reminded that they are also responsible and accountable.

As time progresses, new structures may be warranted. It might be that a middle college serving the last two years of high school and the first two years of college is a better way of attending to the needs of that age group than are present structures. More schools for younger students are in order. It should be possible to omit at least one of the high school or college years; experimentation should establish whether this goal is accomplished through early entrance, a three-year bachelor's program, or college credit for senior high school work.

Central to much reform is the work of schools of education, both for the preparation of teachers and for the preparation of administrators. The schools of education properly based on research should probably be limited in number but more sharply focused with respect to purpose. And schools of education should enter into a new period of close collaboration and cooperation with secondary schools.

This policy document is somewhat strange. It reviews correctly the history of college admissions and points to the pressures that have forced modification of admissions policies and practices. It also reviews the history of secondary education and correctly points to pressures calling for reform. However, in the many suggestions for reform, the report seemingly overlooks some extraordinarily difficult technological and logistical problems. It calls for improvement in counseling and guidance yet does not address itself to how school districts and colleges can finance the expansion of this activity. It urges greater use of testing but does not address the problems of how schools and colleges produce and implement reliable and valid testing instruments. It correctly points to weaknesses in teacher preparation and the preparation of administrators but is not analytical enough to help schools of education move in appropriate directions for reform. It calls for reform in secondary curricula in the humanities and social sciences according to models established in mathematics and the sciences but does not point out that many of those reforms are now being subjected to criticism. The criticisms leveled in California at the curricula developed by the School Mathematics Study Group, a Stanford-based, federally supported curriculum study, is illustrative. The overall reaction to this policy statement is that it may have attempted to do too much. The reform of schools of education would have been an appropriate topic for a full policy report.

Governance of Higher Education: Six Priority Problems

Governance of institutions of higher education differs from nation to nation. The American system is characterized by absence of centralized control, strong public and private segments, trustee responsibility, and presidential and departmental authority. Such a system developed out of a democratic and pluralistic society which sought to keep church and state separate but which employed the Protestant concept of lay control over the clergy in a form compatible with a capitalistic system. Over the years, however, the American system of governance has changed. Presidents gained more power than boards of trustees held. Academic freedom was extended to faculty members. Institutional power over the lives of students declined, and finally public influence and authority, especially over public institutions, grew. That these evolutionary changes have generally worked is evidenced by continued public support, continued diversity of types of institutions, continued educational dynamism, continued responsiveness to public interest, and general freedom from political intrusion into institutional affairs. However, new pressures are forcing more rapid changes in governance, and many of these pressures work at cross-purposes. Thus there is a movement from mass education to universal education yet at the same time a slowing down of enrollments. Faculties are split between those who seek objectivity and those who pursue ideological commitment. The decline in the acceptance of authority throughout the society is reflected in institutions at a time when authority is sorely needed to manage institutions effectively.

Governance of higher education is an exceedingly intricate matter that varies from institution to institution according to the type of institution, the nature of the student body, the composition of the faculty, and the public visibility of the campus. There is no clear theory about governance within institutions of higher education, although the nature of higher education prescribes some conditions such as the fact that a campus can not be a one man, one vote, self-contained democracy. Institutions differ according to function; they should also differ in style of governance. Governance is affected by size, function, and degree of centralization or decentralization of authority.

Since the end of World War II there has been a decline in the independence of campuses from external authority. Although some of this decline was probably warranted (for example, to prevent individual campuses from duplicating expensive programs), in other areas institutional independence, such as academic freedom of expression and the freedom for academics to make essentially academic decisions, should be preserved. What is needed in the future is not complete autonomy of institutions but rather selective independence and a clear understanding of the differences between external influence and external control. If various public agencies rely on influence and not control, institutions must act wisely in selecting from among alternatives. If public agencies possess power to control, they should exercise restraint in the ways control is applied. The temptation, and occasionally the need of public agencies to control institutions has arisen as higher education has consumed larger proportions of the gross national product, as institutions have been scenes of dissent and disruption, and as higher education has loomed larger in the total life of the society. To cope with these developments, public agencies have evolved new techniques of coordinating and controlling institutions, and the evolution of those techniques is likely to continue unabated into the future. The plea for some degree of institutional independence rests on several unproved assertions as well as on several plausible reasons. It is contended but not proved that independence gives rise to diversity, that it allows for innovation, and that institutional independence is a requisite for the academic freedom of individuals. More plausible are the arguments that professional matters should be left to members of the profession, that reasonable institutional independence stimulates a sense of responsibility on the part of various campus constituencies, that independence prevents political intrusion, and that an independent university is a necessary check in a society consisting of many different kinds of institutions. Institutions, if they are to be accorded some measure of selective independence, must demonstrate quality preformance, capacity for effective self-governance, effective use of resources, willingness to abide by law, willingness to account publicly, willingness to remain neutral in partisan politics, and an ability to preserve intellectual integrity, especially from within. A proper balance between public control and influence and institutional independence can be established by assigning rights and domains of influence to both public agencies and institutions. For example, public agencies have basic responsibility for law enforcement, for appointing trustees of public institutions, for requiring reports and data, for auditing expenditures, and for such matters as assignment of missions to types of institutions. Institutions, on the other hand, have the right to independent trustees, expenditure of funds within budgeted amounts, and decision-making about individual members of the various campus constituencies. Generally, with respect to public institutions, states should grant money on the basis of broad formulas, should establish only broad bases for academic policies, and should seek to affect the conduct of institutions through influence rather than through control.

The board of trustees, a peculiarly American phenomenon, was once the dominant authority in institutional affairs. By the end of the Civil War, however, boards had yielded such authority to presidents. Although some critics contend that boards of trustees have outlived their usefulness, they still appear to be an essential institution. Boards hold a trust, serve as a buffer between society and campus, act as a final arbiter of internal disputes, assume basic financial responsibility for the campus, and provide for the governance of the institution. To do this, board members must be independent, free of conflicting interests, competent, devoted, and sensitive to the interests of several groups of people. Thus, politically elected officials should not automatically be made members of boards of public institutions, nor should faculty members or students be board members of their own institutions. In the public sector, board members should usually be appointed by the governor but confirmed by the legislature. Many different kinds of individuals should be involved in nominating board members, but members should not consider themselves bound to any particular constituency. Under authority established by boards of trustees the president should probably regain some of the influence and authority he lost during the 1960s. Both at the end of the Civil War and after World War II conditions were right for strong presidential leadership. Then came an erosion of presidential power. As higher education enters the 1970s, it may be approaching a time for reassertion of presidential authority. Boards should seek active presidents and give them the authority and the staff they need to provide leadership in a period of change and conflict. Boards might consider appointing presidents for specified terms and evaluating them at the end of such periods.

During the 1960s student dissent characterized college campuses. During the 1970s faculty dissent may come to be the characteristic style. Faculty members are concerned about salary limitations, controls over conditions of employment, and such other matters as policies on promotion and tenure. Faculty members in prestigious institutions have long had the power to bargain with administrators and to exert their will. But on less prestigious campuses faculties have lacked some of that authority. In general, faculties at all types of institutions should have the general level of authority recommended by the Association of University Professors; for some faculty members this would not be enough, and unionization and collective bargaining appeal. Generally, sentiment for unionization is strongest in community colleges and among younger faculty. Faculties should have the right to organize and bargain collectively. However, before faculties rush to such a style they should consider all possible consequences, such as the possible strengthening of managerial authority or the possible unionization of students. Faculty members must realize that they cannot have a situation of codetermination of policy formation and the adversary relationship of unionization at the same time. If after careful reflection faculties opt for unionization, representation and bargaining units should be composed of faculty members including department chairmen. Contracts should be restrained, covering primarily economic benefits. Very likely collective bargaining on college and university campuses can be better regulated by separate federal and state legislation than by applying existing labor laws, which were designed originally for industry.

Academic tenure, which has a long history in American higher education, has recently come under widespread attack. Some critics see tenure as protecting incompetence and denying appointment of minority groups and women; administrators see widespread granting of tenure as forcing institutions into inflexible conditions. However, tenure does contribute to a sense of academic freedom. Tenure protects the quality of a faculty and gives faculty members a sense of active participation in the governance of the academic enterprise. Generally, the principle of tenure should be retained. However, appointments to tenure should be made only after a most careful review and should be based on demonstrated merit rather than on seniority. Institutions should be careful not to allow the proportion of their faculties on tenure to exceed approximately 50 percent. When persons are denied tenure they should obviously be allowed to appeal. However, the burden of proof that tenure should have been conferred must rest on the appellant.

Students in early Colonial colleges had little freedom or influence and no power. There has been a rather steady increase with respect to all three over the years. As higher education has moved into the 1970s, students have achieved considerable influence in areas of decision-making. Faculty members have been reluctant to give students influence or authority in a number of areas. Generally, students should be granted greater participation in those areas of governance where they have a substantial interest and adequate competence. They should clearly be given reasonable academic options and should be allowed a voice in discussion of topics of general campus concern. Students should either serve on joint committees or be allowed to have parallel committees dealing with relevant matters, and those who do serve on such committees should be provided adequate staff assistance. Students should be allowed to evaluate teaching performance of faculty members and should have substantial authority over student activities. Most campuses should have an ombudsman or the equivalent. Departmental affairs provide an effective arena for student participation in governance. Students can very likely be more effective in departmental arrangements than in university-wide senates.

The academic world has traditionally evidenced continuity in institutional structures and processes. Suddenly during the 1960s quick remedial measures became necessary as institutions experienced stresses never before foreseen. The new instrumentalities necessary include a formal bill of rights and responsibilities, a clear distinction between dissent and disruption, good consultative machinery, advanced consultation with law enforcement agencies, and a much more adequate and effective mechanism for handling grievances.

Governance of higher education in the United States has never been entirely trouble-free. In the past, however, there was general acceptance of several postulates: governors and legislatures should be quick to help and slow to interfere; boards of trustees should concern themselves with the management of money and the appointment of good presidents; presidents should raise money and protect faculty, students, and alumni; faculty members should make academic decisions; and students should run extracurricular activities, staying out of academic decisions. That consensus broke during the 1960s, and there is some doubt that it can ever be restored. American society itself is going through a period of social transformation. Intellectuals are often in substantial conflict with the society. Higher education is moving from a stage of mass access to universal access. Students have been energized by the problems of society to take a greater interest in the conduct of society, and authority on campus has been subject to serious challenge. It is hoped, however, that a new consensus can be achieved on campus independence, maintenance of the central roles of boards of trustees and presidents, retention of the principle of tenure, and better rules setting forth the rights and responsibilities of members of the academic community. The quest for new consensus is a project of high priority. However, if consensus cannot be achieved, better mechanisms for the handling of conflict must be created.

In this policy statement the Carnegie Commission once again reflects its liberal conservatism. According to this document there are malfunctionings on the part of boards of trustees, but there is a continuing need for such lay boards. The commission values collegiality but recognizes that more constitutionalism is probably required if collegiality is to be retained. In the past, no student voice in academic affairs has been heard; the commission posture is to urge that students be given a voice but that some limitation be placed on that voice. The commission values tenure but maintains that substantial changes must be made in the tenure system if tenure is to remain viable. It maintains that the old-time authoritarianism of college presidents is no longer a tenable posture, but it also sees that presidents must have essential powers to govern. Though the Commission would like to see a return to consensus, it realistically accepts the fact that conflict could become the rule and that mechanisms for dealing with it should be examined. This report will clearly displease aggressive, militant, and paranoid faculty. It will displease the radical element among students. However, it should gladden the hearts of presidents who in the late 1960s found them-

selves in the intolerable position of lacking the necessary authority to govern. One can only hope that the balance that the commission recommends will come to be the prevailing style of governance in the nation.

Higher Education—Who Pays? Who Benefits? Who Should Pay?

The people pay the total bill for higher education but do so through the pluralistic form characteristic of the American society. As of 1973, over two-thirds of all young men and women in the United States are availing themselves of some type of formal post-secondary education; approximately half the direct costs are paid from public revenues. Before considering aggregate costs, several distinctions should be made. There is a nominal price charged for attending college. There are out-of-pocket costs to students. And because all post-secondary education is in some way subsidized there are expenses paid by other than the student or his family. Lastly, there are foregone income opportunities for the student. The question as to who pays for a college education has no simple answer. It must be answered from the vantage point of the user, from that of the educational system, and from that of the economy as a whole. Several income activities of colleges and universities are not essential to the educational purpose of higher education. These are federal research and services, sale of services and related activities, interest on student aid loans, and auxiliary enterprises. Certain categories of income or expenditure are included or excluded according to whether service could be provided as well by a private concern.

The American economy has been devoting an increasing percentage of its total resources to higher education since World War II, and this increase is likely to continue until about 1975 at which time the proportion of the gross national product devoted to higher education will probably stabilize at close to 3 percent. The aggregate costs in 1970–1971 were shared: students and families contributed 30 percent, governments of various levels 60 percent, and private philanthropy 10 percent. This distribution of costs represents a substantial shift from the 1930s, when students and their families paid almost 65 percent of the cost. It should be borne in mind that these are ratios and that the actual dollar outlays for higher education on the part of students and families are three times as high as they were twenty years earlier. When those actual dollar amounts are modified to account for inflation, students and families are spending approximately the same amount that they were paying earlier.

Costs for attending colleges and universities can be determined exclusive of capital outlays. However, it should be borne in mind that if capital outlays were added to the equation, the proportions paid by the three principal sources would be changed somewhat: students and families would be paying an even smaller proportion.

One can question whether the substantial funds provided by government to subsidize higher education were yielding valid societal goals. For example, because many students from upper-income families attend low-cost institutions, there is some inequity to the disadvantage of low-income families. As more and more children of low-income families seek to attend college, the quest for means to eliminate financial obstacles to college attendance will certainly intensify, but programs to do so should not be created if they further weaken the position of private institutions.

In 1970–1971, government contributed approximately 12 billion dollars to higher education; 60 percent of the funds came from the states, 8 percent from local government, and 30 percent from federal sources. These funds went largely to public institutions, which quite logically admitted the largest proportion of students from low-income groups. A question arises as to whether low- or high-income families are gaining benefits or being penalized by this policy. The evidence is mixed and contradictory.

If a student gives up or declines to take a job in order to attend college, he or she has assumed an additional cost over and above actual expense outlays. These costs should be added in order to compute the value of investment in a college education. At present, an annual figure of $3668 should be added to tuition, out-of-pocket expenses, and the like to compute the actual cost of college attendance.

Tuitions and fees are a significant source of income to institutions of higher education. However, this tuition income has declined from 34 percent of total educational income prior to World War II to about 30 percent today. Recently institutions have begun to increase tuition quite rapidly and are tempted to increase scholarship funds at the same time so as to continue to attract students. Currently tuition policy is in flux because development of a new basis for federal student funding would be a force drastically affecting tuition policies of public and private institutions.

Within American society services are usually provided by private or public initiative. However, in higher education services are provided by either private or public initiative with institutions operating together. In the past, the ratio between tuitions in public and private institutions remained relatively stable. In recent years private institutions have had to increase their tuitions to the point where there is danger that they could price themselves out of the market. This widening gap in tuition charges has clearly been one important factor in the decline in sharing of degree credit enrollments. The effects of high tuition have been partially offset through rapidly increasing programs of scholarships and grants-in-aid. If the federal government would assume the bulk of responsibility for providing grants-in-aid, the historic relationship between the tuitions charged by public and by private institutions could possibly be restored.

The benefits of higher education are of several sorts and accrue both to individual users and to society as a whole. Some benefits are quantifiable, but others are quite subjective. One can compute the full cost of education and then the anticipated future income to determine whether an investment in higher education is sound. But there are pitfalls of interpretation in such an analysis. Such calculations are always based on averages and conceal many variations from the average. Defending higher education on strictly economic grounds is a questionable practice, although some economic analyses are desirable. Many more subjective things should be considered in deciding whether college attendance is worthwhile.

Another issue is to determine whether the individual or society gains the greater benefit from higher education. Once again there are serious methodological difficulties, such as assigning economic values to changed societal climates or to dramatic new research for scholarly developments. Individuals at one extreme believe that because the user reaps the major return on his investment he or she should pay for it; on the other extreme are those who believe that social benefits are so substantial that the society should pay a substantial cost of higher education. A related issue concerns which generation should pay the burden for higher education. Traditionally, the older generation has paid for the education of the younger. Some argue, however, that the younger generation should be required to pay through subsequent increased taxes on earnings and so forth. However, in view of the fact that the benefits from higher education are neither all personal nor all societal but a blend of the two, a system of combined individual and governmental financing of higher education is appropriate. A sensible solution would be to ensure all people of relatively low-cost or free postsecondary education for two years, a subvention that could be used at any time in life. The higher the individual went in the educational system, the greater would be the percentage of the full cost expected of him.

While there is a tendency to think of college education as an undifferentiated whole, it clearly is not. There are significant qualitative differences among institutions. The California system is one of the clearest examples of a differentiated system in which some students go to one kind of institution and others to a completely different sort. A question then arises as to who should pay for these qualitatively different institutions. Some have argued that the California system is regressive, in effect requiring low-income families to pay through taxes for the education of children from high-income families who tend to enroll more frequently in the University of California than do children of low-income families. Others contend that children of the lowest classes are the net gainers in the California system. The Carnegie Commission generally tends to support the differentiated system exemplified by California.

The financing of graduate education differs from that of undergraduate education in a number of important respects. It is generally more costly, students are older, and federal agencies have played a key role in the direct support of students. Two distinct philosophies have operated in the financing of post-baccalaureate education, with students in such fields as law, medicine, and dentistry being expected to pay close to full price, whereas graduate students in arts and sciences have been subsidized. The subsidy for graduate students in arts and sciences that crescendoed so markedly in the 1960s is now dropping, and some fear that federal support of graduate students will disappear. Although it seems reasonable to expect advanced graduates to assume some responsibility for payment of their education, it would be a serious mistake to eliminate student support entirely. The great research universities those students attend are a vital national resource, and the support of students is one key element.

The Carnegie Commission believes that access to higher education should be expanded so that in each case there will be opportunity for every high school graduate or otherwise qualified person to pursue post-secondary studies. But this does not mean that all types of institutions in a state system should be of the low- or no-tuition sort. The commission believes that there can be some modification of tuition policy so that more advanced students are required to pay for more of their education. However, there should not be a precipitous shift in tuition policy in that direction. Because higher education is approaching a stationary state and because there is an unhealthy widening of the tuition differential between private and public institutions, the commission believes that public support should be more selective and should be targeted to help those most in need of financial aid. The commission also believes that the division of economic costs that has evolved historically should not be greatly altered but that for at least a generation the effort to provide financial assistance for the neediest section of society would occasion a slightly greater burden on the states. Once that item of social policy is accepted, several other needs derive quite directly. States with regressive tax structures are encouraged to develop more progressive tax systems in the interest of greater equity and adequacy in the financing of education and other public services. Especially, in order to provide for the neediest segments of society, the federal share of support for higher education should be gradually expanded until it reaches approximately half of governmental (state and local) contributions by 1980. Institutions should also change their tuition policies so that tuition would be comparatively low for lower-division students, somewhat higher for upper-division students, and considerably higher for graduate students. More advanced students would, of course, be eligible for loans, work-study programs, and the like. Once such policies are established, and if private institutions can restrain their tuition increases, the ratio between private and public charges should stabilize and private institutions be more viable. When funded, the basic opportunity grants authorized by the Higher Education Act of 1972 will be an important step in the desired direction. However, the amounts should be increased so that the higher-cost private institutions are not placed beyond the reach of students from low-income families. The federal government should attempt to underwrite states' scholarship programs, for example, by assuming the cost of one-fourth of state awards used to make up the difference between basic opportunity grants and the full cost of attending college, especially during the first two years. The Commission strongly believes in maintaining both public and private institutions. Thus it believes that several steps should be taken by federal and state governments to assist private institutions. The first step would, of course, be full funding of basic opportunity grants, which would aid both public and private institutions. Secondly, those grants as a proportion of total cost should be gradually increased from 50 to 75 percent. Thirdly, federal matching of state incentive grant programs would permit states to alter their tuition policies in a manner that would reverse the trend toward a steadily widening gap between public and private institutions. The states could gradually increase tuitions, especially in the upper-division and graduate institutions and at the same time augment a statewide program of student aid. This policy would also aid disadvantaged students and allow greater parity between the tuitions of public and private institutions. Assuming that private education presents some extra benefits, the commission is unwilling to urge that tuitions in public and private institutions be exactly the same. The commission is not unsympathetic with the many experiments being conducted in the states to provide some form of subsidy to private institutions. However, its preference is for grants-in-aid based upon the need of the student. That policy, coupled with some form of additional subsidy to private institutions, should allow the market for college education to operate more freely. Variations in this basic concept would be open to the various states. Thus a state that chose to maintain a low tuition level in public institutions would need to expand direct institutional aid to private colleges and universities. States that allowed public tuition to rise gradually would not need to provide substantial direct aid to public institutions but would have to increase student aid programs considerably. In addition to tuition and grants policies there is still need for substantial loan programs allowing students to repay loans over twenty- or thirty-year periods. An ideal loan program would adjust the costs of repayment to the lifetime flow of benefits and would require a distinct capital market rather than the present reliance on the existing market guaranteed by the federal government. Loan programs should be increased but should not contain forgiveness features nor periods of interest-free obligation. Interest should be charged but amortized over a longer period of time. The commission is inclined to minimize the argument advanced against loans that it penalizes women who would take a substantial indebtedness into marriage. What the commission recommends is that the federal government charter a national student loan bank to serve all eligible students regardless of need. It could be completely self-sustaining, and repayments could be handled through income tax returns.

To bring about the revisions recommended, various agencies will be required to take definite action. The federal government should fully fund existing student aid legislation, especially basic opportunity grants, and those grants could be increased gradually in the next few years. The federal government should also provide matching funds for state scholarship programs. There should also be stabilized federal support for graduate education on reasonably long-term levels including a doctoral fellowship program with selection based upon demonstrated academic ability. Federal sponsorship of research should increase proportionately to the growth in the gross national product, and the federal government should establish a national student loan bank. State governments should assume responsibility for the well-being of all higher education in the state, including the private sector. State tax systems should be revised to make them more progressive. States should provide adequate support for public institutions to maintain their quality through funding formulae. Tuition charges for the first two years of post-secondary education should not be placed beyond the means of low-income families. Student assistance funds should be provided at such a level as to enable students to attend either public or private institutions. Gradually the tuition gap between public and private institutions should be closed, and modest direct institutional aid to private colleges and universities should be created. Institutions themselves should vary tuition charges according to level of education. Tuition levels should gradually be allowed to rise to approximately one-third of educational costs. Private institutions should restrain substantial tuition rise and should also consider differential tuition according to level of education. The burden of Carnegie Commission recommendations is based on several beliefs. A larger proportion of college students will come from economically disadvantaged backgrounds and will require significant expansion of federal and state programs of student aid. Tuition charges in public institutions will rise more rapidly than in the past, and tuition charges in private institutions will follow increases in per capita disposable income. Students and parents who can afford to pay will have to shoulder a larger proportion of educational costs. Students will be expected to increase self-help as they rise in the educational system.

In this report the commission once more reveals its liberal conservatism. It wants to ensure universal access and so proposes low or no tuition for two-year institutions coupled with substantial grants to students. It recognizes the private gains from higher education and thus suggests that the higher one goes in the educational system the more one pays either now or in the future. It values the private sector and has tried to contrive a system so that private and public tuition will once more fall into a rather stable balance. It assumes that the bulk of its recommendations concerning age of students and gradual rises in public tuition will accomplish most of its purposes. However, it does accept the potential need for some direct subsidy by the states to private institutions. In effect, the Carnegie Commission holds that the balance of payment for higher education that has arisen historically is probably essentially valid, given some gradual modifications. It also says in effect that values of higher education that historically have been shared by society and the individual are still valid. Thus the thrust of its recommendations is to maintain the essence of these historical phenomena. The report reflects several weaknesses. First, it is one of the more complicated policy statements and does require a great deal of careful reading before the essentials of the recommendations become clear. Including a data base and analysis in a discussion of policy recommendations contributes to the confusion. Secondly, and more substantively, the report is vulnerable to the charge that the very gradualism it espouses could be detrimental to important segments of the private sector. The report goes further than previous documents in realistically considering problems of private institutions; but a general scheme that anticipates six or seven years to implement may not be particularly helpful to the invisible colleges or to the middle-level private universities located generally in urban areas. One can argue that unless more radical and more rapid changes are attempted, the ratio of students attending public and private institutions will slip to such levels that the private sector will find it difficult to regain lost initiative and influence.

The Purposes and the Performance of Higher Education in the United States Approaching the Year 2000

At the end of the Civil War, the United States underwent great change, and higher education changed equally radically. A century later the society is also undergoing profound changes that will have substantial effects on higher education. Higher education has moved from its elite stage to its mass stage and is now moving to the stage of universal access. New knowledge is becoming more and more central to the conduct of society. Intellectuals find themselves increasingly antagonistic to major strands in the society. The society itself is in the process of reexamining values and life styles, and students are changing as they emerge from increasingly permissive environments and are oriented toward total personal development. Now is the time to examine historic and emerging purposes of higher education and to assess how effectively they have been and can be achieved.

The first purpose is the education of the individual student and the provision of a constructive environment for developmental growth. Colleges and universities can aid the development of students by providing a general understanding of society, helping students find appropriate intellectual environments, developing in students critical minds, training students for suitable employment, and providing a varied milieu in which students of varying interests can find satisfaction. Undergraduate students expect colleges to help them in growing emotionally, getting along with people, forming systems of values and goals, obtaining a general education, increasing their earning power through training for an occupation, and attaining an outlet for creative activities. Students generally have been least satisfied with the occupational training they received. In view of student expectations, a proper question to ask is what should colleges make available by way of direct opportunities for total development of the individual. The primary direct responsibility of the college is to assist with intellectual and skill development. The campus is above all a place where students can enrich their minds by study. Thus the college cannot assume full developmental responsibility for students. No institution of higher education should assume the total domination of the individual personality. What the college or university must do is provide effective opportunities in the classroom and a generally constructive environment in which students can pursue personal development. The campus has a fundamental educational responsibility to provide general education, depth training in a special field, and professional advice and counsel and to maintain high standards of academic performance. Students should therefore be able to develop essential academic skills, career competency, skills for citizenship, and creative interests and capacities. Contemporary students have placed themselves in a paradoxical situation. They have rejected the concept of external authority but are still asking institutions to assume some of that parental role to facilitate their total development. The campus has a basic responsibility to provide good educational opportunities for its students so that they may understand society, develop academic and technical competence, and meet appropriate standards of academic conduct. The campus has a lesser responsibility to provide a campus environment that allows for emotional growth. And, generally, United States colleges and universities have successfully assumed some of their primary obligations. This sort of performance should be perfected, but in addition colleges and universities could do more to create an environment in which students can pursue their own personal development. Higher education could provide more broad learning experiences, more work and service opportunities, more attention to occupational training, and a greater mixing of age groups on campus to provide younger students with appropriate role models. A particularly vexing requirement is for colleges to provide an environment appropriate for individuals climbing their merito-cratic pyramid and for those sliding down it.

A second purpose of higher education is to advance human capability and that of society at large. Higher education is involved in this process through research; service; finding talent; aiding talent; adding to skills of individuals; advancing the level of public health through research, training, and advisory service; providing education and cultural opportunities for the public at large; and generally adding to the capacity of society to adjust to change. Higher education has long been viewed primarily as a technique for increasing economic growth. Attention must now be given to the net social product. The performance of higher education in en-hancing human capability has been relatively superior, especially in some form of research. Recent reduction of funds available for basic research is shortsighted and could blunt this good performance record. In the past, higher education has provided important serv-ices for some segments of the population but has left other seg-ments—for example, labor—unprovided for. Higher education has gradually attracted most young people of top ability, but it is only now trying to serve students of lesser talents. Federal research funds, especially for basic research, should be continued at a reasonably high level, but funds should be concentrated on highly productive centers and individuals. Service should be extended more evenly to all groups. The training of health care personnel presents a par-ticular problem and should be substantially expanded in the im-mediate future. Also, institutions should assume responsibility for providing lifelong learning opportunities for all people.

A third purpose is to ensure educational justice for the post-secondary age group. The United States was the first nation formed with a declared intent of ensuring social justice to all of its students. Achievement of this goal is a responsibility of the society as a whole, not solely that of education. Educational justice means reasonable equality of opportunity to demonstrate ability. Such a definition requires a posture of universal access to higher education such as that created by California in legislation in 1960. Assurance of universal access requires new facilities and more financial assistance. The Carnegie Commission strongly favors universal access but opposes pressures for universal attendance. To achieve this goal, however, specific attention must be given to members of minority groups and women who have in the past been discriminated against. This discrimination is especially marked in the recruitment of faculty. The commission believes that some modification in staffing policy would enhance the likelihood of minorities and women receiving positions. Traditional standards of excellence should of course be maintained. Thus the Carnegie Commission believes that members of minority groups and women should be given special consideration in hiring provided that they be competent and that their employment adds to the effectiveness of a department or college as a whole. The commission opposes quotas or lottery systems. Here the commission is consistent with its earlier view about students. Special consideration is warranted at point of entry, but preservation of quality standards must be insisted upon in actual performance. As higher education attracts more and more segments of the population previously not in attendance, several problems intrude. Universal access could be converted to universal attendance but such a policy would be shortsighted. A better system would provide many attractive alternate channels for the development of young persons. The impact of higher education on social justice becomes more important all of the time. It is a means by which individuals locate themselves among the income classes. It directs people toward various positions and statuses in the technostructure. It has been a way of providing equality of opportunity. It has been a way of facilitating both upward and downward social mobility. And it is being called upon as never before to be an instrument of justice. American higher education has about the best record in the world for providing opportunities for post-secondary education to persons throughout the population. However, it could do more by creating many diverse alternatives for the development of youth. Faculties generally do not reflect accurately the composition of the population as a whole. Higher education has contributed to a narrowing of income differences. Higher education has been an important source of greater social justice, but its task in this regard is far from complete. In the future, higher education should concern itself with the total post-secondary age group. It should improve existing channels and create new channels for entry into adulthood. Open access opportunities should be provided for most of those channels. Admission standards should be relaxed for members of disadvantaged groups, and special efforts should be made to find qualified members of minority groups and women for faculty appointment. When measures along these lines present some danger, higher education must ensure that the quest for equality of opportunity does not destroy standards. Recognition that special talents will continue to require special kinds of education is not an unhealthy elitism.

With respect to pure learning and intellectual and artistic activity, institutions of higher education are the preeminent sources of pure scholarship. Although the validity of pure scholarship can be challenged in the name of ultimate application, it has its own intrinsic purpose. Higher education has a fundamental obligation to preserve, transmit, and illuminate the wisdom of the past; to find, preserve, and analyze the records of the past; to provide an environment for research and intellectual creativity in the present; and to assure for the future the trained mind and the continuing interest so that the store of human knowledge may keep on expanding—all this beyond reference to any current practical applications. The record of American higher education is quite good with respect to pure scholarship in science and the social sciences but is less than adequate in the humanities and the creative arts. To maintain and improve this record it is important that funds be available at a reasonable level to maintain the achievements of American higher education. It is especially important that research funds be substantially increased for the social sciences, the humanities, and the creative arts.

A fifth purpose of higher education is the evaluation of society for self-renewal through individual thought and persuasion. The United States has by now largely completed the initial stages of modernization, although this process is never fully complete. Modern society still, however, has many problems to master, such as reduction of poverty and the end of racial, ethnic, and sexual discrimination. How can a system be created that will assist in continuous reform? Faculty members have an important obligation in this regard because they have the skill and the time to reflect on social conditions; but these particular attributes do not imply that professors as professors should engage in direct political action. Institutional political action should be rejected because it is inconsistent with the free pursuit of knowledge. It could tear institutions apart internally. It is generally likely to be counterproductive. Political positions are likely to be taken during moments of crisis and hence to be ill-considered; and the purpose of higher education is to make good use of truth, whereas the purpose of government is to make good use of power. Thus, in higher education, evaluation of the society should be made through thought, empirical evidence, logical argument, and persuasion by individuals and voluntary groups. Academic persons should pursue truth not power. Unfortunately, in recent times substantial numbers of college and university faculties have rejected this austere approach to criticism of society. Hopefully, those who urge more direct action will change their minds and allow higher education to resume more appropriate functions. Faculty members and students should have freedom and opportunity to engage in evaluation of society through individual thought and persuasion. Unfortunately, the public does not fully understand or accept this purpose, and some elements on the campus have in the past exploited the opportunity. Rectification might come through more public discussion of constructive possibilities of the critical function of colleges and universities and through better rules and more self-restraint on campus. Generally, the principles of academic freedom for faculty members should be preserved and extended where they do not prevail. Further, each institution of higher education should establish a policy of self-restraint against disruptive activities, improper use of campus facilities, improper political indoctrination of students, selection and proposed promotion of faculty members in accordance with their political beliefs, and commitment of the institution to the pursuit of specific external political and social changes.

As higher education reexamines its purposes as it approaches the year 2000, it must do so in the context of a changing society and fluctuating patterns of forces. In the past, higher education in the United States has been superior in the areas of pure scholarship, generally satisfactory in the area of educational advancement of students, somewhat inadequate in the area of ensuring educational justice, somewhat unsure as to how to provide an effective environment for the developmental growth of students, and decidedly unsure as to how to implement its role as critic of society. American higher education has not demonstrated a capacity for responding to pressures for reform and has operated in a golden mean position with respect to changing the society or faithfully reproducing it. In the future, higher education will demonstrate an equal or even greater willingness to reform and to help shape society.

As higher education begins reanalysis and interpretation of its purposes, lessons may be learned from history. The earliest Colonial colleges with their classical curricula and authoritarian doctrine gradually modified themselves; students took over more of the control of their own lives and the curricula embraced needed scientific and technological studies. However, colleges and universities did not give up their role in contributing to the personal development of the students, but rather achieved a bonafide interpretation of that role. Early Colonial colleges had an economic mission to produce certain kinds of professional workers. Gradually institutions have expanded to include appropriate activities in the furtherance of that mission. Colonial colleges also had a political purpose: to provide an educated electorate and an educated leadership. This concept also has been expanded. Graduate colleges and universities assumed a critical stance, and though this role has been resisted at various times, the steady progression has been toward greater academic freedom to allow still more stringent criticisms of the society. With the advent of the land grant colleges, higher education assumed a service responsibility, which also has undergone substantial mutation. Thus the history of higher education is a history of accumulating purposes, accelerating as higher education has increased in size and significance to the total life of society.

Related to those broad purposes are a number of functions of higher education, some performed by accident and some clearly related to essential purposes. Colleges and universities provide general education, specialized occupational preparation, and academic socialization as well as a campus environment reasonably conducive to personal development. Higher education has engaged in research; service; sorting of talent; training in vocational, technical, and professional skills; and cultural advancement. As a means of ensuring educational justice it has created open-access institutions, produced special programs, and facilitated national support for indigenous students. It has provided facilities, personnel, and a favorable climate for the advancement of pure scholarship and has generated a reasonably high degree of freedom within which society can be evaluated or criticized.

Any institution is frequently tempted to take on many more functions than it can effectively accommodate. Higher education is no exception, and once it assumes a function it rarely discontinues it. As institutions assume more and more functions, it becomes more and more likely that some of those functions will be inadequately performed. It is possible to conceive of societies in which many of the essential functions of higher education are handled by other institutions. In American society some of its functions seem ideally suited and should be maintained. But institutions should be careful not to drift into absorbing too many new functions. Examples of functions incompatible with the essential nature of higher education are secret research, operational activities such as governmental developmental laboratories, the running of food services, and the operation of housing facilities. Two tests should be applied to determine whether a given function should be assumed: is the activity compatible with the mores of academic life, and is the activity better done on the campus than by any other alternate agency. Thus each institution should survey the totality of the functions it performs and should move to eliminate those that violate the two criteria. Secret research should be eliminated from all campuses, and campuses should eliminate operational, custodial, and service functions not directly academic or educational. It should be obvious, however, that some functions could appropriately be assumed by some kinds of institutions and not by others. There should be diversity within institutions of substantial size and multiple functions as well as among institutions. Some functions now handled by institutions would be better handled by state agencies. Institutions should seek to avoid and eliminate noncomplementary functions, and coordinating agencies should adopt policies to facilitate clear differentiation of function among campuses. Above all, it should be cautioned that higher education should not promise too much. Some of the excessive promises of the past may well be responsible for some of the failures of higher education.

As the campuses debate purposes and functions of higher education, the significance of fundamental educational philosophy will become significant and should be understood. Generally, three principal philosophic visions have, over the years, been differentially labeled although they are substantively quite similar. The first is an almost Platonic postulant that there are eternal truths and that the quest for them should be the mission of higher education. The second or relativist view holds that truth is emergent. The last view is that schools and colleges are essentially reforming agencies constantly interacting with political and social goals to reform the society. Crossing these three philosophic positions is the continuum of individualism versus centralism; and it is out of the interaction of the three positions and the continuum of individualism versus centralism that the academic battles emerge to be fought. As a general rule the Carnegie Commission has consistently favored the individual over any form of collectivism. It has sought to contrive alternatives allowing the individual maximum freedom of choice. The overall position of the commission is that higher education should serve society by serving the cause of knowledge and should serve the cause of knowledge by protecting the freedom of its members and the essential independence of its institutions. It should protect freedom and independence by responding with consideration to the needs of society and by safeguarding its own universal values of free thought and expression.

In this document, one of the final policy statements of the Carnegie Commission on Higher Education, many early themes are restated: belief in varied but limited purposes for higher education; rejection of the idea of higher education being all things to all people; general satisfaction with the performance of American higher education and optimism that the enterprise can healthfully respond to demands of the future; pervading faith in the individual and provision for individuals to make choices from among the number of clear options; and essential philosophic electicism, which has characterized most of the work of the commission. The commission recognizes the enormous size and complexity of American higher education and is not about to propose doctrinaire solutions. It is at once expansionist and parsimonious. It calls for expanding, strengthening, and supporting some activities but believes that the number of activities in which institutions engage should be quite severely limited. The document, although generally strong, consistent, and clear, leaves at least two matters underdeveloped. The full implication of developmental psychology is given too little significance, and the section dealing with the three philosophic positions is a caricature. Rather than inventing three new philosophic positions, the commission might better have accepted and elaborated on similar trilogies that have been covered rather exhaustively in some of the available literature on higher education.

College Graduates and Jobs: Adjusting to a New Labor Market Situation

Throughout most of American history a college education has been regarded as a major route to a good job. Since the Civil War, and crescendoing after World War II, there has been a high positive relationship between the national economic and educational levels. But beginning in 1969, college graduates began to experience difficulty finding employment. Some people fear that a highly educated unemployed proletariat is in the making and that good social policy would be to curtail college enrollments. This solution does not seem wise. Even if the job situation deteriorates still further, it should be remembered that there are values other than economic values to be had from a college education. Nonetheless, institutions should not be unmindful of economic situations and should adjust programs to changing market conditions.

College graduates have been employed primarily as professorial and managerial workers, and the continued expansion of need for such people during the twentieth century has accounted for the high employment demand for male college graduates especially. The future capacity of the economy to absorb steadily increasing numbers of college graduates can be understood only by examining patterns of occupational change. During much of the first half of the twentieth century, although there was overall rise in the demand for college graduates, there were fluctuations such as percentage shifts away from the traditional professions toward newer fields in social sciences, engineering, biology, and business and commerce. Between 1950 and 1960 there were relatively high percentage increases in the employment of designers, draftsmen, engineers, teachers, and miscellaneous professional workers, whereas in the 1960s, especially in the latter part, there was a decline in the demand for such individuals. Throughout the post–World War II period the number of salaried managers increased and the number of self-employed individuals decreased. Over all, the increase in demand for college graduates in the 1950s and 1960s was probably unusual in extent and very likely will not be repeated. During most of this century, vocational demands for college educated women have come chiefly from the traditional feminine roles: teaching and nursing gave way only gradually in the 1950s and 1960s to other occupations. In the 1950s and 1960s women were in high demand. The demand extended to males with some college work but without a first college degree but did not extend quite so markedly to women having had some college work but without a college degree. Generally it is believed that the labor market conditions of the 1970s are likely to encourage enrollment in the sorts of occupational programs offered in two-year colleges, especially those programs concerned with the health fields. It also seems likely that people who drop out of two- or four-year colleges during the 1970s will be forced to accept lower-level jobs than did dropouts during the 1950s and 1960s. The full implications for individuals should be explored first through more adequate data and secondly through more effective counseling. There is always some question as to whether the utilization of college graduates rested on simple upgrading of job entry requirements or actual occupational growth. Evidence suggests that it was generally the latter. The 1950s and 1960s also were periods when college graduates were paid considerably higher salaries than individuals without degrees. There were, of course, fluctuations according to field: for example, a fairly steady growth in starting salaries for business majors and a somewhat irregular pattern for engineers. However, those increases during the 1950s and 1960s should be reviewed in a broader perspective that suggests an historical narrowing of income gap between most segments of the labor force.

Although in early 1973 there were some indications that the

unfavorable job market for college graduates of 1969 through 1972 was improving, there is little likelihood that employment opportunities for college graduates will again resemble the situation in the 1950s and 1960s. In the 1970s approxmately 9.8 million college educated persons will enter a labor force that demands about 9.6 million, a demand occasioned by employment expansion, educational upgrading, and replacement needs. This saturation of the market for college graduates has also been experienced by other developed industrial nations. In the past, this movement toward saturation has been distorted from time to time by unexpected demands for persons with specific skills or credentials such as, for example, the demand for elementary and secondary school teachers in the 1960s or the demand for engineers by the aerospace industries. It is difficult to tell whether other windfall developments will take place in the future. As the job market becomes more uncertain it is likely that the demand for a college education will lessen somewhat, and enrollment patterns in the early 1970s suggested that such a decrease was taking place. Although it is too early to predict long-range tendencies, this factor should be kept in mind in examining enrollment projections.

Teaching, at all levels, is the occupation that will be most seriously oversupplied during the 1970s. Colleges and universities should therefore counsel teacher aspirants accordingly. However, there are likely to be favorable teaching opportunities in some special fields and in special areas such as urban ghettos and rural districts. School systems might very well make use of the large numbers of available teachers to expand some of their special services such as remedial services for disadvantaged students. Such a suggestion can be countered by some evidence which suggests that remedial services improve neither academic performance nor economic well-being. Such questioning, however, overlooks the fact that schools produce other values substantial enough to warrant expanding the number and quality of special educational services. Also to be kept in mind in pondering the employment possibilities for teachers is the fact that school enrollments may very likely expand in rapidly growing suburban areas while contracting elsewhere. Projecting demands for the 1980s is an extremely hazardous undertaking because no one yet knows whether there is a profound shift taking place in

population growth. The possible decline in demand for school teachers of course affects collegiate institutions that have stressed the
preparation of teachers. Many state colleges and liberal arts colleges
that in the past have made teacher preparation their foremost business are now reducing that emphasis and seeking to diversify. There
is danger of overreaction. Institutions might better concentrate on
improving the quality of the programs offered prospective teachers.
To make a qualitative improvement in teacher education may mean
that the number of institutions engaged in teacher preparation could
be decreased somewhat, and those remaining in the field ought to
develop many specialized programs to meet changing needs. State
government can be of assistance not only in obtaining and publishing
more precise demand figures but also by considering such innovations as lowering the age of entry into public schools to four years. As
a general rule, states should not rush precipitously to increase the
prerequisite for teacher credentials to the master's degree or higher;
but where this upgrading has already taken place, there is need for
qualitative improvement of master's degree programs for future
teachers.

The most serious shortages of teacher personnel are in the
health fields. Informed opinion is unanimous that there should be
large increases in the numbers of medical doctors and dentists; the
Carnegie Commission has consistently urged that numbers be increased but made the proviso that continuous and careful assessment be made to detect any growing imbalance in the supply-demand equation. With respect to nurses some argue that the problem
is one of distribution rather than supply, but when one considers the
growing number of health subspecialties that will require nurses,
either in a subspecialty or in supervision, more rather than fewer
nurses seem in order. Nevertheless, perpetuating the current conditions is not the answer. The nursing profession and schools of nursing must reconsider the role of nurses as well as educational programs designed to prepare various health assistants. Increasingly,
the concept of the health team warrants consideration; there is a
strong likelihood that there will be rather marked differentiation of
function for the various members of the health team. Two- and
four-year junior colleges have recently expanded the number and
variety of training programs for health workers. This expansion has

produced a number of problems such as accreditation and licensing standards. Such difficulties must, of course, be overcome. Generally, states should encourage the development of training programs in nursing and allied health fields, which very likely should be based on a curriculum of basic science. The federal government should provide better information, and universities should undertake major research to suggest alternative ways of using health manpower.

During the early 1970s medical schools and law schools experienced sharp increases in applications. The question arises as to whether the production of lawyers should be increased. Some agencies that have studied the matter indicate a marked increase in demand as lawyers are used more and more in businesses and in public agencies. On the other hand, such developments as no-fault automobile insurance and simplified divorce procedures could very well diminish the demand for lawyers. Even as the question of numbers is studied, law schools are also being forced to reexamine curricula. Revision may possibly involve developing specialty curricula, providing clinical experience for lawyers, developing new master's degrees in law, and even limiting formal law training to two years. Generally, law schools would be well advised to move cautiously both with respect to numbers and with respect to the kinds of reforms undertaken.

Business administration has been one of the more rapidly expanding academic fields, paced by the expanding need for managers. In the 1950s schools of business administration undertook serious curricular reform, and schools of business administration have generally been markedly improved. The long-run outlook for graduates of business schools will be complicated but will certainly be affected by the increased complexity of organizational problems, the impact of technology on the practices of management, and the increasing interrelatedness of business with other social institutions. Thus there will likely be continued heavy demand for graduates of business schools who have developed high competence in some of the newer specialties.

Engineering is a field that has experienced highly irregular supply-demand cycles, and enrollment in engineering programs in colleges and universities is highly sensitive to shifts in the job market for engineers. When the demand for engineers increases sharply, students flock into undergraduate engineer majors. When demand drops, enrollments also drop rather quickly. Since in the early 1970s engineering enrollments have been declining; this decline may very well lead to an undersupply of engineers by the late 1970s, with the attendant increase in demand. Schools of engineering would do well to pay more attention to long-range projections rather than responding to shorter fluctuations in the supply-demand picture.

The scientific fields seem to behave as does engineering, with student enrollments following quite closely the market demand. In the early 1970s, unfavorable market conditions caused students to seek other fields. If that flight from the sciences continues, shortages could develop before the end of the decade. But this suggestion is conjectural because good manpower-needs data are not available.

In the future, professional associations and various governmental bodies should undertake more sophisticated manpower studies. Every professional school should consider ways of increasing minority group representation in the student body. Four-year and two-year institutions must cooperate to provide varied kinds of manpower, and professional schools in universities should give much greater attention than they have in the past to counseling and guidance activities, not only for their own students but for junior college students as well. In all professional fields there is need for a great deal more program flexibility, including arrangements for students to interrupt their education or to prepare for a career ladder.

The market for holders of doctoral degrees was exceptionally favorable during the 1950s and 1960s, but it is likely to be increasingly unfavorable during the 1970s. The imbalance is due partly to expanded graduate programs and partly to the reduction in research and development activities that came about in the late 1960s. The demand will deteriorate still further because of the declining need for college faculty. This situation has caused leading graduate schools to attempt to cut back graduate programs. It has also led the federal government to deemphasize support for graduate students. However, a precipitous retreat from graduate education would be a disservice to the nation. Consistent levels of support are needed so that the strongest universities can continue to produce a fairly steady flow of highly trained individuals. Here again, economic factors should not be the only ones considered. Many people could profit from obtaining a doctorate even in a field where employment possibilities are slight. It would be unfortunate if graduate schools used the occasion of decreasing demand to extend the training period for doctoral candidates. Rather, the demand problem should be met by limiting the number of institutions awarding the doctoral degree. Relatively small doctoral programs are typically deficient in quality and excessively expensive. Better social policy would be served if doctoral programs were limited to universities with high-quality programs in many disciplines. Along with this limitation on institutions granting the doctor of philosophy degree there should be an expansion of doctor of arts programs to provide better preparation for future undergraduate teachers. The doctor of arts degree can be offered by a much broader range of institutions. It would be ideal for many state colleges and universities.

Generally, there is considerable student responsiveness to changes in job opportunities but this responsiveness works within a framework of rather substantial stability in overall patterns of student tastes and abilities. College entrants fall into rather large and loosely defined pools of potential majors, and individuals do a good bit of shifting within those pools in response to changing market conditions. This phenomenon is not harmful, but colleges and universities could ease the plight of students if they were to prepare much better occupational counseling programs. There has been a rather substantial upgrading of many vocations and an increase in the requirements for many kinds of occupational credentials. In general, employers should refrain from increasing educational requirements for positions unless there is a clearly demonstrable relationship between educational requirements and performance. There has developed, too, a growing demand on the part of many young people for alternative life styles and nontraditional careers. It is difficult to indicate the magnitude of this phenomenon, but it is a reality. Some of these changed aspirations could be met if through a reordering of national priorities greater attention could be devoted to attacking the great unsolved critical problems of the society such as those of the urban environment or the seriously disabled. Also, institutions could cope with changing aspirations on the part of the young by encouraging periods of dropping out of college as well as periods of dropping out of school before attending college.

Using manpower data is important, and there is need for better occupational information. However, it would be wrong to defend or plan for higher education on the basis of manpower needs alone.

In College Graduates and Jobs *the Carnegie Commission attempts two principal tasks. It tries to describe factually the market for college graduates and to indicate those fields in which growth is likely and those fields entering a more static situation. At the same time it wants to see education to continue to expand, hence it provides a rationale for a more optimistic view of the job market than its own descriptions provide, and this posture is probably healthy because a commission with the prestige of the Carnegie Commission could cause panic if it adopted a decidedly pessimistic view.*

Of the series of recommendations, two seem to be salient but difficult to achieve. Throughout the report there are pleas for better data regarding need and utilization of manpower and pleas for more effective counseling and guidance. Each of these has proven intractable in the past. So important are they, however, that the commission might have considered separate technical reports indicating precisely how counseling and guidance could be improved and how selection and dissemination of accurate data could be enhanced. Throughout the document the commission is quite careful to separate itself from any single justification of education for manpower reasons alone, and this stance is healthy so long as such institutions as liberal arts colleges do not take the broader conception of higher education as a justification for ignoring vocational concerns.

Toward a Learning Society: Alternative Channels to Life and Work

American colleges and universities have evolved to their present stage of development through the gradual alteration of many widely held assumptions. The evolution of higher education in the last decades of the twentieth century will be affected by a number of assumptions held contrary to fact. It is assumed that colleges and universities are for young people, yet more than half the students are twenty-one years of age or older. It is assumed that higher education comes directly after high school, but more and more people seek to learn throughout their lives. It is assumed that dropouts are failures and seldom return, whereas actually many dropouts do return. Because it is assumed that higher education is for the young, it is assumed that financial assistance should be provided exclusively for the young. In reality, financial assistance should be provided throughout life. It is assumed that colleges and universities are the principal providers of opportunity beyond high school, but actually they are not even the largest part of the total system of post-secondary education. These incongruities can be resolved, and as they are the society can move toward becoming a truly learning society.

American higher education is now organized basically to serve the young full-time learner who begins his postgraduate career in the fall after graduation from high school and terminates it in the late spring four years later. This pattern has persisted for several reasons, including the availability of parental support and the fact that education at that age can be obtained without disrupting careers. However, increasingly there are large numbers of other sorts of individuals who could and would like to profit from formal education. These would include those who find traditional instruction inaccessible, inconvenient, or unappealing; those who work full time; those who need to update their training; and those who would like to follow educational activities as a leisure-time activity. These new learners represent an expanding market for educational services. However, they encounter a number of barriers. There are procedural barriers, environmental barriers, financial barriers, and institutional barriers. For example, much testing and advising is designed to use high schools and high school counselors. Many institutions regulate their campuses to fit the life style of the young. Many older people cannot afford to pay the full cost of an educational program, and institutions themselves find that new students represent a serious financial drain.

Post-secondary education, and especially the education offered by colleges and universities, has been extended rapidly during the twentieth century to many new segments of the population. Colleges and universities have demonstrated their capacity to adapt to social needs for trained manpower. College degrees have come to be symbols of social status. The incomes of college graduates have been higher, and non-collegiate post-secondary education has a rather poor public image. This fact is unfortunate because for many people college or university is not the most appropriate form of post-secondary education. About one out of every ten students in college would prefer to be doing something else. Many college students desire job preparation almost exclusively. In the future the nation's heaviest manpower needs will be for individuals who have skills unaffected by traditional college programs. Colleges and universities are preoccupied with cognition, yet many students are concerned with affection and personal growth and development. Collegiate education is offered in tightly structured blocks, whereas many people need more flexible arrangements.

Currently a new emphasis is being placed on broadly defined post-secondary education. This new emphasis derives from the needs of many new kinds of students and should result in definite planning at local, state, and national levels. Some of this attention is already being given, as in the education amendments of 1972, which paid considerable attention to vocational education, or in the creation by the College Entrance Examination Board and the Educational Testing Service of the Commission on Non-Traditional Study, which has tried to assess the broad range of educational activity. The range of programs available is indicated by the following incomplete list: colleges and universities; private trade, technical, and business schools; correspondence schools; area vocational schools; public adult schools; educational programs in business and industry; educational programs in government; educational programs in the military; educational aspects of service programs; educational activities in prisons; apprenticeship programs; museums; libraries; television and radio; civic organizations; community agencies such as Y.M.C.A.; churches; and trade and professional associations. Attempts to distinguish between the various activities have proven unfruitful and invidious. Generally the distinction between higher educational programs and other post-secondary education rests largely on whether degree credit is awarded. In addition, college and university programs tend to cluster about a theoretical point on a continuum, whereas noncollegiate programs generally cluster about an applied end of that continuum.

There is need for colleges and universities to accommodate new types of learners. The policy should be adopted that all persons after high school graduation have two years of post-secondary education placed in the bank for them, to be withdrawn at the time in their lives when it best suits them. Colleges and universities should (of course) be privileged to decide whether they will serve older and part-time students; but if they do, they should integrate part-time instruction with that offered by the regular departments of the institution. If an institution wishes to offer nondegree work, it should do so through a separate organization. If an institution embarks on part-time instruction, it should do so in fields in which it is competent and should treat qualified part-time students exactly as it treats full-time students. Fees for part-time students should be no higher per unit than for full-time students.

The needs of many students may be better met through alternative educational channels. For example, it may be that some vocational education is better provided by industry itself than by colleges and universities. In general, college- and school-based vocational education should emphasize general knowledge common to broad groups of occupations, whereas industry should concentrate on specific skills; there should be closer cooperation between educational institutions and business and industry. Similarly, collegiate institutions and the military can work more effectively for educational purposes if collegiate institutions are more flexible and if the military can indicate more specifically what sorts of programs are needed. Operating outside the orbit of formal education are the private specialty schools, of which there were approximately 5000 in 1973. These fulfill a needed social role, but they should be reviewed periodically to ensure that their educational practices are valid and that the rights of students are safeguarded. Apprenticeships in the past have served the work force well and can do so in the future. However, apprenticeships, internships, and in-service training programs should involve systematic instruction as well as work experience. Citing these examples indicates a much broader domain for post-secondary education than is generally conceived of. However, for that domain to be effectively exploited, better information about educational opportunities must be made available, and counseling and guidance services must be greatly improved. Further, much broader planning efforts should be made, especially at state levels, so that the potentialities of the many different educa-

later elected to reopen Old Westbury and decided that the college should serve primarily local needs. The new curriculum was organized around a single guiding theme—justice. Admissions policies prescribed that at least half the students be from Nassau County and that half be nonwhite. Admission was to be by lottery from categories of students, and considerable financial aid was to be provided. The earlier problems of governance were to be solved through recognition of the necessary powers for the various constituencies and through the provision of representative bodies, which could act more efficiently than the total community in making decisions. In retrospect, Old Westbury I made its major contribution by introducing students into full partnership in the academic world. Old Westbury II may make its major contribution by breaking the lockstep of education in order to serve a different population in new, more appropriate ways.

During the 1960s the University of Pennsylvania probably made greater strides than any of the nation's older universities, largely because it had further to go. Faculty personnel policy has changed as new and capable faculty are recruited to replace older, mainly Pennsylvania-trained faculty. Serious recruiting efforts have been made to upgrade the student body, and these efforts have been largely successful, attracting students from the public schools more frequently than from the private schools. Admission standards were tightened, and enrollment dropped; but while admission standards were raised, a major effort was made to increase the proportion of black students on the campus. By the 1970s student interests had shifted to social action activities. Students were given a great deal of personal freedom and freedom to organize their own group affairs. New structures were created to foster the feeling of a true university. A major effort was made to improve the quality of education of undergraduates, and their needs influenced faculty recruitment programs. The institution began to think about long-term goals and to bring about the administrative, curricular, and service acts essential to achieve those goals. Especially significant was the early movement to bring faculty and students into governing organizations and to democratize the decision-making apparatus. Thus as the University of Pennsylvania faced the onslaught of student protest it did so from an expanded and strengthened base. The first incident, involving Defense Department contracts, was quickly contained. A second incident concerned recruiters from the Dow Chemical Company, and a third concerned the expansion of the physical plant of the university into regions previously occupied by the poor. In each event the new administrative structures, the growing feeling of loyalty toward the institution, and the willingness of the central administration to innovate allowed responsiveness without destructiveness. Serious movements into the community by the university were highly significant but occurred with full community awareness and participation. As the institution looks to the 1970s there are serious financial problems to be solved, but the base established during the 1960s seems strong enough to support the institution through the next years of difficulty.

The disruptions of the late 1960s manifested at Stanford University had a particularly dispiriting effect because no university, public or private, had made a more intense effort at organized self-examination and reform. Much of the expansion, especially in research and graduate education, resulted from two policies that were to have later repercussions. The first was to permit classified research on campus and to include federal money in funds used to pay faculty salaries. At the same time, faculties were encouraged to develop relationships with the growing technological industries along the San Francisco Peninsula. In 1968, at a time when campus dissent had begun to intensify, university administration was notably weak. The institution was torn by a series of episodes that were met not flexibly but with extraordinary vacillation. Dissent focused, as it did elsewhere, on civil rights issues and on a number of incidents related to the Vietnam war. A major cause of protest was university involvement in defense research frequently being conducted at the Stanford Research Institute. Students demanded that the institute be brought under university control and that defense contracts be eliminated. Their insistence on this solution split the faculty. However, the episode was eventually brought to a close. The Reserve Officers' Training Corps was another focus of protest; violent demands were made that it be eliminated. When the Cambodia, Kent State, and Jackson State incidents took place, the Stanford reaction was intense and, for the first time, included large numbers of faculty and students. Even as these episodes were transpiring, the university undertook an improvement of its educational program. The report of the major self-study was issued under the title *Study of Education at Stanford*. Virtually all the programs came under scrutiny, and the many recomendations relatively quickly adopted into practice included eliminating requirements and changing the grading system. At the same time, the university facilitated a reorganization of student government and created a faculty senate to replace the burdensome academic council. The university also acted relatively early to increase the proportion of nonwhite students and to provide them financial support. In spite of these impressive developments, problems still persist. The judicial system is still in flux, and the university is facing serious financial constraints. Whether the reforms of the 1960s at Stanford will be adequate to the challenges of the 1970s depends on imponderables. There is a general resolve that the imponderables shall be overcome.

Antioch College in 1972 is one of the most lively and stressful experiments in higher education; it is a network of several campuses, more than a score of centers, and widespread job and foreign study linkages. The growth of the Antioch system has caused substantial unrest on the original Yellow Springs campus. Faculty and some administrators believe that the creation of off-campus centers has been too rapid, has been too haphazard, and has drained resources from Yellow Springs to outlying centers. These many centers have been created in the expectation that some will fail and some succeed and that the doctrine that each branch pay its own way is viable. Critics of such policy argue either that requiring economic self-sufficiency is at odds with social change or that in reality the Yellow Springs campus will support the branches. Democracy pervades Antioch College, where students have long had a significant voice in governance, especially in a powerful administrative council. That council worked quite satisfactorily when Antioch was simply one campus, but there is some question that it is sufficiently flexible to govern an empire. Antioch began aggressive recruitment of black students quite early and equally early encountered the wave of black nationalism. White students have been uneasy over the deployment of funds for such activities, and white professors have been equally concerned over seeming dilution of quality. The efforts to provide black students highly unusual programs and to evaluate performance by new and possibly less rigorous techniques are in sharp contrast to the press toward academic excellence that characterized the college during the 1950s and 1960s. Intergroup and intragroup conflicts rose to the surface in 1965 with the adoption of the new first-year program at Antioch, which allowed freshmen to use the Yellow Springs community in any way they saw fit as an educational resource. All requirements were abolished as were all prescribed activities except for pre- and post-freshman-year advising and evaluation sessions. Faculty debate quite naturally focused on the potential drop in standards that such a program implied. Evaluation of the Antioch system is difficult and confusing. There is reason for concern, for withdrawal rates have increased significantly on the home campus, and the number of acceptances has fallen off sharply. Several centers have run into financial difficulties because of inability to meet enrollment projections. There are problems of establishing equity among campuses on such matters as salary, financial aid, and supportive resources. There is also difficulty in defining academic credit for the enormously varied experiences that the branches provide. Basically, Antioch is seeking to do with private resources what has heretofore been the function of low-cost public education. There is serious question as to whether such an empire can be rationalized into any coherent whole.

San Francisco State College was peaceful and quiet in the early spring of 1971, just two years after it had undergone the longest strike in American college history and had acquired a television image as one of the most convulsed campuses in the country. The strike in 1968–1969 was the culmination of a series of disruptions at the college that were intensified by a polarized faculty, weak leadership, and vicious attacks on the institution by political leadership. The first act of violence in that sequence occurred in 1967 when black students invaded the offices of the campus newspaper, attacked the editors, and left the offices in shambles. Then followed months of escalating demands by black students met with vacillating administrative response. From this milieu came a student strike— eventually compounded by a faculty strike—that was finally ended in March 1969. The few gains made had ironically been in the process of development even before trouble began. The peace and quiet on the campus in 1971 may be deceptive, for few of the conditions that produced the turmoil have been alleviated. Daily faced with a pluralistic population, with youth from many of the cultural subgroups seeking to rediscover their cultural heritage, the institution was faced with the imperative to conform to those expectations but to do so within constraints imposed by a state system of institutions. The master plan of 1960 created a specific system of state colleges under an independent board of trustees and headed by a chancellor with full administrative support. An elitist mission imposed by that same master plan, muted the efforts of the institution to provide for various minority groups. Thus at a time when demands for pluralism intensified, the power of the college over its own programs was seriously diluted. No longer could decisions be made quickly in response to strident demands. This general structural defect was aggravated by changing and frequently weak presidential leadership. By the late 1960s, faculty morale was low, strong efforts were made toward student power, and demands of third world students become strident. Questions arose as to the central purpose of a university, questions especially difficult to answer for an institution existing in the shadow of a distinguished research-oriented public university and an equally distinguished research-oriented private university. As San Francisco State College enters the 1970s, a number of issues remain. There is always the danger of incipient violence. There is some question as to the viability of the concept of academic freedom; there is continued flirtation with unionization and collective bargaining, and there are problems of close scrutiny of the institution by political powers. Probably the worst problem remaining is the polarization of the faculty over the president and chancellor. The need in the present and future is for leadership, support of the state, and freedom to initiate change.

Swarthmore College has been very little altered by the waves of change that swept higher education during the 1960s. Its faculty has stood firm on various requirements, and even during the emotion-laden days of the Cambodia invasion and the tragedy at Kent State most classes continued. The college did experience some violence when black students seized the admissions office. During that incident the president died of a heart attack; that tragedy left the college chastened and subdued. Weaknesses in the educational structure began to appear as students came to question the limited choice of seminars, as the elitism of the honors program came under question, and as the college began to recruit less-qualified black students. A quite serious threat came when faculty were attracted by larger institutions offering higher salaries, lower teaching loads, and a chance to teach graduate students. A major self-study was conducted in 1966 by a commission on educational policy. The report of that commission, *Critique of a College*, put forward 165 specific recommendations, most of which were adopted verbatim. Still, like all colleges, Swarthmore has had its internal dissensions, disaffections, and general militance. Faculty and students began to distrust each other. The Quaker tradition precluding the use of force or violence eventually prevailed. The crisis of 1969 involved the Swarthmore Afro-American Student Society protest of a sensed lack of concern for black students. Initial demands that had escalated to demands for student power quickly collapsed—and the entire crisis ended— with the death of the president. His successor was able to heal most of the wounds and to engender considerable faith in the administration until it was discovered that members of the campus community had been supplying information to the Federal Bureau of Investigation. The president resigned, and a committee of students, faculty, administration, and board members began the search for new leadership. As that new leadership assumes office it will have to cope with several new conditions. Some faculty members are experimenting with newer kinds of problem courses. There has been a drastic decline in the number of graduates entering graduate school; the number of seniors graduating with honors has declined; and the enrollment of women has declined. There is a danger that the faculty will remain complacent because although the college faces problems they are not insuperable.

The University of Wisconsin, Madison, is a volatile combination of a large cosmopolitan student population, a distinguished graduate school, and a tradition of radical student activism that proved so potent as to prevent the university community from dealing effectively with the challenges of the 1960s. The University of Wisconsin is a large university substantially committed to graduate education but located in a relatively poor state. During the 1960s, however, growth was a watchword and no one foresaw the retrenchments that were to come in the 1970s. Many of the problems that affected the University of Wisconsin were due to national forces such as the Vietnam war, but increasingly there was dissatisfaction with the academic environment of the Madison campus. These feelings were intensified in the late 1960s and early 1970s, and a strike was undertaken shortly before the Cambodia–Kent State crisis on campus. At the end of the strike the student organization signed a contract with the University. The contract was a declaration of independence from subservience to faculty. The faculty is one of the key elements in the Wisconsin crisis. Despite a new governance structure, senior faculty members have been unwilling to relinquish any real power, and there has emerged bitter factionalism. For the most part, however, central administration still represents and reflects the interests of senior faculty members. There is such a high degree of decentralization of decision-making authority that needed reforms bog down when they reach the departmental infrastructure. The crises at Madision began with student protest over university cooperation with the selective service system and over job recruitment by the Dow Chemical Company. The first episode resulted in student arrests; the chancellor paid their bail. The first large-scale disruption in the fall of 1967, over job interviews by the Dow Chemical Company, resulted in student occupation of facilities, the use of police to clear the buildings with tear gas, and finally massive student protest. The faculty divided with respect to support of the administration, and the legislature demanded that the regents evaluate administrative policies of permissiveness in handling student demonstrators. The next crisis arose over thirteen black demands, supported by all white radical groups, calling for a strike. Occupancy of classroom buildings was followed by the use of police. As generally happens, the use of police expanded the student protest group; the faculty this time supported a harder line on the part of the administration, although some of the demands were subsequently met. Wisconsin experienced severe dissent following the Cambodian incursion, and the institution closed for the rest of the academic year. It was the Cambodia–Kent State crisis that brought the faculty squarely in support of student protest and somewhat in opposition to the administration. The bombing of the Army Mathematics Research Center, although apparently not connected with the protest movement on campus, nonetheless threw the movement into tactical disarray. The majority of students, many of whom were sympathetic to the radical movement, were outraged by the bombing. The faculty was both outraged and demoralized and sharply increased its opposition to radical students; the administration and regents intensified their posture. In sum, restrained handling of crises produced a hardening of the stance of the regents and the legislature; there was relatively poor communication between administration and students and younger faculty; the decision-making apparatus was too cumbersome; the sense of community among faculty declined and serious cleavages developed. Most of the university community's responses to crisis have been without great conviction. Because of this failure to respond the governor of the state consolidated higher education in the state under a single Board of Regents. The Univesrity of Wisconsin enters the 1970s without direction and in a state of substantial crisis.

In the early 1960s, Rutgers, the state university of New Jersey, seemed destined to evolve steadily toward the status of a large, full-fledged state university. Such an evolution was made possible by growing state interest and state assumption of substantial financial responsibility. Planning for Rutgers presented unusual complications related to geography. In New Brunswick there were four campuses, with other campuses located in Newark and Camden. Orchestrating those into normal university growth proved especially vexing. Then in the middle 1960s Rutgers encountered unanticipated challenges. There were undergraduate rebellion; black students' demands; and faculty reexamination of values, goals, and structures. The University responded rather unsystematically. Admissions criteria for disadvantaged students were modified and efforts made to provide remedial work for the culturally disadvantaged. A similar effort to increase the number of black faculty members brought into the open the clash between meritocratic values and grading standards and reduced somewhat the general education requirements. Many departments offered new courses. Greater freedom in personal lives was provided students and greater attention given to the out-of-class environment. While the administration accepted in principle the right of orderly dissent, it arrogated to itself the right to call police when necessary. Faculty members disputed that arrogation. Similarly, faculty members began to dispute policies regarding auxiliary services, student discipline, physical plant expansion, the Reserve Officers' Training Corps, disciplinary power, and military-related research. Student demands for power were generally accepted in form, but in substance the faculty opposed student representation in groups concerned with critical academic and personnel matters. Cross-currents produced by these disagreements came to light in the founding of a new college within the university structure. Livingstone College was to be a unique liberal arts college with special emphasis on such contemporary problems as urbanization and racism. The college was to challenge almost every element of the normal university creed. The vexations thus engendered were intensified as the legislature began to take a more direct interest in the functioning of the university and began to examine ways of dismembering the institution by 1972. Those kinds of debates were still in progress at the time this Carnegie Commission document was published.

Within two months of the opening of Federal City College in the District of Columbia, there began a series of incidents that has kept the college in almost constant turmoil. These crises of the institution are unique. The college is a unique black, urban land grant institution and is the first comprehensive public college in the nation's capital. Created by Congress, it was intended to meet critical needs not only for the sort of technical vocational education that a junior college could offer but for more advanced training in the liberal arts and professions as well. The new institution embraced simultaneously junior college education and graduate education. To be of maximum utility to the residents of the District of Columbia, the college was to operate on low tuition and through an open admissions policy. There were many more applications than there were spaces. Hence the first class to be admitted was selected through a lottery, but selection by lottery meant that an extraordinarily large range of student ability would be represented and that it would be extremely difficult to devise an appropriate curriculum. Impetus for unrest came from within the faculty and administration rather than from students and focused on decision-making powers: who should run the college, who should teach, and what should be taught. The first faculty had a majority of academically trained whites, and the eighteen blacks shared their academic values. One of the early faculty decisions was that all subsequent faculty appointments were to be Negroes. Implementing such a policy, however, proved vexing. Much use was made of part-time faculty members, and each part-time faculty member had a full vote in faculty meetings. The result was that decisions were made by a majority consisting of white radicals and black separatists. Only when an issue touched upon faculty power was there anything like unanimity: no one could be fired the first year, heads of divisions were to be elected, and administrative perquisites went to elected positions. With respect to educational issues, the cleavage between the group of radicals and black separatists and the rest of the faculty was significant; on political issues the division was generally strictly according to race. For example, blacks favored a program for Vietnam veterans aspiring to teach in inner city schools, but radical whites objected to war machine money on ideological grounds. To complicate matters, most of the faculty were relatively young and inexperienced in the ways of academe. Into this complicated structure was injected the demand for black studies, a demand approved so quickly that faculty members had little chance to prepare curricula. There came a proliferation of black studies followed by demands for administrative autonomy for a black studies program; as the program developed it became more and more radical and demanded complete autonomy from institutional restraints. It was this demand for complete separation of black studies and white studies that called into question the very philosophy of the college. Eventually the militant blacks resigned and set up a center for black education in the District of Columbia, and the institution moved into its second year. That second year witnessed the answer to the question of who should teach. The resounding answer was that blacks should teach. However, the newly appointed blacks came largely from the southern Negro colleges and reflected an academic conservatism. What should be taught, then, were traditional courses. During the second year it was still undecided who should govern. Rivalry between the races continued, and conflicts with the Congress persisted.

Student protest at Massachusetts Institute of Technology climaxed in November 1969 when several hundred students and three or four faculty members staged a march to protest the Drape Laboratory involvement in military-related research. Police were called, the march was disrupted, and one protester was arrested. The events precipitated serious discussion of how the institution had reached that point. There had been a major shift in engineering and science education. Students were required to deal with much greater complexity and abstraction. Secondly, students had changed. They were more mature but much more bitter. Thirdly, political goals were more seriously challenged than they had been in the past, and faculty and students were fiercely divided over a number of issues. The gradual reform characteristic of the institution did not keep pace, and the highly prescribed curriculum became vulnerable. Prior to the November 1969 confrontation, there were a number of debates related to the war in Vietnam and to the role of science and engineering in national public policy. There was, of course, disagreement as to what should be taught. In response to the November crisis a number of new procedures emerged, all directed at improving the quality of communication. A new faculty organization came into being to communicate more frequently with administrators. But the November episode raised other issues such as the consequences of gradual versus sudden reform; dehumanization, which leads to the use of reason without humility; and the need for new processes and modes of education and some understanding of their probable effects on administrators and students. Students are now allowed to take courses on a pass/fail basis, departments have undertaken curricular revision, and university-wide faculty groups have begun to sponsor reforms. In addition, there have been changes in the ways financial aid is awarded, and students have been added to various governing and policy committees. Even before conflict erupted, the humanization of education was in full flower, but after the confrontation rectification actually took place. Although the episode was relatively small compared with dissent on other campuses, it was of tremendous significance at that university. It suggested that something was wrong fundamentally and motivated faculty, students, and administration to return to more humane and rational discourse over the conditions of education.

The University of Toronto has traditionally looked to England for its educational ideals of elitism and espousal of high culture. Students have become dissatisfied with the narrow curriculum stressing British politics, history, and social thought, and leaving untouched third world matters as well as Canadian interests. In addition, many are critical of what they sense to be an Americanization of Canada and Canadian institutions. The president appointed a committee to examine undergraduate studies and urged sweeping reforms. The committee's report recommended the abolition of distinctions between the general and honors programs and the development of an elective system that would allow students to choose not to specialize and to finish in three or four years. Requirements were minimized, although departments were still left free to impose prerequisites for advanced courses. The committee also recommended drastic curtailment in formal teaching as well as an increase in interdisciplinary programs of study. Reactions were mixed, with university professors unwilling to become overly involved in undergraduate affairs but with students pleased to be able to take more university courses. Generally, recommendations regarding teaching were ignored, and no student force developed to pressure faculties to change. At the time these events were transpiring, the federal government shifted the entire burden for financing onto the provinces to allow each province complete control over its educational system. The University of Toronto was forced to do more careful planning in order to maximize financial support and still keep the institution moving in directions favored by its faculty. Such planning required a new governance structure and the president again set in motion a study device to produce this new structure. Students operating within the system were insistent upon and successful in gaining a larger share in the decision-making process. (Canadian students thus differ substantially from American students, who have sought to bring about changes through a power base outside the system.) The faculty was slow and somewhat reluctant to spend the time necessary to change the system of governance. When the proposals were announced, the faculty closed ranks in opposition to the concept of faculty-student parity of representation. The ingredients of a confrontation had emerged. Sit-ins brought together several different dissonant groups. When the confrontation did not produce the sorts of gains students were seeking, some of the more radical created a free university, which did not last long. It proved that university governance could not be decided within the university. There was growing sentiment that if the province was to provide 80 percent of the budget, provincial interests should be safeguarded in any new governance structure. Further, at that time the youth vote was being courted. The students were given careful attention at hearings on a new board structure. The compromise board that was finally produced broke faculty hegemony, and the Oxbridge type of elitism disappeared.

Since 1964 the name of the University of California, Berkeley, has been synonymous with crisis and change. A multitude of crises had produced months of intensive and bitter controversy, physical confrontation, thousands of arrests, many injuries, and a fatality. An intriguing question is why this happened first at Berkeley. Part of the explanation rests with a number of changes in the larger society, such as the emergence of the civil rights struggle and the opposition to war. More particularly, Berkeley has long been regarded as a center of political activity. The campus is located close to a nonuniversity population of indeterminate size and consisting of a shifting mixture of culturally alienated people. During the decade before 1964 the composition and size of the campus changed rapidly; it increased in size but fragmented in function. There was a certain jurisdictional ambiguity between the president and the chancellor with respect to the administration of the Berkeley campus. The outbreak in 1964 was the immediate result of an administrative decision to revoke, without apparent cause, privileges that students had formerly held. After the outbreak, formal authority was quickly restored. However, any protest of the magnitude of the one at Berkeley creates other issues or a climate in which dormant issues can be brought to the surface. This, indeed, is what happened and during the ensuing years central administration and faculty were constantly off balance trying to cope with student dissent on the one hand and political pressures and social demands on the other. The various constituencies on the Berkeley campus formed constantly shifting alliances depending on which issues arose, and conflict arose over such questions as the kinds of political activities to be authorized on campus, the degree of direct and official campus involvement in political activity, the degree of authority held by others than the campus administration, and the relationship between campus authority and civil authority. The physical plant, the curriculum, and the administration organization of Berkeley have not changed much. The political consequences were much more salient, the most direct effect of political backlash being the curtailment of the budget. The board of regents has intervened on the campus more directly. Faculty response to crisis has become predictable: the events from 1964 to 1970 have forced the moderate majority into frequent alliance with the Right. This alliance has produced such things as a representative assembly and the adoption of a code of conduct for faculty that includes obligations as well as rights. Immediately after the 1964 outbreak, a study of education at Berkeley set forth many recommendations. Most have not been enacted. The few that have, such as the creation of a board of educational development, an experimental college, and a department of ethnic studies, have had momentary significance but in the long pull their influence has dissipated. Despite the turmoil, Berkeley continues to be a strong university. Faculty resignations have been few, and the ranking of the graduate school has remained high. There has been no appreciable improvement in undergraduate education: the typical undergraduate still does most of his work in arts lecture courses, although he does find that requirements have been somewhat minimized, and doesn't participate very actively in departmental governance. There is still a wide array of opportunities for individual and social development. The student radical movement is splintered over many issues, the chief of which is whether to work through established forms of student government. The future of the University of California at Berkeley is fluid and unpredictable. If the institution continues to be harassed on many fronts, the results can be disastrous. On the other hand, favorable modification of just a few factors might produce an essentially healthy restoration.

At Princeton University the Cambodian invasion was met with a university-wide strike and a number of other protest actions, for the most part legitimate. The fact that the university was able to respond in a legitimate way is attributable to profound changes brought about gradually during the 1960s. Before then Princeton had combined a first-rate educational system with an antiquated social system. By 1971–1972 the university had become coeducational; there were substantial numbers of black students, black administrators, and professors; parietal rules had all been abolished; the outdated grading system had been abandoned; students were participating in university decision-making groups; and the social system had been modified substantially. When Students for a Democratic Society initiated a teach-in in opposition to the Vietnam war and staged a sit-in at the Institute for Defense Analyses, calling for its separation from the university, it was revealed that the university decision-making processes were not sufficiently responsive to strong feelings of the university community, and steps were taken to rectify that situation. A special committee on the structure of the university produced significant new governance structures. The committee on governance recommended the establishment of a council of representatives of all constituencies of the university, as well as the formation of a larger assembly of the Princeton University community. These two instruments became legitimate means for the total university to respond to crisis rather than allow a small group of radicals to determine the course of events. These instruments were severely tested by a number of episodes, the first being demands on the part of black students and Students for a Democratic Society that the university divest itself of investments in companies dealing with South Africa. Appointed study groups made recommendations; the one adopted stated that the university should not divest itself of securities on its books but should refrain in the future from investing in companies doing the bulk of their business with South Africa. The Princeton community was generally supportive of the measure. Some of the more vigorous disruptions pointed to the need for a new judicial agency, and this measure too was adopted without serious disruption. Therefore when President Nixon announced the Cambodian intervention the university was able to respond quickly, and it possessed instantly the procedures that prevented its responses from being dominated by extremist elements. The various legitimate groups met, discussed, and passed resolutions on the basis of which the university could take action. Similarly, when an SDS attempt was made to picket the Institute for Defense Analyses, university rules were imposed and respected. By the fall of 1970 things had calmed substantially on the Princeton campus, so substantially that even the presidential announcement that the university would not divest itself of the Institute for Defense Analyses caused scarcely a ripple. Factors in this orderly change were several. The president had been able to shift from a conservative posture to one of flexibility in a relatively short time. There was a solid group of moderate

students and faculty who allowed moderation to prevail. Students
had initiated pressure for change but had at no time pressed beyond
the bounds of propriety. One essential element that should not be
overlooked is that Princeton is a relatively small institution. Its
faculty can be called together on very short notice and can meet comfortably in a room holding 400 people. The faculty-student ratio
is very high, and there is a genuine sense of community on the
campus. The institution is experiencing serious financial difficulties;
there is concern about such changes as the increases in minority
group students with an attendant lowering of academic standards.
However, as compared with other institutions of similar quality, the
future of Princeton looks good.

After the occupation of University Hall at Harvard in April
1969, followed by police action and a strike, Harvard has come full
circle. Apathy, inwardness, and individualism have displaced mass
political action. If anything, Harvard student attitudes had become
more radical by 1972 than they were in 1969; therefore the critical
question is why this return to normality has occurred. There has
been, to be sure, a series of episodes attracting varying degrees of
student support. The Center for International Affairs was invaded
in the fall of 1969 but attracted no strong feeling. The October 15
peace moratorium received no special notice at Harvard though the
faculty had voted, by a narrow margin, to condemn the Vietnam
war. Students for a Democratic Society protested allegedly racist
hiring practices but individuals causing obstruction were promptly
punished. Students apprehended for illegal activities in some of
these episodes were given relatively light sentences, a fact that attracted critical comment from the president. The most spectacular
event of the 1969–1970 academic year involved relatively few Harvard students and alienated the majority because the activities consisted of willful and unfocused destruction of property. Early in the
fall of 1970 there was a small blast in the library of the Center for
International Affairs that apparently was caused by a radical group
including militants for women's rights, but this episode did not
escalate. Some radicals challenged the Harvard Admissions Office
on grounds that it was selectively excluding potentially militant students; this charge was effectively denied by presenting data to show
that there was little shift in the makeup of succeeding freshman

classes. The same pattern prevailed during the academic year 1971–1972. There was a new president who surrounded himself with experienced administrators, and this group seemed likely to be able to maintain stability. Their ability to do so was tested in several incidents, one of which was the fairly steady protest about and harassment of Professor Richard Herrnstein who had written on the possible genetic basis for intelligence. The second issue involved changes in the basis for financial support of graduate students. The third concerned university investment in a large bloc of Gulf Oil shares. These issues were never linked, and though each protest was vigorous, activities generally did not escalate. Black students did occupy Massachusetts Hall over the Gulf Oil controversy but eventually vacated the building; the university punished the leaders but suspended most punishments. The most militant of Harvard students had apparently turned away from tactics of confrontation and violence, even with respect to the volatile Vietnam issue. The question is why those potentially divisive episodes have not produced another 1969. Apparently, Harvard students are even more radical in their attitudes than were the students of 1969, and generally Harvard students are little different in the 1970s from those in the late 1960s. One major reason is that each of the episodes existed almost in a vacuum and was not linked to the other issues. In sharp contrast, the April 1969 controversy linked a cluster of issues. Among them were abolition of the Reserve Officers' Training Corps, rent rollbacks, housing for workers displaced by university expansion, a black studies program, and amnesty for the protestors. The radical community at Harvard has been split, and the ensuing factionalism has prevented mobilization of students. Administrative responses have been less harsh. The sentiments of the faculty have shifted considerably, in part because apathy has replaced involvement. Faculty meetings have actually been canceled for lack of business. More important, however, the faculty saw in the attack on Richard Herrnstein an attack on academic freedom and hence an attack on the total faculty. Previously the faculty had supported the goals of student dissenters but not their tactics. The Herrnstein controversy exposed important differences in goals, thus diminishing faculty support for student demands. Harvard students in 1969 were relatively satisfied with their education, and in 1972 they were similarly satisfied. Over all, then, it would appear that there is little chance for another spring at Harvard like the spring of 1969. The Left has splintered, and administrators have begun to respond politically to political demands of students. Hence the blunders of three years earlier are rarely repeated. One may therefore expect a continued high level of political activity at Harvard because of students' frus-trations, but one may also expect that demands will be met with negotiation and strategic compromise rather than confrontation.

This document is an important series of vignettes of college campuses during the late 1960s and early 1970s. For the most part the writers are acute observers and have been able to reduce highly complicated events to reasonable generalizations. It is agreed that considerable quiet has descended on university campuses, although observers on a few campuses are not prepared to say that protest and violent dissent are indeed gone. Though each reader of these vignettes will of course make his own generalizations, several are drawn so frequently as to deserve comment. The presence of increasing numbers of black and minority students stands as the greatest unresolved issue. The role of black students in the various protests indicates that large critical masses of students, many underprepared, pose problems which may yet strain the viability of American institutions. The second strain that runs through these vignettes is the observation that when central administration began to bring about reforms of governance and of regulating students' private lives early enough, it was possible to create instrumentalities and institutional loyalties that facilitate coping with even the most grievous of events. Those campuses where this steady evolution of reform was not present experienced the most violent disruption, the most extreme polarization of the campus community, and the poorest prognosis for complete recovery. Thirdly, the role of the faculty emerged as paradoxical. Faculty members were reluctant to concern themselves with reform in the early years of student dissent. They later began to create new and effective instrumentalities but by 1972 seemed generally to be in retreat from active involvement. The instrumentalities remain and can conceivably be utilized should protest again intensify. But the faculty barons are retreating to their feudal estates.

Several weaknesses should be noted because they do narrow

the breadth of this series of profiles. The first weakness is the highly selective sample of institutions included. Less widely known institutions have experienced equal if not more intense dissent and confrontation. It may be that parallels exist between events at Stanford, Berkeley, Harvard, the University of Wisconsin, Wesleyan, and Swarthmore on the one hand and Virginia Polytechnic Institute, Kent State, Long Beach State, Notre Dame, and Virginia State on the other, but it is conceivable that different dynamics were at work. The second weakness is that the essays reflect no consistent theoretical framework or consistent format for describing events. The variety of style makes for engaging reading but also makes it more difficult to draw conclusions from the rich data the profiles contain.

IV

Organization and
Governance

People who have lived or worked in American colleges and universities have sensed that even relatively small institutions were highly complex organizations. The nature and extent of this complexity is delineated in the works of the Carnegie Commission that follow. Though the university as an organization possesses some attributes shared by other complex bureaucracies (executive officers, hierarchical alignment of positions, and policy-forming groups), in major respects it is sufficiently different. It has no clear-cut purpose comparable to the balance sheet in a profit-making organization. Its spokesmen claim that it seeks three or possibly four major purposes, one of which is frequently antithetical to another—for example, research versus teaching. This paradox provides support for labeling a collegiate institution an organized anarchy incapable of being directed by even the strongest of presidents. Indeed, presidents are capable academics who achieve high administrative office relatively

210

early in their careers and who devote their remaining tenure struggling in an ambiguous situation to achieve some measure of success at activities for which there are no satisfactory criteria of success. The very complexity of larger institutions in particular, coupled with the ambiguous role of the chief executive officer, makes educational decision-making almost impossible. Some individuals are convinced that with existing forms of governance the limits of collegiality have been reached and large-scale institutions are nearly ungovernable. This difficulty is particularly pronounced when institutions seek to deal with state governments. Because there is no one legitimate voice for even a single public institution, legislators and fiscal officers do not know whose authority to accept. This syndrome has contributed in the minds of legislators to the desirability of a state-wide coordinating or controlling board.

The documents offered under the heading of "Organization and Governance" make one of the truly unique contributions of the entire effort of the Carnegie Commission. Much of the exhortative literature about higher education pleads for adapting theoretical information from other fields, such as business or organizational theory. Several of these works demonstrate for the first time how that application might be made.

The University as an Organization

James A. Perkins, editor

Although universities are usually described in simple terms, they are in fact among the most complex structures in modern society, in part because of their conflicting missions. The university assumed approximately its present form during the twelfth and thirteenth centuries as a location for convenient interaction of master and student. It was early recognized that this interaction required a degree of freedom to enable thorough examination of orthodoxies. Custodians of this freedom were variously students, professors, or, ultimately, boards of trustees. As enrollments increased, universities became established as physical fixtures complete with properties, endowments, and the like; the growth of administration paralleled the growth of faculty organization as curricula proliferated. Thus governing authority, faculty, and administration all appeared in the earliest universities in primitive form. Medieval universities gradually developed residence facilities as the need for close connections between teacher and student came to be realized. This relatively simple organization, devoted primarily to teaching, became more complicated as the university assumed a new mission of research. Prior to the nineteenth century the primary rationale for scholarship or research was its impact on teaching. Gradually, however, scholarly attention turned from the transmission of truths to a search for new knowledge, so that by the end of the nineteenth century it had become clear that research was an end in itself. By the late twentieth century, teaching and research have emerged as separate missions with distinctive styles and different and often contradictory organizational requirements. The ascendance of research has clearly produced a different view of undergraduate and graduate instruction, with research professors preferring to work with more mature students on research projects and research techniques. Further, the ascendance of research brought about different relationships between members of the faculty, for presumably the scholar is not dependent on the judgment of his institutional peers but rather on that of other scholars around the world working along similar lines. This independence clearly has undermined departmental meetings and faculty assemblies as methods of conducting academic business. Then, too, as research expanded, significant new organizational requirements emerged, such as specialized libraries or laboratories; this expansion obviously resulted in growth in organizational complexity. Eventually, of course, research demands transcended institutional conditions. Hence, an increase in new structures outside the university paralleled the growth in complexity of organizations on campus. These new structures were, of course, outside the pale of departmental or institutional control, and thus further weakened the autonomy of departments and individual institutions. Thus universities must cope with decisions on research programs made elsewhere but must cope without appropriate organizational devices to do so. The creation of multi-campus universities was an attempt to find such a device, but their functioning is still relatively primitive. To these two functions, teaching and research, has been added the mission of service to society. The traditional university structure devised for instruction is largely irrelevant to research and is almost antithetical to serving the needs of society. Early expressions of this mission were the agricultural programs of land grant institutions, but by the late twentieth century pressures mounted for universities to perform many more complex and devisive public services. Public service requires institution-wide commitment, yet institutions cannot offer this commitment because research activities transcend university boundaries. Another complexity is that the rendering of public service implies the right of the recipient to judge its effectiveness, but this implication runs counter to the concept of the university as an autonomous institution. Generally the public has grown to the point of allowing freedom for teaching and research; but with respect to public service, measurable, practical results are expected. The degree to which university performance is measured by nonuniversity institutions is the degree to which university autonomy has been compromised. As though three were not enough to break the organizational back of a university, a fourth function has emerged, the achievement of an ideal democratic community within the institution. This mission derives from the notion that the policies of universities should conform to the social aspirations of its members. As this new mission has expanded, drastic changes have been required for its overall functioning and organic structure. The concept of an ideal democratic community runs counter to a number of traditional concepts of university organization; among them are faculty independence guaranteed by academic freedom and appointment of a chief executive by an individual not elected by the local community. Instrumentalities of an ideal democratic community thus cut across traditional organizational forms created to handle the other three major functions.

Further understanding of the organizational complexities of the modern university may be facilitated by examining the emergence of the corporate form of universities, the changes in the nature of the presidency, and twentieth-century expansion of higher education and efforts to consolidate its new organizational structures. The modern concept of an educational corporation derives directly from efforts of the medieval church to insure cohesion and freedom of its various appendages. The central idea was that each cathedral chapter, collegiate church, religious fraternity, or university constituted a free corporation. This concept of a corporation meant ultimately the end of the guild system and the emergence of a form of academic governance still in existence. The concept was strengthened in England during the fifteenth and sixteenth centuries by being an effective legal means by which the King and later Parliament could delegate authority in an orderly way for designated activities. Ways were established by which freedoms of corporations could be maintained yet still allow some degree of supervision and visitation by representatives of the state. This English model was evident in the founding of Colonial colleges and clearly revealed in the language of founding charters that conferred corporate powers. However, in the Colonies, corporate powers were conferred on an independent board rather than on a faculty. The idea of a lay board of control was originated in Italy, adopted by Calvinists in Geneva, and ultimately applied by Scottish universities. Its first American expression was the legislative charter given to a board of trustees, partners, or undertakers. English patterns implied that whosoever granted the charter could withdraw it. However, a Colonial modification based on a philosophy of natural law held that charters were issued in perpetuity. This concept was given its clearest juridical definition in the Dartmouth College case that held that a charter was binding on the state as well as on the trustees. Although in theory the concept of corporate autonomy lodged in an independent board of trustees still exists, in practice the powers of boards of trustees have been steadily modified and eroded. Throughout the nineteenth century, faculties expanded their influence over academic affairs, and alumni also began to express influence. Of special significance was the unique role the presidents of institutions came to have, often conferred explicitly by boards of trustees but still eroding the power assigned boards by corporate charters. The office of president emerged as the central force that gave United States higher education a distinctive character. Also during the nineteenth century American institutions shifted from a programmatic emphasis on discipline and piety to an emphasis on utility. This shift produced specialized departments and professional schools as basic units for academic affairs. It also made collegiate education more popular and thus led to enrollment expansion, which in turn required new organizational structures. Presidents found they had to diversify their offices and employ associates who could take charge of such things as student discipline or raising of funds. The presidency proliferated its bureaucracy in the United States but not in other western nations largely because of the unique managerial responsibility of presidents to their boards of trustees. The nineteenth century elaborated a number of instruments invented earlier that in the twentieth century came to be strained by radical expansion of institutional size. There has been proliferation of managerial services and creation of hundreds of new administrative academic subspecialties with autonomy concentrated in departments. Departmental autonomy, while a logical outgrowth of size and specialization, served to challenge the authority of presidents. Boards of trustees, still legally in power, were removed farther and farther away from the locale of actual administrative decisions. At the same time, individual faculty members moved into academic governance, reducing both presidents' and trustees' authority. These developments were further complicated as students sought a voice in governance and as alumni groups attempted to expand the bridgehead of their own influence. These changing organizational structures have come in time, and American universities have proven themselves to be effective organizational devices, but there exists a sense of uncertainty as to how well universities are likely to fare in the future. At least three pervasive organizational inadequacies are perceivable—the first attributed to size and complexity, the second to specialization and departmentalization, and the third to the shifting pattern of institutional government. American higher education is so diverse as to make classification extremely difficult. There are public and private institutions subdivided according to level of government or kind of private sponsorship. These can be further subdivided according to type of student served and type of instructional program offered. Cutting across these categories are other differences such as quality of instruction, level of financial support, and number of campuses in a basic academic unit. The United States Office of Education classifies according to control, program offering, and type of student body served. The Carnegie Commission on Higher Education has developed a classification scheme of seventeen elements, and a financial study supported by the Carnegie Commission employed six categories. Each of these systems is partial, and there has been developed no generally appropriate classification scheme. The majority of public institutions are state sponsored, and the majority of private institutions are denominationally sponsored. These institutions are widely distributed through the fifty states, with California having the largest number of public institutions (113) and Alaska and Hawaii having one each. Even more critical than the geographic location of institutions is the extent to which differences in type result in differences in operation. In terms of mission the most important distinction is that of degree program offered to students; there is considerable question as to whether academic or career objectives should predominate. One point of view favors knowledge for its own sake, and another holds instrumentally that institutions should prepare people for vocations. This conflict is seen in liberal arts colleges when faculties debate institutional missions and in universities when the kind and amount of research to be undertaken are discussed. The conflict is further expressed in two-year colleges as faculties divide over whether college parallel or technical vocational education should be stressed. There is substantial diversity in the financial support available to institutions of higher education, with the essential distinction being between those having public and private sponsorship. The difference in source of instructional income is reflected in charges made to students but is not reflected in any presumed dichotomy between affluent public institutions and poor private ones. Financial support for research derives from different sources and results in still further confusion with respect to classification of institutions. The federal government and private philanthropy have been the primary suppliers of research funds. Public service activities have more frequently characterized public universities than private, and various levels of government have provided the necessary financial support. Both public and private institutions have assumed that many of the services provided students should be self-supporting. However, both public and private institutions have involved themselves heavily in providing some measure of financial aid to students. This diversity in American higher education is also reflected in structures of governance, wth the most important difference being the modes of selection of members of boards of trustees. Boards of public colleges are usually appointed, whereas boards of private colleges may be selected by the board itself, appointed by a constituency, or elected by various constitutencies. In theory, boards of both public and private institutions have similar authority. However, the board of trustees of a public institution is related to the locus of political power. Private boards are similarly limited by the social setting in which they operate. Thus in public institutions the crucial issue is the relationship of the board of trustees to the political process, whereas for private institutions the crucial issue is the relationship of the board of trustees to an external social process. Private institutions do have greater freedom to do such things as limit size or conduct educational experimentation. A last dimension is that of communication and consensus; once again institutions differ widely with respect to this matter. Both size and quality seemingly affect feelings of community and consensus but in frequently different and asymmetrical ways. Thus one would presume that a highly selective institution would have a greater feeling of community, yet dissent and disruption have more frequently appeared on those kinds of campuses.

Universities are communities in which to varying degrees there are shared sentiments and values, reciprocal roles, and acceptance of a system of authority. One way to test the existence of a community is to find out the degree of acceptance of shared sentiment and cherished values. These should be expressed in statements of purpose and goals. For a time on American campuses there was considerable agreement. As conflicting missions emerged, that agreement became diluted. On many campuses there is now a clear dichotomy of interest between administration and faculty that has virtually destroyed the traditional sense of community. That split is complicated by splits between younger and older faculty or between faculty, students, and administration. Such splits are exacerbated as society increasingly views the university as a certification mechanism. These cleavages are expressed in substantial differences of attitude toward other values, an important one of which is the right of a scholar to inquire freely into matters that interest him. Recently various groups on campus have assailed this right when it was exercised in reviewing socially controversial materials. Another value traditionally has been the concept of the professor as master of his classroom. Students began to contend they had rights of determination as to what went on in classrooms. Still another value based on tradition was that of loyalty to the institution, a value that has been assailed as professors, administrators, and even students place higher loyalty to external institutions or value configurations. The research-oriented professor, more attuned to his discipline than to his institution, is exemplary. As these values are challenged there emerges increasing disagreement about the character of an institution that effects such things as admissions policies or the relative importance of teaching, research, and service on campus. On many campuses there does not exist common agreement about goals and purposes nor about emphases of daily operations. In addition to common values, a community implies a set of statuses or positions. The idea of a community of scholars carries with it the notion of collegiality marked by a sense of mutual respect for the opinions of others, by agreement about the canons of good scholarship, and by a willingness to be judged by one's peers. But those ideals that once could be accommodated by a ranked faculty are jeopardized by increasing specialization and inequitable levels of support for different specialties. Thus humanists may so resent support given to scientists as to lose feelings of respect for scientific colleagues. At one time there seemed to be general agreement as to the role of professor and the role of student; but increasingly students develop expectations that may differ from those of their professors. This clouding of roles is intensified as colleges recruit students from more varied segments of society. It is also clouded as students demand the right to evaluate a professor's performance, whereas formerly only professorial peers evaluated each other. Nor have the roles of faculty and administration remained constant. As the educational bureaucracy expanded, a separation of interest between administrators and faculty was bound to develop, with neither group accepting clearly understood roles for the other. In a sense the university community consists of three networks: faculty, administration, and students. Decreasing understanding on the part of any one network of appropriate roles for those in other groupings is compounded by the tendency for alliances between networks to shift. This confusion of role has occasioned the challenge to accepted systems of authority that is essential for a community. Authority needs legitimacy if it is to be accepted by the community, and traditionally that legitimacy has existed on college campuses. However, legitimacy has recently been challenged by various groups on campus that seek to restructure the authority system. Various attempts have been made to approximate the traditional model of campus government. As various new groups have arisen on campuses to challenge legitimacy, such new models as that of conflict have arisen. The weakening of these three elements of community has been furthered by two additional facts. One is the relationship of the campus to the surrounding local community, and the other is the attendant confusion of academic governance with problems of larger political governance.

Understanding of the governance of American institutions of higher education may be deepened by comparing it with the governance of selected foreign institutions. The University of Paris exemplifies the Napoleonic university grafted onto the medieval guild of masters. The University of Freiburg is research-dominated along the lines of the University of Berlin. Cambridge follows the model developed at Oxford, and The University of Toronto represents a combination of formative influences. These four institutions have traditionally emphasized research, and all are currently large. The governance of the University of Cambridge embraced several traditions. It is composed of houses or colleges that traditionally ruled the university. Those colleges resembled a guild in the sense of being societies of masters and scholars, each having a voice in governance. The University of Toronto was born out of religious dissent; the government drew several denominational colleges together and secularized them. It was hoped that the University of Toronto might reconcile differences between denominational institutions by assuming degree-conferring powers similar to those exercised by the University of London. And, in point of fact, the University of Toronto does dictate curricular offerings of the constituent colleges. Thus the colleges figure only slightly in the power structure of the university and serve primarily as communities. The university itself has a two-tier system of governance with a lay board and a senate composed largely of academics and with the president serving as a link between them. That two-tiered system was changed in 1971 in favor of a single governing board. At one time the federal government of Canada provided considerable resources for universities, but recently provincial governments have assumed responsibility. Earlier the University of Toronto was the most powerful of very few institutions in the province, but it now faces competition of many others; this development has necessitated the imposition of suprainstitutional control over the university. The University of Paris, the oldest of the exemplary universities, has undergone such profound transformation that it no longer exists as a single university. In 1968 it was dismantled, and the 5 original faculties were broken down into about 200 units comparable to American departments. A common framework continues to govern, but the new structure also reflects a substantial break with the past. Separate disciplines are presumed adequate to set their own directions. The university is no longer elite. The Ministry of National Education no longer has the right to determine curricula and degrees, and universities were given great flexibility in determining course offerings. The University of Freiburg, though one of the oldest in Germany, does not occupy a position in the nation comparable to Cambridge, Paris, or Toronto. Since the beginning of the nineteenth century it has been research-oriented, with full professors enjoying enormous power and freedom. The expansion of university enrollments that began in the late 1950s put pressure on that system and produced an expansion in the number of assistants, who then began to assume responsibility for most teaching. The university was financed mainly by the *Land* (state or province) government; more recently the federal government has assumed powers for developing guidelines for university expansion and has attempted to initiate educational reforms. Although these four institutions are different and stem from different traditions, they are developing along similar lines. General administration has been strengthened, and the central administrative bureaucracies have grown. Senior teaching staff have generally lost power, both to administration and to middle- and junior-level staff. Senior professors are losing ground even with respect to their most cherished tasks, the personal supervision of advanced students and the pursuance of research. Increasingly, all four institutions have made greater provisions for student participation in university governance, but the actual changes have been more widely publicized than real. As all four institutions have increased in size, complexity, and expense, new suprainstitutional systems have come into existence to regularize higher education, which is now being offered to larger and larger segments of the population.

Another way to understand university governance is to compare it with other complex institutions. One of these is the corporation; there are both similarities and differences between universities and corporations. The business corporation has a clearly defined common interest group with ultimate power possessed by the shareholders. It produces clearly understood results and resolves dissent in authority by elimination of dissenting voices through purchase of dissenting shareholders' interests. Thus the corporation for profit is always an authoritarian structure. The university has no single homogeneous constituency such as shareholders. It is responsible in different ways to students, faculty, legislators, or a sponsoring church. Authority is often fragmented and the board of trustees handicapped in exerting strong leadership. The board of trustees does not possess complete authority over the academic structure and cannot therefore delegate complete authority to a university president. Further, the university does not engage in a unified activity to produce a perceivable product. The sort of authoritarian control that characterizes corporations is therefore effectively precluded. Corporations possess a well understood criterion of success, dollar profits. The university has no such single criterion. Corporations can generally evaluate individual performance, but university professors engage in so many different activities that evaluation of total performance is virtually impossible. Corporation research can be judged by the profit criterion, a technique unavailable to universities, which engage in research for different reasons. However, universities could do more than they have done in utilizing the cost accounting procedures of corporations. Within corporations there is a well understood training program by which individuals advance to the highest administrative ranks. Universities rarely select their presidents from among those who have advanced step by step in the administrative hierarchy. Generally, within corporations, presidents are selected from subordinate officers in the corporation, whereas universities generally select their leaders from other institutions. Corporations generally do not accord permanent tenure to individuals, whereas universities do; hence corporations have greater power to control the activity of people employed by them. Corporations build buildings which are functional and cost-justified, whereas universities will frequently build a physical plant for such nonfunctional purposes as to satisfy the desires of a donor or the desires of a president to be remembered as a builder of a campus. Universities have frequently found themselves with more physical space than they needed or with the wrong kinds of space. Generally, corporations are able to compute economies of scale and regulate growth accordingly. This device is simply unavailable to universities, which must operate under different financial constraints. Although corporations and universities differ substantially, a number of techniques used by corporations could be modified successfully for university activities. Most of these concern the management area and are not applicable to actual teaching and research.

The university may be compared with a government bureau. Once again there are similarities but great differences. Both form and supervise budgets; both must deal with personnel; both must worry about organizational design and management of space; both are concerned with leadership and with external trends. Universities and government bureaus are multidivisional organizations and have both superordinate and subordinate structures. Both must deal with external clienteles that shape purposes, procedures, and structures. Thus in many respects an individual can move from a governmental bureau to a university without modifying appreciably his style of operations. The size of the organization is more important than any basic difference between a university and a bureau. In addition to the structural similarity, universities and government bureaus possess contextual similarities. A context of moral implications and self-righteous passions constrains both governmental and academic institutions. Both suffer the ebb and flow of financial largesse; both have recently faced the context of changing view about the legitimacy of authority; and both have had to learn to deal with independent scientific and professional personnel who dislike hierarchical governmental arrangements. But there are important differences as well as similarities. Most government bureaus live with dynamic tension caused by executive/legislative competition. They conduct their business within the constitutional context of federalism and overlapping powers. They conduct their business in the glare of publicity and are tremendously influenced by the impact of elections. Governmental bureaus, by definition, have the ultimate sanction of force, and they must deal with an almost infinite variety of goals. Universities are staffed by people more responsible and loyal to themselves than to the hierarchy. They generally operate with a flat organizational pyramid; individuals at the lowest level have rather quick access to the apex of the pyramid. Power is generally decentralized, and solution of conflicts is arrived at through mediation and slow achievement of consensus. In substantial areas of collegiate activity, individuals are effectively immune to accepted standards of accountability. The clientele of universities (youth) is unique, and the institutional product (the production and transmission of knowledge) is also unique. These two give the university a distinct flavor. In spite of these differences, distinctions between government bureaus and universities may be disappearing with real power in both lodged not at the apex but someplace in the middle of the organizational pyramid. Increasingly both government and universities must deal with highly trained personnel who expect treatment similar to that of professionals regardless of the organization. Increasingly also, government bureaus and universities are inseparably involved in certain areas of activity, such as research. Most importantly, both government bureaus and universities now face the public conviction that what they do is not worth the cost.

The university may also be compared with the large foundation. There are some apparent similarities, such as common concern with research, dissemination, and application of knowledge and with the development of skilled personnel. Large numbers of people who work in foundations come from universities and have attempted to employ the idiom of academic life in foundation life. They have frequently sought a collegial style of operation, and they have tended to organize themselves along disciplinary subject matter lines. With respect to decision-making, foundations differ somewhat from universities; there is an axiom that in a foundation anyone can say "No" but it takes everyone to say "Yes." However, boards of foundations behave frequently as do the boards of universities, relying on the professional recommendations of the staffs to decide on proposals and indeed to set overall policy. Increasingly there has been interaction between foundations and universities; support for individual professor-entrepreneurs rather than support for institutions has been of particular significance. Generally, foundations have used universities to serve national needs and international policy and have tended not to support institutions as institutions. They may have distorted to some degree university mission and university deployment of resources in pursuit of their own concerns. Foundation structure has been affected by close relationships with universities; for example, there is often a weakening of actual foundation control of overseas projects when they are staffed by university personnel having their own professional aspirations. At the administrative level, once again, there are differences and similarities betwen universities and foundations. Presidents of both tend frequently to speak in the name of the total organization. However, a university president must be responsive to much more complex constituencies. Presidents of both have the opportunity to implant their own ideas in the organization, but once again the university president probably operates with more constraints than does the president of a foundation. In general, boards of trustees of foundations may seek a more activist role in determining the nature of foundation activity. University trustees tend to allow the institution to evolve as long as things are going well. University trustees have very definite constituencies to which they are responsible, whereas the trustees of large foundations have only clients. As a matter of fact, in many respects the true constituents of a foundation are their trustees. By and large, the popular view of close resemblance between the structures of foundations and universities is confirmed. There is a similar collegial process within each moving toward a consensus and a comparable influence on each by a board of governors.

The organizational charts of universities and other institutions demonstrate marked similarities, but there are differences as well. All formal institutions have some form of guiding charter. However, the univerity charter states purposes so vacuously as to provide little guidance to members of the organization. This vagueness exists because of the many approaches to the discovery and transmission of knowledge and because of the varied concerns of the several factions that make up a university. Most other organizations can make reasonable plans for a logical evolution, a level of planning virtually impossible for universities because of the vagaries inherent in the nature of teaching and research activities. All organizations select personnel according to the kinds of activities the organization undertakes. These personnel then help shape the organization and its modes of functioning. This procss is complicated in universities by the several differing and frequently conflicting activities, such as teaching and research, and by certain intractabilities inherent in guarantees of academic freedom. The significance of professorial freedom insured through the doctrine of academic freedom and through the high degree of specialization that characterizes professorial work is reflected in the governing structures of institutions of higher education. The lay board exists to represent the concerns of society and to insure professorial freedom. Below that is a dual structure: one element is the academic concern with the substantive contribution of the institution and the other is the administrative concern with supporting services and business affairs. Both of these elements portray a relatively flat organizational profile indicating the considerable independence accorded individual scholars. The processes of academic decision-making are highly diffused. Colleges and universities possess the unique character that derives from their purposes and activities. Academic life is generally satisfying, in part because of social approbation assigned such activities as shaping the values of an oncoming generation. However, some of that satisfaction may be diluted as institutions take on the character of public utilities and lose some of their autonomy. As yet that tendency has not proceeded far enough to destroy the concept of an institution as a total community, loosely structured but cohesive. Within this community several categories of individuals pursue their activities and derive varying degrees of satisfaction. Trustees are attracted to their posts by social status, a desire to contribute to the public good, or an emotional attachment as an alumnus. Academic administrators derive satisfaction both from scholarly discipline and the power and influence of the administrative position. Faculty members, especially in prestige institutions, gain their satisfaction from academic discipline. Students gain satisfaction from the academic community. Although faculty loyalties are chiefly to disciplines and student loyalties are varied, the two groups claim a greater part in governing institutions than do their counterparts in other institutions, but neither the training of scholars nor the limited experience of students fits them particularly to succeed in dealing with specialized administrative problems. Thus academic administration and governance are often quite amateur; were it not for the bonds of shared values, the college or university as an organization might fall apart without the tighter structure afforded by trained administrators. A major current threat to the structural integrity of institutions is the decline of shared values on collegiate campuses because of increased size and complexity and increasingly heterogeneous student bodies. The current struggle for new organizational forms is an attempt to compensate for this loss of shared values. Prestructuring, when it does occur, will probably include five elements: recognition of the relative independence of subunits, establishment of processes to facilitate consensus, representation of all elements of the campus community, strengthening of the authority of the president, and establishment of a system of accountability.

The structure and autonomy of collegiate institutions are being significantly modified by a steady proliferation of laws reshaping the university by creating new roles, new organizational designs and relationships, and new concerns; the sources of this enlarged law are court decisions, administrative rules and regulations, and legislation. The law articulates power and structural relationships, defines legal status of institutions, describes the range of permissible activities, and affects the nature of authority exerted on campus. Legal activities are equally concerned with social and individual interest; for example courts have ruled that a college education is a necessity, and legislation has been enacted to specify the kind of education to be provided those whom the state will credential. The legal power of an institution is almost always vested in a governing body that alone is legally responsible for final institutional decisions. But this total authority is expressed differently in different states. In some the powers of governing boards are listed in the state constitution, whereas in others the legislature confers the powers of boards of trustees; private institutions derive their authority from a corporate charter that confers virtual perpetual autonomy. However, none of these types operates independently of other law-making activities. States are the most significant sources of laws impinging on institutions, but federal law is fast becoming as influential.

The increase in legal attention given higher education is due to rising costs, growing enrollments, and changing social expectations. Recent laws have conferred powers over institutions to existing state agencies and have created new agencies such as state-wide coordinating boards. The power vested in them varies considerably from state to state, but all are seeking to achieve a legitimate role between institutional governing boards and the executive and legislative arms of state government. Of perhaps even greater significance are state budgeting agencies, which not only control dollars but have begun to inquire into the propriety of many institutional activities. In some states that inquiry is so thorough that the budget office has assumed many of the prerogatives previously held by boards of trustees. Such shifts in power are occasioning increased litigation as agencies seek legitimate roles. Scholarships and loan agencies, civil service systems, building commissions, and public works commissions are other state agencies that have powerful influence over institutions. Their authority derives from legislative power, which can but generally does not exclude collegiate institutions from the purview of state agencies. State legislatures are beginning to deal with broad social questions such as discrimination, collective bargaining, and voter residency, all of which influence collegiate institutions. Although the United States Constitution has no provisions clearly sanctioning federal legislation dealing with any federal institutions of higher education, federal law is rapidly setting conditions and regulations regarding federal funds; federal law applies general legislation to specific institutional activities, for example fair labor standards, minimum wages, and campus disorders. As higher education enters an era of scarce resources, the federal government is bound to exert considerably greater influence on universities. Over and beyond legislation, various administrative agencies responsible for the administration of statutes develop procedures, guidelines, and regulations that further weaken the autonomy of institutions presumed to derive from the founding charter. Courts have been increasingly involved in questions of due process, academic freedom, tenure, admissions, and political activity. Further complications of the legal environment of higher education are the growing number of contractual relationships institutions must make with other social institutions, the emergence of consortia or other multicampus organizations, the growing significance of voluntary accreditation (which has begun to take on a legal character), the emergence of large numbers of institutional associations based in the national or state capitals, and the regional and national compacts that have legal permission to involve themselves in institutional affairs. The decision-making power in the academic community is increasingly shared by a variety of interests both inside and outside the university. The growing interdependence of the university and the society is bound to dilute the sense of community that has been the prevailing characteristic of higher education. As the interdependence of the university and the society increases, inflexibility of operation increases. Institutions become more and more hierarchical, with an attendant heightening of the organizational structure replacing the generally flat organizational structure. As this change transpires, conflict is likely to increase, institutional autonomy begins to erode, distinctions between institutions become blurred, and legalization of certain basic values such as academic freedom appears necessary. These results lead to a situation ripe for unionization of higher education and the emergence of collective bargaining as a part of the policy-making process.

The complex way in which university governance has had to adjust to the accumulation of missions on the one hand and constituencies on the other is especially evident in the operations of governing boards. The board of trustees had the original role of an agent of its creator. To that were added the role of bridge between the society and the university and the role of agent for the university community and court of last resort for the ultimate resolution of conflict. The board, as an agent of church or state, was conceived in medieval times and expanded in the United States as churches founded colleges to extend churchmanship and as secular authorities founded or assumed responsibility for college as devices to produce citizenship. But this concept comes into question through examination of charters that seemingly confer a degree of independence from the creating authority. The Dartmouth College case was decided in support of such a contention, and the degree of independence of a board from its creator is still under contention. As boards become more independent from their creators, they bridge the gap between institutions and the larger society. As bridges they interpret institutions to the society and societal needs to the institution. Sometimes they serve instead as barriers to protect the academic community. The question is whether an instrumentality can be both a bridge and a barrier, a dilemma that continues to produce significant conflicts. To ensure that boards can function as bridges or as barriers, protective devices such as lengthening appointments of members or creation of self-perpetuating boards have been developed. If boards are to interpret institutions adequately to the society, they have to understand higher education and hence have involved themselves with many details of administration. As a result of evolutionary forces, boards have moved into a third domain, that of agent for the university community. Boards have had to adjudicate conflicts within the university community, and this responsibility has led to broader representation on boards so that justice could prevail.

At one time boards of trustees of colleges and universities stood relatively unchallenged in their exercise of their legitimate authority. However, along with other agencies of the social establishment, board members, board functioning, and even the very existence of boards of trustees have been assailed. Part of the challenge relates to the ways trustees are chosen, the length of time they serve, and the nature of the responsibilities they assume. Over several generations board members have become almost a race apart from the university community. Trustees have also been assailed for a number of specific decisions despite the fact that board members have generally acted honestly and generously in a time-consuming role. In recent years boards have been accused of excessive conservatism and unwillingness to confront critical social needs. In times of conflict it is well to rethink the many contributions that boards make, such as defending academic freedom and interpreting the peculiarities of institutions to the public. Campus constituencies often suspect that trustees can not interpret academic life properly and that board members are unsympathetic to campus peculiarities. Students and faculty have demanded representation on boards of trustees. Despite the plausible argument that representation of specific campus constituencies on boards could produce potential conflicts of interest, it should be possible for trustees, faculty, and students to reach consensus without representation. For example, boards might be improved by using committees having wide representation to recommend policies on specific issues. Ultimately boards of trustees must still make final decisions; to ensure sensible decisions a great deal of staff work must be done, and the opinions of various campus constituencies must be presented in the context of generally understood and shared purposes and goals for the institution. To acquire the needed insight, it is imperative that boards of trustees meet quite frequently and that members conscientiously attend meetings. Further it is imperative that board members view their participation on boards of trustees not as representatives of specific pressure groups but as agents acting in the best interests of their institutions. Trustees are inevitably the last appeal in matters related to university independence and integrity. They must understand that their reactions to external pressure inevitably influence the ability of an institution to function effectively. But they must also serve as interpreters of an institution to the larger community. It is imperative that individual board members realize that they do not have an individual voice in such interpretation but only a corporate voice. When important policy decisions are made or when institutional statements are issued, they should be in the name of the full board of trustees. The tendency for individual board members to make individual pronouncements is stimulated during times of crisis and public dissatisfaction with institutions. It is especially important at these times that board members exercise great self-restraint. Clearly the most crucial relationship of trustees is with the president. Both presidents and boards need to make intensive reciprocal efforts to create a feeling of community and to facilitate decisions for the most part through consensus. Overall, the bases for a sound relationship between trustees and the rest of the university community are a common understanding of educational purposes, a common dedication to those purposes, a deep loyalty to the institution, a realization of what role is appropriate for each constituency, a sensitively fashioned system of sharing ideas when decisions are being reached, and, above all, a full commitment to the protection of the independence of the university and its preservation in the face of impending erosion. The concept of trusteeship is sound. What remains to be done is to refine the functions of trusteeships until they more nearly match the concept.

The purpose of structure in a board of trustees is to provide a framework that will support the board's function. But the matters that come before boards are varied and frequently in conflict; therefore different boards have adopted different structural postures. Working boards involve themselves greatly in day-to-day administration, and policy boards tend to delegate decision processes to the management. The formal structure of boards of trustees is easy to describe. There is a chairman of the board, but whether he is the leader of the board or simply the presiding officer is left largely to individual interpretation of the role. Some board chairmen become almost copresidents, whereas others tend to defer always to their equals on the board of trustees. In addition there is usually a vice-chairman who serves in the absence of the chairman but who generally does not have much authority. Boards generally maintain a secretary who keeps records and provides staff assistance. Financial matters of collegiate institutions were early vested in a treasurer chosen from among the trustees. However, with the growth of financial administration this office has changed character. Relating with the board of trustees, of course, are the chief executive officer of an institution and his principal associates. General practice is for the president alone to report directly to the board of trustees, but in some institutions some of his associates also have that prerogative. Much business of boards of trustees is conducted by standing committees of the board; there is usually an executive committee that can act for the total board on some matters. Boards tend more and more to use special committees effectively to deal with specific problems. These committees may be composed of one or more board members as well as individuals from other constituencies. How a board functions is influenced not only by its structure but by other characteristics such as size, frequency of meeting, and the background of individual board members. Further, board functioning is affected by the frequency of conflict situations and by such matters as whether faculty and students are allowed to serve on boards. In theory, boards of trustees have the power to make all decisions concerning the institution. However, in practice there is a division of decision-making authority, a division increasingly described in written rules and policies. Perhaps the most significant factor in determining how a given board of trustees will function is the relationship maintained between the president and the board of trustees. Here the president has clear responsibility to orient board members, to provide for clear communications, to develop appropriate but not excessive written materials, and to encourage participation of individual board members.

Universities have found themselves in organizational trouble because they have accepted multiple and conflicting missions. These difficulties could be reduced by eliminating one or more of the four major missions: teaching, research, public service, and the achievement of democratic community. A case for maintaining or removing each of these missions can be made. However, elements of all are likely to remain but in modified form. Thus instruction will remain the central mission, and research will be practiced, but large-scale research will gradually shift to nonuniversity institutions. Service to the public will likely decline dramatically in areas such as defense and space but increase in urban affairs, ecology, and international organizations. The democratic impulse will dominate systems of governance, and the locus of power to plan and allocate resources will continue to rest with the managers of systems and to shift from private to quasi-public and public coordinating boards. Several observations can be made concerning the future. Boards of individual institutions will become less and less powerful. University organizations representative of various internal constituencies will emerge. Presidents will become elected officials for limited terms. Chief administrative officers will also be selected through participation of subordinates. Administration will become more simplified as the missions of research and public service are reduced in scope and as the residential features of the university are progressively abandoned. The university will become less a community as a geographic and social entity as it becomes more a community of professional interests. The university will take many new forms, once freed of its geographic definition.

The American College President

Michael D. Cohen, James G. March

The American college presidency is a reactive, parochial, and conservative job, important personally to each incumbent (who normally is and has been an academic). In a sense the presidency is illusory in that it purports to govern an organized anarchy. An organized anarchy seeks problematic goals through fluid participation of individuals using an unclear technology. The American college or university is a prototypic organized anarchy. Its goals are either vague or in dispute; its technology is familiar but not understood; its major participants wander in and out of the organization.

American college presidents are commonly middle-aged, married, male, white, Protestant, and academic; they come from relatively well-educated, middle-class, professional-managerial, native born, small town families. The average age of college presidents is about fifty-three, an average that has varied only slightly over the years. Typically presidents accede to the office in their mid-forties after an earlier career in academic life. The most fruitful academic sources of college presidents are the fields of the humanities, education, and religion. It is of special significance in understanding the presidency that incumbents have rarely had significant nonacademic experience. It is also of likely significance that the average president came from a more affluent, better educated, and longer-resident family than does the average student in his institution. Though some presidents move into office directly from professorial posts, most achieve the office by moving up the hierarchy of professor, department chairman, and dean. This ladder is not climbed in a single institution. Presidents normally enter office from a subordinate administrative post in another institution of the same general type and in the same general location as the new one. This homogeneity of background and this filtering process produce presidents strongly and conservatively committed to academic values who, for the most part, do not wish to make major changes. The conservative character of the presidency can be modified significantly only by sacrificing a structure of recruitment, selection, and socialization that is itself ingrained in the traditions and values of academe.

The college president is expected to be involved in decision-making and governance, but to understand his precise role there are a number of relatively distinct ways to regard the governance of universities. It may be regarded as a purveyor of certain goods in a free market. Governance thus takes place as a result of the operation of that market (for example, the market for students, for faculty, for donation, and the like). A second model assumes that the university has well-defined objectives specified by some formal group and that the institution is organized into a hierarchy most suitable to achieve those goals. The third model, which could be called a collective bargaining model, assumes fundamentally conflicting interests within the institution that are resolved through bargaining between representatives of the major interests and then enforced by formal contracts and social arrangements. In a democratic model the university can be seen as a community with an electorate consisting of the many campus constituencies. In this system the president operates almost as an ethnic politician. The related model of consensus requires a great deal of time as people of diverse interests seek to reach consensus. There is an anarchy model that assumes various individuals making relatively autonomous decisions. The decisions of the system are a consequence of the system but are intended by no one and decisively controlled by no one. The reverse of the anarchy model is that of an independent judiciary. Whereas in the anarchy model there is a constituency without explicit leadership, in the independent judiciary model, leadership is assumed without an explicit constituency. A plebiscitary autocracy model assumes a ruler chosen by some arbitrary process to govern so long as the actions of the leader are tolerable. Generally, presidents can be expected to accept some mix of these various models, probably preferring a combination of administration, participation, and collective bargaining. However, these models may be somewhat misleading in that several models are commonly used and others such as anarchy are rarely used. Each model assumes a primary presidential role: on the competitive market the president is an entrepreneur; in democracy the president is a hypothetical candidate for office; in anarchy the president is a catalyst.

The orientation of a president and his associates to the presidency is important to understanding the problems of leadership in contemporary universities. When asked to indicate successful presidents, presidents normally select those from their own region who preside over higher status institutions. In aggregate, presidents do not agree as to what is persuasive evidence of success, nor do they typically agree as to what presidents should actually do. There is, however, more general agreement on activities with short-run effects than on activities of longer significance. When administrative associates of presidents are asked to gauge the activities and successes of presidents, expectable differences of perception appear; chief academic officers may stress educational program development while business officers stress fiscal stability or fiscal growth. Greater variance of perception of presidential activity and success is reflected by student leaders who think the presidency should be an activist interventionist role to be judged successful if it promotes and embodies values held by students. Further confusion is added by the fact that trustees do not display consensus as to what constitute the core objectives of the presidency. While there is general agreement on some broad, important presidential attributes, there is no consensus that any particular attribute is essential. There is no clear core of objectives that presidents should pursue and consequently no set of attributes that will insure success. A paradox exists in that presidents are nominally in the public eye, yet most presidents are nearly invisible to the larger community in which their institutions are situated. Newspapers rarely mention the president except when printing news releases issued by the institutions themselves and dealing with presidential speeches or presidential announcements. The president is rarely an important public figure; he is hardly a public figure at all in the mass media sense. The college president is parochial, honorific in that the status of a president rests more with the status of the institution than with the president's own performance, conventional, and heroic in that the role is seen as important by both incumbents and their associates.

In one sense an organization is a collection of choices looking for problems, issues and feelings looking for decision situations, solutions looking for issues, and decision makers looking for work. Organizations must deal with problems, solutions, participants, and choice opportunities. Theoretically, one might suppose a sequential relationship between problems, choice opportunities, and solutions, but that presumption disappears on closer examination of the ways colleges and universities actually function. Colleges and universities can appropriately be described as organized anarchies in which decision-making is an almost random activity. Thus problems, choices, and solutions are necessarily related to each other, a phenomenon that does not solve problems but does enable choices to be made.

How decisions are actually made in American colleges and universities may be viewed by examining decisions about operating budget, educational policy, academic tenure, and long-range planning. The operating budget is normally determined by the rates and patterns of enrollment, the general institutional reputation, and the research reputation of the institution. These are such powerful determiners as to restrict considerably presidential influence over the budget. He can affect enrollment trends slightly, and he can also theoretically affect institutional reputation. However, the research reputation rests with and is controlled by others, hence it is not really subject to presidential influence. If this be true, a strong research faculty should result in a weak president, the prestige of an institution should affect student influence, and public institutions should constrain presidential discretion over the budget. Nor is the situation better with respect to academic policy. Presidents as academicians should have a special concern with academic policy decisions, but for the most part they do not have much to say. Formal conventions lodge academic responsibility in the faculty, but this responsibility is exercised chiefly in countless small actions taken by many different individuals within the institution. In reality most colleges leave the conditions of education to informal bilateral negotiations between students and faculty. These negotiations very likely would include agreements that teachers and students work very hard and corollary agreements to restrict work. Because such agreement is so important, the setting of general policy by the faculty tends to be fairly straightforward. Logrolling, for example, occurs: the price of a requirement in foreign languages is a requirement in the natural sciences. Presidents are unwilling to intervene in those negotiations. Thus they rarely make or affect academic policy. The granting of academic tenure should be an important fiscal and symbolic act requiring close attention of the president. However, in recent years conditions have minimized the substance of tenure decisions. A long-term tenure contract becomes the problem of a subsequent administration. High faculty turnover means that the contract is not a long one; inflation and expansion allow easy absorption of tenured appointments, and costs of tenured appointments have been frequently borne by external agencies. Most presidents have thus never rejected a tenured recommendation that came through an internal faculty and administrative reviewing process; but because conditions are changing, presidents may interest themselves more seriously in tenure decisions, a fact that very likely will produce complaints of personal favoritism. Planning is a primary responsibility of executive leadership, and most presidents accept in theory this responsibility. Closer examination indicates that little planning actually goes on. Many schools have fiscal plans of one sort or another. Some schools have academic plans, but these are not generally regarded as significant in academic decision-making. Plans tend to become symbols, advertisements, gains, or simple excuses for interaction of the many constituencies on campus. None of these manifestations is significant to motivate intense presidential involvement or community-wide commitment to execute what has been written. Once it is established that the president plays a far from dominant role in these four conspicuous areas of decision-making, it becomes necessary to examine the degree to which the president possesses or uses power. Here three types should be considered: legitimate power, actual power, and perceived power. The significance of these depends on presidential perception of each. This, if a president overestimates his legitimate power he may alienate his board of trustees; if he underestimates it other constituencies may assume power postures. Presidents are more likely to overestimate power in early years of office, and they may consciously underestimate power in times of serious crisis such as those that characterized some campuses during the late 1960s. The concept of power leads to another phenomenon: university governance is simultaneously a system for making decisions and a system for certifying status. For many people the process and structure of university governance are more important than the outcome. Much argument over governance is really argument over symbols of governance, over who has the right to claim power. Academic governance is crowded with instruments of participation to allow claims of victories: committees, faculties, specialized groups, reviews, memoranda, and conferences. Generally, these instruments are not widely used except where validation of status position is involved. All of these observations point to a decidedly limited presidential role. A president probably has more power than other single individuals, but he generally does not dominate decision-making.

College presidents are busy and constantly complain of lack of time. Most presidents work about the same amount of time and sense frustration from misallocation of effort. They generally work fifty to fifty-five hours Monday through Friday; about 47 percent of the time is spent on campus, 14 percent in town, 16 percent at home, and 22 percent out of town. Most of the time is spent talking to people, reading, or writing reports or other documents. Presidents do not spend much time talking with students or faculty but rather spend it with administrative associates, politically important people, or off-campus individuals. Presidential use of time is generally determined by others. However, his use of time is rather regular, week after week, and the kinds of subjects a president will be discussing during particular parts of a week are reasonably predictable. The matters discussed in the early part of the day and the early part of the week are relatively clear-cut matters concerning which some decisions can be made. Less structured activity such as reflection or broad discussion, which theoretically should be most important, is generally relegated to the latter part of the day or week. The differences in the ways presidents spend their time (differences based on the size, wealth, or region of the institution) are relatively slight. Although presidents feel frustrated about the use of their time, they have difficulty turning down requests from others because they have no normatively legitimate basis for the allocation of time. Thus they make themselves available to whoever seems to presume a legitimate need to talk with a president.

> The college president is an executive who does not know exactly what he should be doing and does not have much confidence that he can do anything important anyway. His job is the pinnacle of his success, and he has been by the standards of most of his contemporaries and colleagues a quite successful person. Consciously or not, presidents organize their time in such a way as to maintain a sense of personal competence and importance in a situation in which that is potentially rather difficult. They make themselves available to a large number of people whose primary claim is simply that they want to see the president. Counter to most other

evidence, such interactions remind the president that he is the boss. Similarly, presidents preside over otherwise pointless meetings, for the process of presiding involves a subtle reassertion of primacy.

If this be true, several recent proposals for reform of the college presidency are misdirected. Reducing presidential overload would reduce the opportunity for presidents to feel that they are doing important things; and substituting subordinates in many activities would similarly produce a loss of self-esteem. Most presidents would prefer a slightly different world but not at the cost of undermining their conceptions of themselves as competent and important individuals.

There is and has been much confusion as to length of presidential tenure and as to where presidents move to when they leave office. During the troublous times of the 1960s there were sharply attenuated presidential tenures. There have been studies purporting to show marked increases and decreases in average tenure at different periods of history. Using more complicated modes of analysis it is possible to generalize that tenure expectations are now about what they have been throughout most of the twentieth century. During most of the century the median college president has served about ten years. Presidents depart through death, retirement after age sixty-five, death before age sixty-five, transfer to the presidency of another college, resignation, or dismissal. It would be a mistake to combine these modes into a single statistic. The most significant mode for analysis is that of resignation or dismissal. Very few presidents are officially dismissed. Rather, departure results from a mixture of pull and push that is the result of a relatively long-term, subtle procedure of accommodation between the president and his environment. When presidents leave office before age sixty-five they generally go to academic jobs other than the presidency or to jobs having less social status, prestige, and power. The result is that institutions fairly routinely make workers out of middle executives. Most presidents who achieve the presidency at a relatively young age and for whom the presidency is the capstone of a career serve that role until sometime before a normal date for retirement and then prepare to leave the presidency; but there are no better places

disproportionately large numbers of younger and less favored academics and paraacademics. In any system-wide election the "have-nots" will invariably defeat the "haves." Such an eventuality would alter dramatically the texture of higher education.

V

Reflections on
Higher Education

The original design of the Carnegie Commission intended to present a number of different reflections about the nature of American higher education as recorded by informed scholars from a number of different nations. It is unfortunate that that intention was not fulfilled because the informed and insightful foreigner can perceive nuances to which the American observer is blind. For example, participating daily in a rapidly expanding system of higher education and coping with never-ceasing demand blinds one to the fact that American institutions have historically had to compete vigorously to recruit students and that this tradition is likely to persist into the future. And the envy with which American scholars view the more highly selective and restrictive systems of European higher education while those scholars struggle to accommodate the enormous American heterogeneity blinds them to the social cohesiveness that an egalitarian educational system helps contrive for the society.

American Higher Education: Directions Old and New

Joseph Ben-David

The most conspicuous characteristic of the United States system of higher education is its size. It enrolls a much higher percentage of the relevant age group than does any other country. It has reached this size by almost continuous increase, with enrollment doubling every fifteen years from 1870 until the 1950s. An element of this size and rate of growth is the egalitarianism which has characterized American higher education. In spite of evidence of many inequities, the system historically has provided space for every student who wished to attend. Such a policy of course required that higher education be comprehensive and willing to cater to a great diversity of demands. Hence the system has historically offered much work not subsumed under higher education systems in other nations. The structural characteristics that set it apart from other systems are a combination of differentiation, standardization, and integration. Differentiation is achieved through the three primary and discrete degree levels (bachelor's degree, master's degree, and doctoral degree) along with the associate's degree. Standardization is achieved through a general awareness of what constitutes each of these degrees. And integration is achieved through the relative ease with which students can move from one institution to another and from one degree level to another.

Another highly important characteristic that differentiates American higher education from the education of most other nations is the high degree of individual institutional autonomy. In the United States there was never a state religion, and colleges were founded by different religious denominations. In European countries that maintained state religions, the church created institutions in a centralized mold, and when churches were disestablished the educational structure was simply transferred intact to the state. Although recently there have been movements toward greater centralization within the American system, autonomy of individual campuses has in part been preserved because of the responsibilities assigned administrations actually to conduct the affairs of institutions. In nations having a centralized system that includes a centralized system of finance there is no need for an elaborate system of institutional administration, for the most important function of administration— the acquisition and allocation of funds—is performed outside the university. In the United States system administrators have those responsibilities; that factor is of enormous consequence for the form and substance of American higher education. Related to the autonomy of each institution is the power of the department as the operating agency within an institution. The department is really an American adaptation of the European concepts of a chair and a research institute. With the existence of departments there is an administrative mechanism linking the actual conduct of teaching, research, and service to the elaborate central administration. And the existence of the department has made American institutions capable of somewhat more rapid change than are European institutions. Both Europeon and American institutions maintain the concept of academic freedom, but it is expressed in different ways. European professors derive their academic freedom from being members of an estate, whereas in the United States professors have gained academic freedom through controversy with central administration and boards of control and more recently through contractual relationships.

The most important condition of the American system, composed of independent units, is that institutions have had to compete for community support, students, and faculty. Competition has forced American institutions to be attentive to the changes of opinions and attitudes among the diverse groups whose patronage they have sought. The imperative of competition has produced several strategies that are manifest in virtually all American institutions. The first is not to antagonize anyone, and this strategy has produced an atmosphere of liberalism that can accommodate many different points of view. Such an accommodating posture has generally resulted in weakening pressures from any one constituency for changes that would alienate other constituencies. Occasionally, however, when a professor or activity threatens to jeopardize the liberal consensus, the institution has taken steps to eradicate the disturbing element. The second principle is to solicit the goodwill of as many groups in the community as possible. This strategy has been responsible for the amazing responsiveness of American institutions to the demands of varied constituencies for new kinds of activities or services. The third strategy is for institutions to monopolize the loyalties of at least one important constituency whose support would be invaluable in case of a threatened breakdown of consensus. For most institutions the one highly important public group has been the alumni, although the significance of that group may have deteriorated recently in view of the enhanced significance of the federal government in institutional affairs. Using these strategies and others, American institutions have engaged in serious competition for students, resources, and faculty. In the United States there has always been a scarcity of students, which is a substantially different phenomenon from that which has existed in Europe. Competition for students has meant that every institution has, from time to time, compromised standards of admission to ensure an adequate supply of students. The quest for competitive advantage has also resulted in the continuous attempt on the part of American institutions to build prestige that will attract students; and competition has also produced institutional leadership constantly seeking to determine the educational mood of the country. Competition for students, of course, produces some danger for the equally important competition for faculty, and institutions have generally tried to produce educational programs to attract students and yet give faculty opportunities to pursue their own interests whether through research or specialized courses. Thus at various times institutions have stressed the goal of producing well-educated and well-mannered gentlemen and yet have allowed room for faculty scholarly expertise; they have offered broad service, as did the land grant institutions, but have still provided conditions for faculty members to develop intellectual excellence. It is this need to satisfy several constituencies (for example parents, students, legislators, and faculty members) that has led American institutions to combine liberal undergraduate education with graduate education in the arts and sciences and with a wide variety of professional education and professional services.

Until the end of World War II, most institutions maintained at least two strands of prestige, the liberal arts college and the graduate school; these were maintained in some degree of balance. However, the prestige of the graduate school of arts and sciences gradually achieved hegemony in spite of a series of experiments designed to maintain the prestige and intellectual validity of undergraduate liberal arts education. Prior to the secularization of higher education in the 1860s, the aim of college education had been to shape the character of the student according to a rigid model of a pious, righteous, and educated gentleman. Secularization and the impact of science broke that hegemony. For a time it seemed likely that an alternative ideal—that of scientific, scholarly, and technological education—could replace the earlier synthesis. That ideal proved inadequate for the large number of undergraduate students who were not seriously interested in science and scholarship. Not willing to alienate any group of students, American education opted for a free elective system that allowed students to choose from an increasing variety of courses. In practice, the free elective system, related as it was to the scholarly interests of faculty, gave the advantage to scientifically and professionally oriented students. It soon became evident that specific provisions for other students were necessary. The general education movement attempted through a prescribed core of courses to provide a liberal culture that was intended, among other things, to facilitate character formation. The general education movement was relatively short-lived because of failure to solve several intractable problems. The first of these was the content of the curriculum, a problem requiring faculty agreement on that education which was most important. Faculties were unwilling to agree, nor were students inclined to accept prescription. Further, a prescribed curriculum was premised on a vision of an ideal person but without a religious synthesis. That ideal proved to be illusory. Though the general education movement did not gain an intellectual hegemony, it did slow for a time the precipitous movement toward overspecialization.

General or liberal education to be effective required a common body of shared values that for a time could be achieved in the United States. Liberal intellectuals tended to support the political arm, and the western tradition provided an intellectual synthesis. The historic role of a college provided a rationale for prescription. Each of these three conditions came to be challenged. Intellectual faith in political goals deteriorated, the impact of nonwestern cultures broke the western synthesis, and the increasing permissiveness with respect to youth broke the rationale for prescription. Hence the conditions were present for the breakdown of the general education movement in the 1960s.

A major determinant in the shape of American higher education of the 1970s was the steady rise in significance of the graduate school. Graduate education came to be valued as the most desirable form of professional activity, and this prestige produced a shape of undergraduate education most sympathetic to graduate needs. American graduate education has differed somewhat from European graduate education. In Germany, from whence many American ideas came, a professor maintained two roles: one as a holder of a chair and the other as a director of an institute that was the means by which the professor expressed his research interests. In the United States these two roles became one, and research took on many of the attributes of a profession itself. This research emphasis spread from arts and sciences to the professional fields, and training in those fields became as research-oriented as was training in the arts and sciences. Because of the all-pervasive value assigned to research, American universities developed a great deal of quasi-disciplinary research not found in European institutions (the study of statistics is a case in point), and the research interests of professors were reinforced by demands of industry and government for more and more university-based research. Thus research, rather than being a corollary of teaching, became in the large universities the most important activity and the main source of finance.

For almost a century American colleges and universities have been engaged in the diffusion and the marketing of liberal, gentlemanly education, specialized knowledge, and creative research. They have educated a minority of the population destined to middle- and upper middle-class careers. However, that mission is being seriously questioned. An overemphasis on research has encouraged institutions to neglect the education of the average student. The research emphasis has also led institutions away from the vocationalism many prospective students desire. It produced a new class, the intellectual Bohemian proletariat, composed of graduate students and subordinate research workers who gradually felt themselves to be exploited. This new class contributed substantially to the politicization of the American university in the 1960s. Unless the problems posed by that phenomenon are solved, the character of American institutions could be radically changed.

Of the several interpretative essays commissioned by the Carnegie Commission on Higher Education, this document is the most insightful and the most understanding of American conditions. It interprets validly the elaboration of administration, and it senses properly the tremendous significance of competition in American institutions. The analysis of the rise and fall of the general education movement is one of the more perceptive elaborations available in the literature. Only occasionally does Professor Ben-David's knowledge fail. His contention that nonwhite students may have the edge is not supported currently by available evidence. But over all the errors of fact or interpretation are so minor as to be discountable. Clearly, this work is not a handbook for faculty or administrative use. However, if faculties could but be persuaded to read this interpretation, much of the rhetoric of faculty meetings could perhaps be muted.

Any Person, Any Study: An Essay on American Higher Education

Eric Ashby

Two questions can be asked about American education: Does the system fall short of its frequently enunciated ideals and aspirations, and do the ideals and aspirations themselves need revision. Answers to these questions are difficult because American colleges and universities are so diverse, because there is such a voluminous literature on higher education, and because the world of higher education is in a state of crisis and rapid change. On the basis of present trends American higher education seems to be moving inexorably toward universal higher education, equality of opportunity, proliferation of graduate education, research, and corporate involvement in helping to resolve the dilemmas of society. These trends seem inevitable because during the past century most indexes of higher education have been increasing exponentially. Obviously, projecting exponential growth to infinity leads to absurd results, and exponential growth is coming to an end. The critical problem facing higher education is to maintain excellence in a system that, for the first time, is not expanding. As the system faces an end to exponential growth, the enterprise must face the short-term problem of how to plan and finance one last phase of expansion and the long-term problem of how to preserve innovation, initiative, and adaptation in a system that has reached its peak in size and support.

The institutions that provide higher education in the United States are not a coordinated system but a constellation whose units influence one another but are not subject to any master design. There are the community colleges, the most rapidly expanding segment, which serve as an important distributing point for students; there are the four-year colleges, which represent an enormous diversity; and there are the universities, which offer doctorates and maintain a number of professional schools. These universities in a sense provide characteristic values and aspirations for the entire system, valuing as they do graduate education, research, and the service orientation that derived from the land grant idea. In aggregate, these types of institutions yield several impressions. There is a range of quality that allows mediocre institutions to coexist in a system with quite excellent institutions. The very existence of mediocre institutions protects the standards of the stronger ones. Secondly, American institutions have historically had a higher drop-out rate than have systems of higher education in other countries. In part, this factor is beneficial for it allows institutions to serve as screening devices; but in part it is a luxury that even the United States can scarcely afford. A third impression is that though the American system has tried to eliminate class orientation, it has not done so successfully.

Much thought about the future of higher education in the United States is concerned with two questions: How can a continued expansion of higher education and of research be financed, and how can opportunity of access be equalized. Those who wish to provide universal access to higher education are clearly in the ascendancy. The next spurt in enrollment will come from the less talented segments of society because enrollment of the most talented persons of college age is almost at saturation level. As this spurt of growth occurs, attrition (which has always been relatively high) is likely to increase. Attrition can be reduced only by erecting formidable achievement barriers to entry or by introducing several modest steps in certification at which students could leave the educational system with honor and a sense of achievement. Because of the diversity of types of institutions, the United States could adopt a policy that would make no attempt to reduce attrition in junior colleges but would modify policies for other kinds of institutions. If the United States tries to remove all financial barriers in the way of higher education, there will be a danger that the proportion of poorly motivated students in universities will increase to such an extent that the entire system could break down. This danger is especially acute because traditional higher education and other kinds of post-secondary education are not segregated into different categories of institutions. However, a requisite thin stream of intellectual excellence has been maintained through the existence of the highly selective university and the prestige graduate school. For the system to remain viable there must be stratification based on capacities of students; otherwise all higher education will become watered down.

The next question is what should be taught. In the United States as contrasted with England or Western Europe, the formal curriculum is and has been enormously important (though not all curricular plans have proven satisfactory). The general education movement has had its ups and downs. However, general education requirements have provided a somewhat more broadly educated graduate than has the English system which has concentrated on a high degree of specialization in a single subject for undergraduate students. A possible compromise between the high degree of specialization found in English universities and the broad and occasionally diffuse general education of American institutions would be a model based on the Scottish universities of the nineteenth century, which combined general and special work in a more felicitous fashion than do universities in the United States. To solve the question as to what should be taught, the powerful influence of the graduate school must in some way be modified yet at the same time retain its mission of setting standards. More attention can be given the preparation of teachers through doctoral programs. The solution to the undergraduate curriculum might be attained by eliminating the associate of arts degree and assuming the bachelor's degree to be a generalist degree. Some divorce of certification from the bachelor's degree would be possible, but room would be allowed for using more advanced degrees for certification. Such a proposal would allow modification of examination and grading for the bachelor's degree but would still allow graduate professional programs to exercise rigorous testing and examination as a basis for certification. The United States system is admirably suited to do this because the standardizing power of the Educational Testing Service and its various programs can be used for quality control.

Another question is who should teach. The recent tendency of universities to attract professors by reducing teaching loads and substituting teaching assistants or junior faculty members is not a healthy development. The pressure to publish should be removed, and at least two routes to high professional achievement should be established, as is the case in England. Under such a system a highly capable individual could opt for a teaching role or a research role. The conditions under which these professors serve is, of course, set by systems of governance and administration. In the United States the roles of boards of trustees and central administrations have been the more dominant. Recently faculties have been gaining legal power to participate in governance, and this progress is wise and healthy. Students as well should be given a legally sanctioned role. Research, if the term is broadly conceived, is essential for effective college teaching. American universities have achieved an enviable reputation for research. However, the professionalization of research in the United States may have gone too far. A better policy for the future would be for universities not to require research from anyone who does not feel compelled to do it. Unless research is relevant to teaching, it makes no sense to require a faculty member to pursue it. This radically changed posture may be a distinct possibility in view of the leveling out of external support for research. Thus there may be a decidedly healthy concomitant to the depression facing higher education. The hothouse growth of research during the 1960s produced some diseconomies in American higher education. The scale of scientific research was abnormally inflated. Universities by accepting the contract system of funding research lost some initiative, and the heavy research support produced an overdevelopment of graduate activities at the expense of undergraduate activities. If research funds are cut back and if a more equitable system of distribution of support for higher education is worked out so that universities are treated more alike as they are by the University Grants Committee in England, American higher education will be well served.

The future of American higher education may be predicted by extrapolation of present tendencies. There will be universal access by the year 2000 with enrollments of around 14,000,000 students. Those students will be taught by an army of about 900,000 faculty, whose teaching loads will be inversely proportional to the distinction (measured in research terms) of individual faculty members. There will continue to be striving for status as institutions try to change. By the year 2000 there will be no more expansion, and there is a danger that there will be no funds to support educational and curricular innovation. However, that picture could be changed if one of three other alternatives were adopted. One of these would be a moratorium on expansion by replacing socioeconomic barriers with barriers of meritocracy or motivation. This could allow funds for a flowering of quality of secondary education, which might come to be viewed as the normal terminus for most people. An option favored by the New Left is the replacement of presently existing forms of education by something quite different. A third option would be to identify the dangerous features in the present system and to eliminate those systematically through slow evolutionary change. Neither of the first two options seems reasonable or likely. For the third option to be adequately accepted, several issues must be resolved. The first of these involves the source of finance for the system. Here a pluralistic system of grants, loans, contracts, and institutional grants seems best suited to meet the needs of all constituents. The second issue involves clarification of the purposes of higher education. Because the several purposes may be mutually contradictory, resolution of this issue may result in many types of institutions functioning under a broad system of higher education. The third issue involves the relationship of the university to the society. There is considerable temptation for institutions to become adversaries with respect to social and political issues. For this to happen would be highly dangerous, and a policy that takes that danger into account would be advantageous.

In this work, Sir Eric Ashby is able to see clearly the effects of growth on the educational system and the dilemmas which that growth has produced. He sees both the enormous contribution of research and the baleful effects that the research emphasis has had on undergraduate education. Generally, his suggested reforms are reasonable and politically feasible. Thus he sees a deprofessionalization of the bachelor's degree, probably accompanied by a decrease in the length of time required, as a desirable way out of an impasse. He thinks that universities have been demanding too much research on the part of faculty and that some curtailment of the pressure to publish is in order. He sees that the undergraduate curriculum for the bachelor's degree is in need of reform and that this reform is likely to take place as the growth of higher education slows down. Yet two other opinions of the author are antithetical to this reform of the undergraduate program. Sir Eric Ashby believes that faculty should generally be allowed to follow their own interests and that they should have a much greater role in governance of the institutions. It was through allowing faculty members to follow their own interests that the collegiate curriculum lost its integrity from the late nineteenth century onward. And it is in those institutions in which faculties have had the greatest voice that there has been the least educational reform. The author uses as a model the British tradition that makes students and faculty both part of the corporation which is the university. Yet it may be this very syndicalism that has resulted in British universities being somewhat unresponsive to the larger needs of the society. It is entirely possible that it is in some degree responsible for the industrial and technological lags that have weakened Britain's power to compete with other developed nations in the world.

The American College and American Culture: Socialization as a Function of Higher Education

Oscar Handlin, Mary F. Handlin

The American college was formed through a variety of motives by the colonists. The religious motive emphasized the need for a learned clergy and had a missionary element as well. The professional motive was reflected first in the preparation of people for the ministry and then gradually in the preparation of people for law or medicine. Colleges were also created for utility and for social mobility. But even more important than these was the belief that colleges facilitated socialization of individuals into adult society.

Although colleges were early formed in the colonies, by 1770 (when Harvard was 134 years old) there had been relatively slight growth of higher education in America. The principal tasks in the colonies were the establishment of settlements, the advancement of the frontier, and the development of a viable economy, none of which required higher learning. Nevertheless, during this quiescent period colleges passed through a significant phase of development. These colonial colleges were unexpected products of a peculiar combination of causes and were not in the least an inevitable development. Puritanism was certainly a factor, as were colonial chauvinism and missionary zeal. These forces produced an ideal rather than an actual collegiate structure, for though members of the colonies argued the reasons for colleges they did not support them well. During the formative period colleges relied on student fees. A degree was essential for the ministry in the solidly established churches, and a degree came to be a requirement for entry into the professions of law and medicine. Even more importantly, exposure to a college course of studies was assumed to produce a cultured individual who exemplified gentlemanly ideals. Parents, for their part, were willing to pay tuition in the hopes that colleges could discipline their sons more effectively than could the parents themselves. This very realistic desire resulted in a preoccupation of early colleges with discipline rather than with affairs of the mind. Colleges were not well supplied with faculty, for the role of tutor was a generally undesirable post. The president in the early colleges assumed virtually all educational, moral, and disciplinary duties. A major duty, of course, was to develop reliable sources of income, and to do so a rhetoric indicating the values of college attendance had to be developed. Utility became the keystone of such rhetoric although utility was clearly not reflected in the curricula.

Between 1770 and 1870 substantial changes in higher education had taken place. In 1870 some 500 institutions (more institutions than in all of Europe) were awarding bachelor's degrees. Such rapid growth was a reaction to complex impulses rather than to specific student demand. There was the need for trained leaders, a feeling that education was positively related to the economic well-being of society, a nationalistic desire to have institutions as good as those in Europe, and a desire to accomplish the two contradictory goals of producing an elite and maintaining an open society. There were, of course, contradictory forces serving to limit the expansion of colleges. It was relatively easy in a fast growing nation for young men to get ahead quickly by exploiting the frontier. In some respects then, students who attended college were either those who wished to enter the learned professions or who wanted an extension of adolescence or late childhood. A powerful ingredient in the expansion of a number of institutions was the pervasive sectarianism of American religious life, with each new denomination desiring to create a college in each new region of the country as it opened. The numbers of colleges increased, but only a minority of those created survived; those that did survive were characterized by poverty. A yearly college budget of $6000 was sizable. Endowments were pitifully low or nonexistent; again tuition was the primary economic resource. To attract students, spokesmen for colleges had to engage in an endless routine of self-justification. Partly to justify colleges to students and partly to accommodate an increasing desire on the part of faculty for greater specialization, changes in the curriculum seemed warranted, and there were serious attempts to invoke the elective principle and to intrude science and practical subjects into the curricula. Most of the early attempts quickly failed, and by the mid–nineteenth century most colleges had drifted back to the prescribed classical curricula, which produced declining enrollments. As was true of colleges during the earlier period, nineteenth century institutions had to concern themselves with inculcating moral discipline; that goal required maintenance of rigorous control over student life yet a sufficiently lax control that overt student rebellion could be prevented. This ambivalence gave students enough room to organize themselves and eventually control much of their own private behavior. Fraternities were allowed to develop as a means of meeting student needs for freedom but also as a means of controlling student behavior and incidentally of getting colleges out of the housing business.

Between 1870 and 1930 the number of American institutions of higher education increased from somewhat more than 500 to above 1400, with enrollments increasing from 52,000 to more than 1,100,000. The economy of the country had shifted from an agricultural base to an urban industrial base at the same time the nation was struggling to accommodate new social and intellectual development. There was the need to accommodate the point of view expressed by Darwin and also to accommodate new attitudes toward morality. As colleges struggled to reach a compromise between religious tradition and the dictates of science they became even more vulnerable to external pressures. Parents wanted an education for their sons to ensure upward mobility in an increasingly industrialized society. Colleges had to offer preparation in the professions that would lead to actual credentials. As education became linked more and more closely to credentialling, the regularization of program length, the age of students entering and leaving the program, and the curricular requirements had to be regularized. But vocational preparation was still not the only function of the college. College students were assumed to receive a general culture. This concern with general culture manifested itself not only in the colleges but in the growing number of land grant institutions and, before the end of the century, in the complex research-oriented university. It was an uneasy relationship that has persisted into the present. The concept of the college man was involved in the rise of athletics as a focus for college life and as a means of ensuring student and alumnus loyalty. Athletics and other extracurricular activities provided a regimen that allowed the undergraduate to develop the characteristics of a college man while at the same time allowing an increasingly specialized faculty to concentrate on its own scholarly interests. Colleges did allow the intellectual young person to browse and satisfy his curiosity, but in general the lives of the faculty and the lives of the students proceeded along different courses. There were strains in a system that drew together scholars presumably intent upon the pursuit of knowledge and students without a clear sense of purpose. These tensions produced student outbreaks and considerable vacillation of institutional policy.

The evolution of higher education from 1930 to 1960 presents a number of paradoxes and some quite contradictory developments. The Depression underscored the vocational value of a college degree and accounted for escalating college attendance. After World War II the values of college attendance became codified in such documents as President Truman's Commission on Higher Education. Attending college became the desirable means of upward social mobility; the demand was of such magnitude as to allow college faculties to move toward hegemony with respect to teaching and the curriculum. There were attempts to preserve some of the elements of the older idea of general culture—general education represented one such attempt—but such reforms proved to be of short duration. In a sense 1957 is a watershed date, for that year (the year of Sputnik) introduced profound changes in the purposes of colleges and universities and in the nature of support of higher education. Education in the 1960s became a growth industry that in addition to socializing students, was called upon to undertake many other activities.

> From generation to generation . . . the university was also the home of men for whom learning—the pursuit of truth—was an end in itself and for whom the service of rearing the young was the price paid for the tolerance to pursue their own interests. A full history of the university might well balance the two elements; and in any estimate of future prospects a significant question will certainly be the extent to which the obligation of socialization will remain compatible with scholarship [p. 85].

The Handlins have made several important contributions in this document. They have attempted successfully to get below the rhetoric of higher education and to examine functions. They clearly reveal the function that higher education plays of screening people into preferred positions regardless of the substance of the curriculum. The Handlins have come close to showing how a collegiate institution has been able to accommodate the conflicting interests of faculties and students seeking quite idiosyncratic goals. Very likely someone could reanalyze the several interpretative volumes that the Carnegie Commission on Higher Education has sponsored and produce a reasonably definitive taxonomy of the function served by American higher education as contrasted with the various purposes claimed for it.

Recent Alumni and Higher Education: A Survey of College Graduates

Joe L. Spaeth, Andrew M. Greeley

The college graduating class of 1961 is a rather diverse group of people. However, its members had many things in common. Seven years after graduation, eight out of ten were married and had an average of two children. Seventy-one percent of those working were in professional positions, and slightly more were earning at least $10,000 a year. Slightly over a third had enrolled in graduate school immediately after college, and seven years later a third of them held some kind of higher degree. The vast majority expect their children to attend college, and they seem much more concerned with the quality of education their children will receive than with how much it will cost. Over a third made financial contributions to the colleges they had attended. Three out of five alumni believe that state taxes should be raised to provide more money for higher education, and almost half believe that federal financing should be provided all institutions. As a group, the alumni class of 1961 recognize the problems of financing higher education and have begun to take realistic steps to pay for the education of their children. As compared with their parents they are liberal politically, but only a tiny proportion place themselves on the radical Left.

When asked to assess comparatively the goals of higher education, alumni overwhelmingly endorsed general education over a career-oriented education. When a number of values were combined into three (personality development, career training, and intellectual development), graduates from all kinds of institutions endorsed similarly intellectual development, but graduates from less prestigious institutions tended to rate personality development and career training higher than did graduates of higher quality institutions. The relationship between fields of major and strength of support for general education was that which would logically be supposed. Those in the social sciences and humanities were most likely to be enthusiastic about the intellectual goals of higher education; those who received highly specialized career training in postbaccalaureate programs were similarly supportive of general intellectual education.

One reversal of logical expectation is that men tended to stress general education goals, whereas women stressed career training and personality development. Very likely the masculine emphasis results from the professional orientation of many men who received little career preparation during their undergraduate years. In general, it appears that alumni emphasize as important goals of higher education precisely those attributes they find important in their own particular life positions.

Although the majority of alumni claim to read serious fiction and nonfiction occasionally and to listen to classical music occasionally, the involvement of alumni in cultural activities is not pronounced. Alumni do not have a "know-nothing" attitude for science and scientists. There is relatively little relationship between the quality of college attended and cultural activities. Sex is a far more significant predictor; women are considerably more likely to participate in cultural activities than men. There is also a strong relationship between career choice and cultural activities, with those having graduated in engineering and business less involved than those active in humanistic careers. Educators faced with the generalization of the lack of relationship between school quality and cultural activities tend either to reject the data or to claim that colleges and universities have other more important missions to fulfill than to direct graduates into cultural activities. College quality is, however, related to attitudes toward experts; graduates of lower-quality colleges are more suspicious of science and technology than are graduates of high-quality institutions.

Over all, graduates of the class of 1961 liked the colleges they attended but lacked strong positive feeling. Their enthusiasm tended to diminish over time. When asked how college did affect them and how college should have affected them, they revealed that a substantial gap exists, except with respect to training for jobs and forming friendships. For example, almost a third believed that the production of a well-rounded student should have been of absolute top importance, but only 14 percent believed that it actually was of absolute top importance. Another example is that alumni do not believe that their colleges were powerfully influential in their cultural lives. Once again, neither the size, control, or quality of institution makes much difference in alumni attitudes. There is a slight tendency for graduates of private universities and liberal arts colleges to be strongly attached to those institutions. A particularly disturbing result is that in the minds of alumni actual college accomplishments were the relatively unimportant ones, but important outcomes were judged not to have been achieved. One significant variation from an otherwise consistent pattern is the critical attitudes of graduates of Catholic colleges toward their institutions; yet they feel deep attachment for and want to send their children to the colleges they attended. The flavor of alumnus attitudes can be found in several quotations. "After four years of teaching I realize most teachers know little of life and transfer their hang-ups to their students as much as they can. Remedy human beings as teachers. My own teachers rarely broke through to my soul—and it can be done, even in a class; but I doubt if college can prepare people for teaching or if most teachers can help people to feel honestly." Or "I regret that my university provided so little intellectual excitement. Faculty members went about their academic interests and professional business in craftsmen-like ways but seldom brought any possibility for the life of the mind to their classrooms or the campus at large." Alumni, in retrospect, seem to value the humanities highly and would like to have taken more such courses. Once again, however, there is a strong relationship between what one needs in one's life pattern and how one values college courses. Thus, doctors and lawyers tend to overvalue undergraduate work in the humanities as compared with businessmen and educators. The alumni of the class of 1961 were only somewhat sympathetic to the demands of contemporary college students. Once again there is a career relationship, with alumni in the humanities and social sciences most sympathetic with student involvement in campus affairs and those in business and engineering least sympathetic. Although alumni plan to send their children to college, they are by no means convinced that going directly from high school into college is a desirable practice. But if their children do go to college, alumni would like them to receive a good general education and some career training; general education is still the most desirable prospect for children of college graduates. Over all, it would seem that alumni want their children to receive the kind of education college catalogues say is being provided. The disquieting thing is that in aggregate the alumni do not feel that their colleges did for them what they might have done.

Generally, alumni reported political affiliations in about the same proportion as the political affiliation of their parents. However, between 1961 and 1968 political affiliation shifted away from the Democratic party and toward a primarily independent posture with a slight upswing in the number of Republicans. There is, however, a fairly clean division on a liberal/conservative continuum, and this is reflected in attitudes toward a number of specific issues. At least half the alumni were in sympathy with black and student protesters; graduates of private universities and high quality colleges (frequent locations of protest activities) were considerably more sympathetic to student protest.

Patterns of alumni donations to their institutions are not unexpected. Graduates of private colleges who feel strong attachments and who come from affluent families are the most likely to make financial contributions to their institutions.

College attendance has had a considerable impact on occupational choice, but that impact derives from a sorting function rather than from a specific training function. As alumni progress through the educational system, bright individuals exhibiting good performance are drawn into the more intellectually demanding occupations; the reverse is true for those (especially men) with poor records.

Recent Alumni and Higher Education *provides documentation highly consistent with other studies of the impact of colleges and universities on students. With respect to attitudes and intellectual development some impact is perceivable, but it is not of the magnitude academic apologists claim to want. Institutions do not differ markedly from each other with respect to impact on student lives, although occasional variant patterns do emerge. The tenor of the report suggests a parsimonious set of actual collegiate accomplishments. Colleges and universities may very well have consistently claimed to do too much. Quite possibly they might reduce their claims and in the long run achieve more.*

Higher Education in Nine Countries: A Comparative Study of Colleges and Universities Abroad

Barbara Burn

From 1950 onward higher educational development in eight industrial countries has followed similar trends. Enrollments have expanded greatly to meet the demands for higher education. Nations have expanded numbers of institutions, have created new kinds of institutions, and have become more concerned with educational planning. Partly or perhaps even largely because of rapid increases in institutional size, higher education in all developed nations experienced considerable student dissent during the 1960s. Though the evolution of higher education in eight industrial countries followed parallel lines, there are of course significant differences.

In France most higher education is publicly sponsored and supported and was controlled by the government; before 1968 the number of universities was limited to one for each educational district. The University of Paris, by far the largest, had one-third of all university enrollments. After 1968, however, various new institutions were created with the firm intent that there should be more comprehensive and interdisciplinary institutions than specialized ones. There are a limited number of privately supported institutions, but attendance was somewhat limited before 1968 because conferral of degrees was limited to public institutions; public institutions no longer reserve that right. Enrollments in French universities increased from about 134,000 in 1950–1951 to about 650,000 in 1969–1970. Attrition rate for those enrollments resembled generally the attrition rates in the United States. These increases in enrollment were obviously accompanied by increases in the numbers of faculty members. However, as was true in the United States, there developed a tendency to use assistants and advanced students to teach. Before 1968, public higher education in France was highly centralized, with the national government appointing professors, determining curricula, setting examinations, and allocating facilities and financial support. One of the aims of the Orientation of Higher Education Act of 1968 was to decentralize that system through a variety of techniques, one of which was the creation of something resembling the American department. A second technique to achieve some decentralization was to strengthen the authority of the chief executive of each campus. Most authority had been lodged centrally, but great individual freedom was provided the individual professor to determine how and what to teach. As did other nations, France increased support for both public and private higher education during the 1960s and increased funds available to students. Because of the student disturbance of May 1968, French higher education tried to involve students in academic governance and tried to produce educational reforms such as modernizing curricula, reducing class size, and encouraging closer contact between teachers and students. Exemplary specific reforms were the establishment of intermediate degrees and actual planning for some kinds of institutions to tolerate high attrition rates while seeking to reduce attrition rates in other sorts of institutions. This movement is quite similar to the movement in the United States that tolerates high attrition rates in junior colleges in the hope that attrition rates will decrease in the universities. As to the future, France deviates somewhat from the United States in that the major problems of the future will be finding enough qualified staff members and building enough physical facilities.

Higher education in Great Britain has been highly selective and has forced students to make decisions and to be evaluated quite early in their educational careers. The system in Great Britain now includes 42 universities and about 175 colleges of education. Oxford and Cambridge have historically dominated the British system, but currently much of the expansion, innovation, experimentation, and advanced work is taking place at new institutions. In the past, teacher training institutions were not considered part of higher education, but colleges of education are now becoming more like universities with respect to admission standards, curricula, and graduation requirements. To provide diversification of educational opportunity, Great Britain and Wales have created a large number of local and regional institutions, each dealing with specific technical and vocational programs. Most universities, however, offer a great deal of adult education, especially through the device of examinations to validate education obtained off-campus. Within universities the honors degree is still potent, stressing as it does concentrated study in one field. However, one element of university reform is to provide greater breadth of study for more students. Enrollments in higher education have increased substantially, with enrollments in the various local and regional institutions exceeding growth in university enrollments; specific policy tends to restrict enrollments in universities. Generally, first degree courses at British universities take three years, with university enrollments experiencing relatively low attrition rates. Though limiting enrollments in universities produces lower attrition rates it also produces strictures on experimentation in secondary schools, which must prepare students to pass rigorous entrance examinations. Although British universities are autonomous by virtue of royal charters, the bulk of their income is allocated from governmental sources through the University Grants Committee. Universities are free to recruit the professors they want to teach the subjects they want to the students they choose to admit and are limited only by conditions set by the University Grants Committee. British faculties, operating through a number of different instrumentalities, have considerable say in the governance of individual campuses, although the powers of institutional vice-chancellors or principals are expanding. These officers coordinate the system through a national committee of vice-chancellors and principals with expanding professional staffs. Although student financial aid through state scholarships, local awards, and university awards is considerable, higher education in Great Britain is still class-related, with the proportion of children who reach full-time higher education being about six times as great in the families of nonmanual workers as in those of manual workers. Nevertheless, there is growth in heterogeneity of student bodies as well as overall expansion of enrollments. These trends have been accompanied by some student protest and dissent. Compared with institutions in other nations. British colleges and universites did not experience much violence, partly because of the predominant form of tutorial education perfected at Oxford and Cambridge and adopted by many of the new institutions.

Higher education in Canada consists of 62 degree-conferring colleges and universities and 250 other institutions, many of which confer degrees through one of the degree-conferring institutions. There are significant structural and substantive differences between higher education in Quebec, which follows the French model, and higher education in Canada generally, which combines elements of British, Scottish, and United States higher education. In general, the curricular programs of Canadian colleges and universities are more specialized and more oriented to the professions than are American institutions. However, they tend to resemble American institutions with respect to the substantial attention given to research and public service. Enrollments are rapidly expanding, and the expansion seems to be producing a steadily increasing rate of attrition. Enrollment expansion has also produced a significantly higher ratio of students to faculty. Generally, Canadian higher education is the responsibility of the provinces, although recently the federal government has become more involved, especially through assuming responsibility for research, cultural affairs, and adult education. To facilitate provincial assumption of responsibilty for higher education, some federal taxing powers have been transferred to the provinces (a Canadian equivalent to the intent of the United States concept of revenue sharing). With respect to governance, Canadian institutions are similar to those in the United States in that authority in academic affairs is vested in a faculty senate, and other authority is vested in a lay board of trustees. Presidents, principals, or vice-chancellors have powers comparable to presidents in the United States. Some of these powers are being attenuated through more formal faculty instruments of governance. As is true in the United States, provinces earlier made the principal financial contributions to institutions, and recently there has been an increase in federal support, not only for capital development but for research, student aid, and actual program development. Most Canadian students enroll in institutions in their own provinces, although there is some increase in student mobility. Canadian colleges and universities have shown remarkable capacities for adaptation to enrollment pressures and rapid expansion. They have, however, lagged somewhat behind United States institutions in providing financial aid for students, developing graduate programs and research, and coordinating institutions within the provinces.

Higher education in Australia grew rapidly from only six universities in 1945 to fifteen universities and two university colleges at present. More recently, university growth has slowed down partly as a result of governmental policy restricting university enrollments and redirecting most high school graduates into colleges of advanced education. These institutions resemble United States junior colleges and are characterized by the preponderance of part-time students, high attrition rates, and a mixture of college level and subcollege level courses. Teacher preparation is handled mainly in teachers' colleges maintained by the several states. Universities have historically been highly professional in achieving their chief function of providing graduates for government service, teaching, law, medicine, science, argiculture, engineering, dentistry, and veterinary medicine. Australian institutions tend to resemble British institutions in the high degree of specialized work that undergraduates are required to assume. However, universities have not been primary suppliers of scientific research, which in Australia has developed largely outside universities, although in recent years there has been some increase in the research function of universities. Australian enrollments quadrupled between 1950 and 1969, but large numbers of those students were enrolled in nondegree courses. There is considerable difference of opinion as to whether continued expansion is desirable; those seeking to restrict university enrollments are seemingly in the ascendancy. Although the central commonwealth government has no stipulated responsibility for education, it has been more and more involved, and state responsibilities have been reduced. Internal governance in Australian universities is similar to British governance: faculties have a great deal of autonomy. Recently faculty authority has come to be shared with students and with the growing number of agencies intended to coordinate higher education. There has been very little increase in student financial aid since the mid-1950s. As a collorary, university students come mainly from middle-class and upper middle-class families; this situation is likely to remain unchanged as Australia copes with the demand for postsecondary education through nonuniversity teachers' colleges and colleges of advanced education.

West Germany's university-level institutions have an elitist tradition that gives extended and flexible opportunities for learning to highly qualified students. Typically, students who enter West German universities have completed four years of primary school and nine years in gymnasium, which is presumed to provide the student's general education. Recently, mature young people who did not attend gymnasium can qualify for admission by attending evening schools or subuniversity institutions. The West German system consists of twenty-three universities, nine technical universities, three medical colleges, three specialized universities, fifty-four pedagogical colleges, and seventeen theological institutions. As in the United States, nonuniversities move steadily toward university status. Research has long been important among German universities, but much of this research is conducted through institutes that are part of a university structure or closely related to a university structure. In the 1950s and 1960s an enormous enrollment increase was facilitated in part by making more flexible the ways of entry into mainstream higher education. Recently some sentiment has developed to limit enrollments on the ground that existing capacity can produce the needed professional and technological manpower. Such proposals are called into question when it is noted that universities are not producing the numbers of needed college teachers. In fact, West Germany has adopted patterns similar to those in the United States of using assistants for a good bit of undergraduate instruction. Higher education is the responsibility of the various *lander* or states, but the federal government is increasingly involved through direct financial support or indirect support of research. The lander incorporate individual institutions and stipulate the powers and prerogatives of faculties and administrative officers. Earlier there was a tendency for those stipulations to grant too much power to faculties, and currently serious attempts are being made to increase the powers of chief executive officers. Universities are financed almost entirely with public funds; student fees support only about 3 or 4 percent of institutional expenditures. University education in West Germany is not yet widely regarded as an avenue for upward social mobility. Hence it is even more class-related than in other industrial nations. The operative model is still the ideal of the traditional German university. Yet this ideal has encountered demands on the part of large numbers of young people for postsecondary education. West Germany is currently attempting to develop nonuniversity institutions to absorb those numbers.

Swedish higher education consists of university-level institutions and some university institutions that offer specialized and professionally-oriented training in such fields as journalism, agriculture, education, commerce, and the like. A student who enters a university-level institution must have a certificate of completion of a general or technical school, whereas this qualification is not required by subuniversity institutions. Nearly all postsecondary education in Sweden is public or state sponsored, and there has been in increase in the number of institutions recently created. Swedish professors spend a large share of their time on research, leaving the training of practicing professionals to nonuniversity institutions. Although all of Swedish higher education has enjoyed a remarkable expansion, enrollments in universities have been limited largely through the right of individual faculties to accept only those students they wish to. What expansion has taken place has been accommodated by greater reliance on lower-level staff who assume the principal teaching responsibilities. Individual institutions in the past had considerable autonomy under the overall supervision of the Ministry of Education and Ecclesiastical Affairs. Recently there has been an attempt to create a higher educational system through the creation of the office of the Chancellor of Swedish Universities, which has its own board of trustees and its own professional staff. However, thus far faculty autonomy has remained strong. Swedish institutions are supported almost entirely by public funds, which are used in substantial amounts to support research and a no-tuition policy for students. Almost half of all students are engaged in part-time work. Student unrest has been relatively limited in Sweden, and reforms in Swedish higher education consist chiefly of removing relatively minor problems, such as reducing the time spent by students to acquire degrees.

Japanese higher education represents a unique blend of Japanese and American concepts. There are four kinds of universities: national, prefectural, municipal, and private. Prior to World War II, Japanese universities were highly elitist, and institutions were ranked in a rather rigid hierarchy. Curricula were highly specialized, resembling British honors degree work. As a result of American influence, Japanese universities after World War II adopted general education for lower division students and more recently have developed junior colleges as an appropriate intermediate step in the system. Japan resembles the United States in the large number of private institutions involved directly in the system or closely related to the system. The private institutions reveal the problems of finance and reliance on tuition that characterize American private institutions. Japanese universities have major responsibilities for basic research, whereas industry is more responsible for applied research. Research is generally conducted in national universities and is concentrated in research institutes. Japan has mass higher education and is constantly seeking to expand capacity. The number of applicants still substantially exceeds capacity; hence admission is rationed through entrance examinations. These are apparently successful, for attrition rates in Japanese institutions are substantially lower than in other nations. In spite of efforts to decentralize, both public and private Japanese institutions are controlled by the central government, which approves appointments; determines salary levels; establishes personnel criteria; and decides on the creation of departments, research units, levels of students fees, and budgets. The central government is assisted by various advisory committees and is attempting to allow greater institutional autonomy. Internally, Japanese universities follow the German model, with a great deal of freedom allowed the individual professor. For the most part, Japanese students rely on their own or parental resources to meet higher educational expenses. There are some scholarship and loan funds, but the student himself is the biggest contributor; this factor produces class-related higher education. Japanese students have been among the most politically active in recent years, with activism and dissent continuing even after it began to decline elsewhere in the world. Activism brought about the closing of Tokyo University, the largest and most prestigious of Japanese institutions. Japanese higher education faces the serious problem of enormous growth in enrollment, which has resulted in the overcrowding of facilities and a serious limitation of personal and intellectual contact between students and teachers. The pronounced problem is that higher education is struggling with confusion of aims, a struggle which is particularly vexing to the private sector.

All institutions of higher education in the Soviet Union are public institutions operated, financed, and administered by the state. The system is made up of universities, polytechnical institutions, and a variety of specialized institutes. Contrary to the patterns found elsewhere, the total number of Soviet institutions has been reduced somewhat recently. The universities concentrate mainly on training teachers and researchers, leaving to other more specialized institutions the training of various kinds of practicing professionals. Soviet higher education experimented with insisting on work experience before entry into college or universities. That attempt proved abortive, and the Russian system has moved once again into patterns similar to the American. Russian higher education is characterized by a high degree of specialization, there being no equivalent to the general or liberal arts education that lower division United States students receive. Graduate training is offered in almost half of the institutions and leads to any of several different categories of degrees. The government has tried to encourage university-based research, but there is still considerable separation of undergraduate professional education from research. Higher education is clearly an instrument of state policy. Programs and curricula are determined by the state to meet national needs; and because the economy is clearly expanding, enrollments have increased markedly. But as demands for higher education have increased, so has competition for available spaces. In spite of serious governmental efforts to encourage children of peasant and working families to enter higher education, rationing of spaces still favors students from intellectual and professional backgrounds. Systems of academic governance are highly complex in practice although relatively simple in theory. In principle, higher educational administration is centralized, yet it is affected by a wide variety of interlocking and interreacting committees and commissions. Internal institutional administration is a blend of considerable centralization and considerable faculty autonomy. Because higher education is a public enterprise conducted for the good of the state there are no tuitions, and students receive stipends that are almost the equivalent of wages.

Substantially different from the previously discussed systems is higher education in India, which developed following British models and to achieve British ends. Since independence, India has sought to provide higher education to larger and larger numbers of the population on the ground that a developing nation needed a broadly educated population more than a highly educated elite. The large majority of colleges in India are private; in 1964–1965 there were 1686 private colleges, 527 government colleges, and 147 university colleges. Most of these are relatively small institutions that concentrate on undergraduate education. Graduate departments and professional schools are lodged in the larger institutions, with professional education being somewhere between a graduate and an undergraduate concern. Higher education is constitutionally the responsibility of the various states. However, the constitution also assigns limited roles to the central government. Patterns of internal governance in Indian institutions are fairly uniform throughout the country; there is usually a senate, a syndicate, and an academic council, all broadly representative of a number of constituencies. The principal, president, or vice-chancellor is similar to the American president in that he still maintains a key role in determining the directions in which his institution moves. Indian higher education has been marked by extraordinary quantitative growth, but there is fear that quality may have suffered. This possible deterioration of quality may be involved in the somewhat higher attrition rates in Indian institutions than in others. Financing has been a particularly vexing problem, for India does not have the resources necessary to support universal access to higher education and qualitative improvements. A particularly serious and indigenous question facing Indian higher education is the official language. For generations collegiate instruction has been conducted in English. Now, however, there is an attempt to have each institution adopt one of the fifteen official languages of India. Graduate education, however, continues to be offered primarily in English.

This volume is one of relatively few cross-cultural studies of higher education. It not only provides comparative data for the Carnegie Commission but also stands as one example of what could be a growing field of comparative higher education. The two serious weaknesses of the document are the unavoidable fact that it is dated and the fact that many details of a given national system use terminology and concepts indigenous to each nation without pointing out comparabilities with developments in other nations. Most nations have tried to accommodate increased demand for higher education by creating less demanding institutions. The reader must, however, probe rather deeply to find that the junior college movement in the United States parallels movements to create subuniversity institutions in most other nations.

VI

Education for
the Professions

The documents in this section stress several themes. The enormous expansion of graduate and professional education will likely continue. However, continuation of traditional modes of curriculum development, instruction, or even financing will no longer be appropriate. Within most of the professional fields, and especially in the fields of law and medicine, there is considerable ferment and innovation. It is too early to determine which of these innovations will emerge, crystallize, and become the prevailing pattern for the future; but it seems reasonable that such a crystallization is not far off.

Professional Education: Some New Directions

Edgar H. Schein

Recent social and technological change has forced both growth and change in the professions, which have always been the

302

medical specialties. The process of becoming a doctor involves not only socialization; not only learning the skills, knowledge, values, mores, life-style and world view of the medical profession; but also initiation into a club and brotherhood. This initiation is facilitated by heavy workloads and demanding routines but also by the sources for historic recruitment of medical students. They have been predominantly young, male, white, and relatively affluent. Attempts to increase the number of minority group members and women become distorted: testimony from blacks, Puerto Ricans, and women in medical schools indicates that they feel a great sense of isolation. Strong forces such as finances are likely to ensure that medical education continues to be class- and sex-related. Although medical students while in school are somewhat skeptical of the curricula, the fact that as a group they come from similar backgrounds and enter similar life roles suggests that once they become practicing physicians they will not insist on substantial changes in medical education.

Legal education, which for decades has remained substantially unchanged, is now being critically reevaluated. During the early history of legal education, apprenticeship was the prevailing mode. Gradually universities developed courses in law and law schools until by the mid-nineteenth century the nation was ready for a revolution in legal education. That revolution started at Harvard, which developed the case method of instruction taught by the Socratic method. Some felt that concentrating legal education in universities was antidemocratic. Their objections were overcome by the floodtide of professionalism that gained strength in the late nineteenth century and has continued to the present. Though university law schools gained the bulk of control over the preparation of lawyers, they did not gain control over entrance into the profession; that role was assumed legally by the profession itself, which administers the bar examinations. The American Bar Association not only gained that victory but gained control over the curriculum of law schools through the power to credit. This close relationship between the profession and the law schools produced a common pattern of legal training in which students, regardless of the institution attended, would likely have similar experiences. In the early part of the twentieth century there were challenges to the prevailing mode of legal education such as the legal realism movement, which charged that there was little relationship between appellate opinions and what was happening in the real world. Nonetheless, the form established in the nineteenth century has prevailed until quite recently, as has the tendency to demand more and more undergraduate education as a perquisite to entry into law school. In part, this homogeneous form of legal education rested on the myth that all lawyers were generalists and capable of practicing all forms of the law. In reality, lawyers specialize as do medical doctors. Therefore the question is not whether the practice of law should specialize but rather how specialties should be credentialled and how individuals should be prepared for them. For the most part, the preparation for specialty work has been the responsibility of law firms. Currently there is considerable pressure for the law schools to provide specialty training, even if this means cutting the core legal requirements to one or two years. A few law schools have seriously considered offering a two-year law degree coupled with the opportunity for postgraduate specialty work. All sorts of groups still question specialization in law schools—students on the grounds that it would force premature decisions, and the bar on the ground that specialization with attendant advertising would jeopardize ethical canons. Further, if specialization became legitimate the murky relationships between lawyers and other professional groups rendering similar sorts of services would become even more cloudy. Very likely law schools will ultimately be required to take cognizance of a variety of professional and subprofessional specialties and to assume some responsibility for the preparation of them. When this happens, the monolithic generalist training program will disappear, and law schools will offer some paralegal training while working with other institutions, including community colleges, to prepare other needed paraprofessionals. Of course, such developments are still theoretical, and lawyers themselves fear precipitous movement into specialization, partly on ecomonic grounds. Specialization and growth of paraprofessionals will bring about redeployment of fees. Although lawyers ideally claim to be concerned with public welfare, in actuality they are concerned with the problems of the reasonably well-to-do. The poor are penalized because they are poor and because they lack the knowledge to exert legal rights. In the past, law schools themselves have been biased toward the wealthy, even in the substance of the curricula. Law students were rarely introduced to the economic and legal institutions shaping the experiences of the poor; the legal profession has tended to define service to the propertied as its sensible or true work, and law schools have made their curricula conform appropriately. This mandate is under serious question as the entire society seeks ways of extending legal services to the poor. The mandate has been challenged by the poor themselves, by activist students, and by various agencies of government. There have been experiments with new kinds of legal firms and with modifications of traditional law firms to ensure that some work for the poor be attempted. Some feel that a new breed of law student will bring about fundamental changes in legal education to expose law students to new kinds of clients and new kinds of problems, such as problems of poverty and of public interest. But law schools cannot move too precipitously into such programs without jeopardizing existing relationships and long-standing practices. There is enough ferment in law schools, partly to prepare law students for new roles and partly to engage them directly in service, as to suggest that in this dimension legal education is changing. Because public interest and poverty law has been the special province of the young, there is of course some doubt about its longevity. Law schools have also been criticized because of their lack of relevance to real life problems, and in recent years there has been considerable experimentation and even more discussion of clinical legal education. It is argued that clinical education provides students with those skills they need in actual practice. There are such counter arguments as the high cost of clinical programs and the fact that the effectiveness of much clinical education has yet to be established. Additionally, stress on clinical education reinforces the class-related system. The poor receive services from aspirant lawyers who are regarded by their professors as menial workers. Law schools must also relate to many other social and educational institutions. One is the profession itself, with controversy arising over how law schools can best prepare students to pass the bar examination. Too much attention on the part of the law school to the bar examination restricts curricular innovation, yet a cavalier disregard of the examination jeopardizes students. If law schools enter the delivery of legal service to the surrounding community they can come into conflict with practitioners, and this conflict can jeopardize definite attempts on the part of law schools to make education more relevant. A related problem is the fact that law school teaching has emerged as a distinct professional career, and law schools have typically not used practitioners. Should law schools seek to become more actively engaged in the delivery of service and provision of clinical experience for students, a change in staffing patterns would be required. Similarly, if law schools should become much more involved in interdisciplinary instruction for students, new relationships between the law school and the rest of the university would be required. Historically, law schools have been in universities but apart from them. There is currently a good bit of discussion of rapprochement between the law school and the rest of the university, but there are still strong forces keeping the law school at a distance. One is that the law school until now has been a distinctively economically viable enterprise. The law faculty is relatively small, classes are large, and most students pay full tuition. Law faculties typically are not expected to engage in research, hence law schools have not been dependent on soft money. As law schools move toward the pattern of other elements of the university, a number of those benefits will disappear. Also due for possible reorientation is the entire experience law schools provide for students. In the past, law schools have developed a distinctive subculture that prepares people to think like lawyers. The first year in particular has been decidedly competitive. There is an aphorism that the first year scares students to death, the second works them to death, and the third bores them to death. During the late 1960s there was considerable student unrest, and there were demands for rather substantial changes in the curriculum, especially with respect to the third year. There has also been increased criticism of law schools because they recruit students from an elite stratum. Although law schools are less restrictive than medical schools, they are still highly selective and have tended to discriminate against women and minority students. There is ferment that more egalitarianism should infiltrate the admissions process. This sentiment may encounter an unexpected problem caused by large recent increases in application for law schools. As the number of applicants per space increases, the strong tendency will be for law schools to select even more rigorously on ability and on ability to pay. Law schools have not been particularly affluent with respect to funds for financial aid to students.

Institutions training clergymen can be classified under three headings: graduate professional schools, undergraduate professional schools, and proprietary schools. From medieval times the preparation for all of the learned professions has been similar. It consisted of studies in the liberal arts followed by apprenticeship with an experienced professional; this pattern held true for the clergy as well as for medicine and law. In the late eighteenth and early nineteenth centuries there came the first effort to reform theological education significantly. In both the Protestant and the Catholic denominations attempts were made to add important elements to the curriculum, even though these changes encountered opposition from conservative churchmen. In the United States there was a proliferation of institutions offering theological training, although those designed for Catholic priests were much more uniform than were those for the Protestant denominations. In general, each type of religious organization has developed its own system for training men to serve in its ministry. It must first discern what sort of a mandate it has from the constituency and then prepare people effectively to meet that mandate. In the Protestant sphere, denominations train their ministers in seminaries sponsored by the denomination to which students are admitted after gaining a bachelor's degree in the liberal arts. At the end of three years of additional study, sometimes interrupted by work, a bachelor of divinity degree is awarded, and the individual is entitled to practice. The majority of ministerial students stop at that point. Recently, however, there has been an increasing number of individuals wanting more specialized work, and this need has resulted in some programs below the three years and an increase in the number of post–bachelor of divinity degree programs. A related way of training religious workers in the Protestant orbit has been the Bible college, which concentrates on training people in literal interpretation of the Bible. For years these were a major supplier of Protestant ministers; recently they have declined in significance. The Catholic system of training for the priesthood is vaster and more complex than the Protestant. The Catholic institutions consist of major seminaries, minor seminaries, and major/

minor seminaries of which approximately 439 institutions now exist. The young Catholic normally enters his training earlier than his Protestant counterpart and is set apart through indicating his willingness to follow the law of chastity. Control of Catholic seminaries is considerably more centralized than is control of Protestant seminaries. During the 1960s there has occurred a great deal of ferment regarding the nature of theological education and the purposes for which it was intended. The adequacy of traditional seminary training was questioned, especially as society became more secular. The traditional role of the clergyman as dealing exclusively with matters of faith and morals came under scrutiny as some clergyman began to deal with critical social issues. Traditionally, clergymen dealt with an ideology, a moral code, and a pastoral role. Not only have new roles appeared as appropriate, but older roles have in part been assumed by other kinds of professionals. For example, counseling has traditionally been an important part of the clergyman's work, yet psychologists, counselors, marriage counselors, and psychiatrists have all entered that arena. Theological education has prepared people to interpret ideology and to deal with liturgy, yet clergymen have historically been entrepreneurs who had not only to raise money but to manage physical facilities and to engage in a host of other specialized undertakings. A question remains for theological education as to whether it should prepare people for these more secular activities or whether there should be specialization and the evolution of subprofessionals within the vocation of religion. Regardless of the particular outcome of that question, it seems certain that criticism of excessively theoretical orientation of the curriculum is likely to continue. Many suggestions have been made as to the future of the practice of theology, a principal one of which is for clergymen to band together in group practice regardless of denomination so that specialized services can be provided. In the past, except for the casual part-time work of theology students as interim ministers, seminaries have not paid a great deal of attention to clinical work. Criticism of that lack has led nearly all seminaries to place field training in their curriculum and also to include collateral training in the social and behavioral sciences. As these elements are added to the curriculum, something must give. Either the programs will be elongated, or such training as preparation in original Hebrew and Greek sources will be eliminated. Theological education has suffered from the same mythology as has education for medicine or law. It was assumed that all seminarians would become pastors and would be generalists, but seminarians were not taught by active ministers, and there was always some discontinuity between curricular content and actual practice. This problem has been compounded as the activities of ordained persons have increased in variety. It is further compounded by the general spirit of the ecumenical movement, which has suggested that much of the restrictiveness of seminary training provided by the denominations was inappropriate to the way life actually was. The responses of seminaries to the growing need for specialization and paraprofessionals have varied according to denomination. The Catholic Church has moved to provide some of this needed specialization through ordaining deacons who do not need to take the vow of celibacy. Protestant seminaries have moved much more informally. In general, enrollments in theological seminaries have not kept pace with enrollments in other parts of higher education. There is a real crisis in self-confidence within the clergy. "The future of theological education will depend upon both the actual careers offered and the conception which people preparing for their life's work have both of the mission of the churches and of the opportunities in it."

Social work is one of the new professions, and it is entering a period of ferment both in practice and in education for practice. In many respects, social work has not yet fully arrived as a profession in the sense that medicine, law, and theology have. This deficiency extends back to the time of Flexner, who pointed out that social work was deficient in professional attributes, both in the area of intellectual knowledge and in technique. It has always been difficult to separate social work as a profession from the problems, policies, and commitments of the wide variety of organizations in which social workers practice. The social work profession does not control most of the organizations that employ social workers, and over three-quarters of a century it has been able to establish hegemony in only a relatively small portion of the broad and diversified field it serves. There is a tendency for the most fully trained social workers to gravitate toward specialized functions and leave much of the actual practice of social work to those of lesser training. The perplexities of social work education have been compounded by an apparent need for increased numbers of people concerned with social problems and by a lack of knowledge of precisely what kinds of people these should be and of how much commitment to professionalization was actually desirable. The response of schools of social work has been ambivalent: There have been increases in both rigor and theory of graduate programs, yet at the same time many undergraduate programs have been created to fit people to enter a number of social work activities. By and large, the proportion entering actual practice from undergraduate programs has exceeded the proportion entering from the master's programs. The fact that people enter from several educational levels does not indicate that there is a hierarchical ladder by which one moves from lower to higher positions. Generally, people tend to stay at the approximate level of entry into the profession. Within the actual substance of social work curricula the most impressive change recently has been a new emphasis on social action. This has meant that social workers not only alleviated distress but actually assumed leadership, often at variance with the desires of their primary employers, to improve the overall lot of their clientele. There have also been some shifts in theoretical orientation, with many new views competing with the traditional psychological orientation. These changes mean that it is difficult to state in any general way what professional social work practice comprises in the 1970s or what should be appropriate training for that practice. The profession of social work is extremely pluralistic at the present time and is likely to remain so as long as can now be foreseen.

This report makes several contributions. It manages, although not in a particularly logical way, to catalog most of the reforms being attempted in professional education, for example, clinical work, interdisciplinary work, attenuation of time, and the like; and it attempts to provide a theoretical explanation as to why the several professional fields are attempting similar reforms. Several chapters develop, for example, the concept of a mandate provided a profession by the larger society; when that mandate is challenged, the profession must modify its practice or else lose viability. In general, the case for challenging the mandate is well made for all four of the professions analyzed. However, it may be that the various authors, writ-

ing as they did in the very late 1960s and early 1970s, overestimated the impact of student protest in bringing about change in professional education. Actually, many of the reforms discussed were receiving serious consideration in a few places at the very time that student protest was approaching its crescendo. Just as the authors may have overestimated the impact of dissenting students they may have underestimated the forces operating to bring changes in the characteristics of the practitioners of the various professions and to bring about profound change in the way professional services are distributed. The authors reflect almost a deterministic posture as they point out the upper middle-class characteristic of the professions and the difficult time minority groups have had and will have in gaining appreciable entry. The authors may be right, especially in view of the shrinkage of governmental support for new ways of providing professional services. But it is also possible that after a brief period of regressive Republican administration the federal government will return to a general liberal posture. Were this to happen, the changes in professional practice would be profound. However, the authors are quite correct in pointing out that many of the reforms are being attempted in only a relatively few places and that trends must be inferred more from rhetoric than from actual performance.

VII

Financing
Higher Education

The documents in this section undergird the financial posture of the Carnegie Commission on Higher Education. The commission maintains that some economies of operation are possible, that pluralistic support for higher education is desirable, and that the federal government must assume a larger burden for particular kinds of educational problems. In each of the reports, support for that posture is perceivable.

Alternative Methods of Federal Funding for Higher Education

Ron Wolk

During the past decade federal support of higher education has become a national policy. Now that the federal government is spending upwards of 5 billion dollars in support of higher education, the debate revolves around the permanent form that federal aid

340

should take. Federal support for higher education began with the ordinance of 1787 and was expanded through the Morrill Acts of 1862 and 1890. Then began a slow expansion through 1917 under the Smith-Hughes Act, which supported vocational education, and the various federal programs of the Depression decade of the 1930s such as the National Youth Administration Program, which provided funds for college students. World War II marked a turning point with the twin developments of support of university-based research and support of students through the GI Bill of Rights. Several landmarks from the post–World War II period indicate the general trend of federal involvement. These landmarks include the establishment of the National Science Foundation in 1950, the enactment of the College Housing Act, the creation of the National Aeronautics and Space Administration, and the passage of the National Defense Education Act, all of which represented a significant broadening of federal support to higher education and thus set the stage for the unprecedented legislation of the 1960s. Federal legislation and programs now authorize funds for developing institutions for the humanities and the arts, for international education, for the training of physicians and other health personnel, for graduate and post-doctoral training, for vocational and specialized training, and for a host of other academic programs. In 1947–1948, institutions received about 527 million dollars in federal funds. By 1964 institutions were receiving 2.3 billion dollars, and in fiscal year 1967 the federal government obligated 4.6 billion dollars for higher education. In 1967 federal grants and loans helped to finance campus construction and the purchase and rental of equipment. Grants and loans affected students at all levels and in all disciplines. Federal funds, usually as part of research grants, paid part of the salaries of thouands of faculty members; institutions received aid to offset the cost of educating federally supported students, to perform various public services, to improve academic programs and teaching, and to finance cooperative projects.

The debate over the ways federal funds should be provided higher education in the future is likely to be vigorous, for different methods of funding are allied with various special interests, and the flow of funds bears directly on the flow of power and monetary benefits. Until very recently, most federal support for higher education has been almost solely in the form of categorical aid, that is, aid designated to be spent in certain areas deemed to be of national concern. Categorical aid was the essence of the land grant movement and the various research projects supported since World War II. Both university and government officials have been reasonably satisfied with categorical grants. There are, however, misgivings. Categorical grants may favor a limited number of institutions or limited regions of the country. Several recent moves such as the development of centers of excellence and the establishment of the National Foundation for the Arts and Humanities are designed to rectify the imbalance that favored the sciences. Construction grants represent another example of categorical aid that has evolved steadily since the end of World War II, when the Public Housing Administration alone spent about 160 million dollars dismantling, transporting, and rebuilding surplus residential buildings on college campuses. That act was followed by the Housing Act of 1950, which provided long-term loans to higher education for housing, and subsequent programs for the construction of academic facilities codified in the Higher Education Facilities Act of 1963.

A second broad type of federal assistance consists of aid to students, exemplified in the past by the GI Bill of Rights following World War II and the National Defense Education Act, which provided for undergraduate student loans and graduate fellowships. Subsequently, aid to students was increased by the Higher Education Act of 1965, which provided federal scholarships for undergraduate students from economically depressed families. Then legislation also provided for loan and work-study programs to be of particular benefit to middle-income students. Further aid to students is contained in a number of different proposals ranging from legislation providing support to all students for at least two years of college, to various long-term, low-interest loan provisions.

Direct grants to institutions is a third method of federal support exemplified by legislation. The National Science Foundation awarded institutional grants to encourage scientific activity, to upgrade science programs, to improve the quality of training and research in various science areas, and to facilitate both undergraduate and graduate instruction in science. The Higher Education Act of

1965 authorized institutional grants to developing institutions, but educational leaders believe that less categorical institutional grants should be adopted for the future. Several such pieces of legislation have been sponsored. The Miller Bill calls for substantial allocations to institutions on a formula basis for support of education and research in the physical, biological, and social sciences and in engineering and mathematics. Although there is widespread agreement in the educational community that some form of general institutional support is needed, there continues to be disagreement over the formula to be used in distributing funds.

Tax relief represents another mode of governmental assistance to institutions. Educational institutions have historically been given considerable aid of this sort; they have not paid property taxes, income taxes, or capital gains taxes on investments. Since 1917, institutions have benefited by laws that allow philanthropic contributions to be tax deductions. Tax relief proposals fall into three major categories: deductions that permit the student or his parent to deduct a portion of education expenses from either his tax bill or his taxable income; exemptions that allow the parents or student to claim extra personal exemptions or increase the size of standard exemptions; and tax credits that permit educational expenses to be deducted from the actual tax owed rather than from the tax base. Generally those who oppose tax credits do so on the ground that they are excessively expensive, that they benefit institutions more than students' parents, that they favor the rich over the poor, and that they favor private institutions over public ones. Similarly cogent arguments in favor of tax credits have not materialized except in the beliefs of some people that tax credits represent a means of granting federal aid without expanding government programs; and they offer a way of facilitating a freer market with respect to access to higher education.

Another approach is through federal revenue sharing and direct federal aid to states. Pressure has been building in recent years for the federal government to return to the states a significant portion of the national revenue to enable them to meet their governmental responsibilities and to help restore the balance of power between the state capitals and Washington. In point of fact, states have been receiving important refunds. Grants-in-aid to the states amounted to 7 million dollars at the turn of the century, 1 billion dollars in the mid-1930s, 4.9 billion dollars in 1958, and 74 billion dollars in 1967. Some 10 percent of all federal expenditures are presently in the form of federal aid of one kind or another, and about 20 percent of that aid goes directly to state and local governments. Debate for revenue sharing proposals is intensive, with at least three types of sharing proposed: tax sharing, which would distribute to the states a designated percentage of the federal tax revenue on the basis of collection; unconditional grants, which would distribute monies for general purposes through a permanent trust fund, with distribution on a per capita basis related to the federal income tax base; and conditional grants, which would be an expansion of existing grant-in-aid programs to finance specific functions. Various formal proposals have been advanced, such as the Heller-Pechman Plan, which envisions the provision of a special trust fund of 1 percent of federal income tax to be distributed by formula to the states. None of the proposals has yet received Congressional endorsement. State and local officials have supported revenue sharing proposals, both the Democratic and Republican parties have supported revenue sharing in principle, and a large majority of the adult population supports the idea in principle. However, opponents contend that the states are not now making efficient use of their revenue sources and that they should be forced to finance their programs adequately. Opponents also fear that increased federal revenues to the states would prompt the states to falter in their efforts to increase income at the state level.

This well-documented and annotated report was one of the earlier publications of the Carnegie Commission on Higher Education. In a sense it is an historical document now, for the Higher Education Act of 1972 has resolved a number of the issues. The report codified existing opinion, brought together documents and statements of opinion relevant to the various alternatives, and may have contributed to a more precise and enlightened discussion of the various options. Though in some respects the report is obsolete, it still is a useful reference tool for understanding how discussions of the financing of higher education have produced the present condition.

Efficiency in Liberal Education: A Study of Comparative Instructional Costs for Different Ways of Organizing Teaching-Learning in a Liberal Arts College

Howard R. Bowen, Gordon K. Douglass

After a decade of affluence and dramatic growth higher education is facing a slowdown of financial support and of utilization. Utilization is actually increasing, with enrollments growing from 7,800,000 in 1969–1970 to 11,600,000 in 1980–1981 and with expenditures doubling; but income is declining, with the net result financial stringency. Some have argued that if colleges and universities would but impose operating efficiences on themselves, costs per student could be quickly reduced by a quarter or even a half. This claim is extreme and unsupportable. Some gains in cost effectiveness might be achieved without sacrifice of standards and even with possible improvement in educational quality. The efficiency problem is to alter favorably the ratio of two variables, cost and quality. Some argue that this modification could be accomplished relatively easily simply by increasing teaching loads. This solution seems to be unlikely because the majority of faculty members are probably working at full capacity already. Through using less simplistic solutions, costs may be reduced or redistributed so as to increase educational yield. The cost output ratio can be modified through a number of different manipulations. Low-cost labor can be substituted for high-cost labor, for example, by replacing faculty with teaching assistants. The intensity of labor usage can be increased by raising teaching loads. Student initiative can be substituted for faculty supervision. Utilization of capital can be substituted for labor; for example, the library or television can be used in place of lectures. Or, capital can be utilized more intensively through using buildings and facilities more fully. Low-cost capital can be substituted for high-cost capital by using more temporary buildings. Cost can also be affected by modifying curricular mix to emphasize low-cost subjects and deemphasize high-cost subjects. Noninstructional services can be reduced, and cost of overhead can be reduced on a per unit basis by increasing scale of operations.

These techniques are variably included in five potential

modes of instruction. There is a conventional mode in which professors give lectures, lead discussions, sign papers, set examinations, and meet with students regularly and frequently in a classroom throughout the semester. Professors working in the conventional mode tend to teach more classes per year than they would in some of the other modes. Hence the conventional plan is highly labor intensive, but capital is required in the form of classrooms and laboratories. This capital is not highly specialized, though, and can be used for a number of different purposes. The costs of producing a unit of educational output in conventional ways are probably moderately high. Recent research suggests that the quality of the product is not particularly high and that the conventional mode does tend to be overly systematized in fragmenting student time. A typical student's program is a semester-long series of often unrelated fifty-minute classes distributed unevenly in time. A second mode, the Ruml Plan (from the Beardsley Ruml and David Morrison book, *Memo to a College Trustee*) utilizes a rational mix of class sizes, with large, low-cost general education courses in effect subsidizing high-cost tutorial and seminar activities. Quality in large courses could be insured by using the best talent available and paying handsomely for the ability to teach large courses effectively. Capital costs could be kept somewhat lower because the space needs of students in large lecture halls are considerably lower than in small classrooms. The net effects of the Ruml Plan would likely be lower cost per unit of instruction and maintenance of high quality. A third mode consists of programs of independent study in which each student would work at his own rate on a carefully prepared syllabus including groups of problems and tests. Students would be free to consult instructors individually but would be expected to work independently much of the time. The time of professors would be reallocated from lecturing to preparing materials and managing the logistics of the course. Programmed independent study would harvest savings primarily by substituting students' initiative for instructors' labor. Capital costs would be mixed, with a possible considerable increase in the use of classrooms and some increase in the use of library and computer services. Experiments with programmed independent study suggest that the greatest gain would be an increase in quality obtained through greater student activity. A fourth mode,

the Bakan Plan, visualizes a limited but relatively unstructured curriculum taught through extensive use of tutorials. Each student
would be free to elect from a list of courses those he was qualified
to enter, and working with an instructor he would develop an in-
dividualized study plan. Instructors would be given great freedom
to offer the course they chose and to teach them according to
whichever pattern they preferred. However, the plan assumes general tutorial work to be compensated by considerable independent
study. The Bakan Plan would probably not reduce instructional costs,
but neither would it necessarily raise them. The cost increase resulting from lower teaching loads and the diseconomy of maintaining standard class size might be counteracted by a constriction of
the curriculum. Capital costs would probably tend to move downward because of less frequent use of classrooms but to move upward
because of greater use of library and computer facilities. Some
students would be comfortable in a tutorial or independent study
setting, but others might require a structured situation. A fifth
mode, the Kieffer Plan, calls for the creation of courses in which,
with the assistance of modern teaching equipment, students can
study at their own convenience and at their own pace. Each course
would be highly organized, but the various activities such as transmission of information, drill, evaluation, and the like would be done
by equipment rather than by a professor. Students might meet with
their professor as a group once a week to receive orientation and
motivation for the work that was to follow. Thereafter, students
would go to a learning station and undertake the various activities
required by using the appropriate equipment—computer, television,
tape recordings, and the like. The Kieffer Plan requires a great deal
of professorial time in organizing instructional units, and it requires
major investments in audiovisual materials including capital costs
for storage control and playback equipment. Immediate costs of
the Kieffer Plan might be somewhat higher than for the conventional plan. However, if durable software and hardware are initi-
ally obtained or produced, costs could be distributed over a number
of years with a long-term savings. The principal source of efficiency
gain in the Kieffer plan would be labor saved in the actual conduct
of courses. Instructors would spend considerable time producing
materials but thereafter would not spend as much time with students

as they would under the conventional plan. Increases in quality would likely derive from more dramatic and meaningful presentations and from allowing students to spend longer periods of time on a given subject. While these five plans differ in cost, actual cost differentials are likely to be relatively small, given present faculty personnel policies and conventional capital outlay policies.

The costs of these various modes can be compared through creating a simulated model of a liberal arts college and computing the differential costs of various kinds of activities and equipment. Too frequently cost analyses have not taken into consideration the full range of costs. First, the full professional work week of the professor should be examined to determine hours spent in instruction, research, administration, public service, and the like. Studies of how faculty members use their time have produced markedly consistent findings. Professional time spent in various kinds of instructional activities (lectures, discussions, examinations, interviews with students, and reading papers and examinations) can be computed. The patterning of these various activities will obviously differ within the various modes. For example, there might be twenty-five hours of lecturing in a semester under the conventional mode, four hours under the programmed independent study mode, and three hours under the Kieffer Plan. The economic values of faculty labor time should then be computed by including such things as faculty rank, faculty salary, costs of fringe benefits and support services, costs of capital outlay (including faculty offices, classrooms, laboratories, and studios), costs of various sorts of specialized equipment, and costs of course materials and supplies. Several other important elements should also be included: the extent, quality, and complexity of library and computer services; and the mix of courses from high-cost (science) courses to low-cost (social science) courses.

Instructional costs of these modes of instruction vary, and obviously the costs of instruction within the conventional plan can vary according to the mix of high-cost and low-cost courses, the standard faculty loads, the size of classes, and the mix of faculty ranks. Costs can vary in the other modes according to similar modifications in patterns. Estimates of costs yield a range of $201 to $442 per student in the conventional mode, with somewhat lower costs for the Ruml Plan. In the programmed independent study plan, costs per student would vary from $114 to $173, depending on how many students were assigned to a particular course. In the Bakan Plan costs would range from $232 to $247, whereas under the Kieffer Plan costs would range from $165 to $586.

Each of the five plans has strengths and limitations; an optimum program would be eclectic, offering large lecture courses, courses calling for programmed independent study (either with or without learning stations and mechanical systems), tutorial courses, and conventional classes. Such a mixture of instructional modes would give a college ample opportunity for experimentation, would give students a healthy variety of educational experiences, and would give faculty a chance to try out promising ways of teaching adjusted to individual style and to subject requirements. Whereas the possible combinations of these plans are almost infinite, some manageability can be produced by imagining low-, moderate-, and high-proliferation models depending on the curricular variety desired. An eclectic plan for a low-proliferation curricular model would yield an average cost per student of $164; a moderate-proliferation model would yield an average cost of $212; and a high-proliferation model would yield a cost of $246.

Thus far, costs considered have been those chiefly related to the instructional program. Educational efficiency should also take into consideration other expenses. Higher education is conducted by bringing students and colleges together; attendant costs are of two classes: costs of getting students to college and keeping them there, and costs of operating institutions. The total cost is the sum of those two. A hypothetical model would show that the costs assignable to students are about $4600 a year and that costs assignable to the college are about $4000 a year; the total cost is $8600. Quests for efficiency should examine ways of modifying each of the two classes of costs. The major part of the cost assignable to the student is foregone earnings to which are added the costs of books, supplies, transportation, club memberships, and the like. The cost for student time is perhaps $3.60 an hour. If economies are to be effected in this sector, the quality of instruction must be raised so that more is learned in a given time or so that the aggregate time needed to gain a given level of achievement is shortened. Generally, however, institutions have not considered the values of student time.

Incentives for institutions have been to save institutional dollars rather than student time. If colleges were required to pay students for their time as employers must do, they would be forced to seek more efficient use of their students' time than they have in the past. When the total cost of a college education is computed to be about $8600 per year, there can be no justification for casual, slipshod, dull instruction or for a slack, spiritless academic environment. The cost of a single conventional course with twenty students is approximately $20,000. Instructors might well ponder whether their efforts really deserve that price. Other factors to be considered include marginal returns from a college education and investment returns from a college education compared with returns on similar amounts invested elsewhere in the economy. Costs will also vary according to the ability of the student; the more able will perhaps be less expensive than the inept. The size of the institution is also involved; economies to scale can be produced in institutions of certain sizes. Noninstructional expenditures should also be examined to determine whether savings can be effected without influencing quality.

Each of the plans suggested is worthy of consideration. By adroit combination it should be possible to increase the course load of the faculty. The curriculum could be simplified. A more efficient mix of faculty ranks could be arranged for. And a better utilization of physical plant should be possible. There probably is no one method of education suitable for all institutions, all subjects, all professors, and all students. Any single plan should be rejected in favor of an eclectic one. An important consideration is that faculty discussions of educational policy should be much more attuned to budgetary considerations than they have been traditionally. Curriculum, mode of instruction, and teaching load do affect costs. They may not spell the difference between institution solvency and bankruptcy, but they may differentiate between institutional progress and stagnation.

Efficiency in Liberal Education *is a refreshingly candid document. Its authors are not preoccupied with costs, nor are they persuaded that miracles can be accomplished through cost analyses and economies. However, they are persuaded, as any reasonably sophisticated observer must be, that too much educational discussion has been carried on without reference to cost factors. Courses and curricula are developed and adopted without full realization of either immediate or ultimate costs, a fact which is likely involved in the present financial crisis of higher education.* Efficiency in Liberal Education *indicates a relatively straightforward method of analysis that faculties could use as they discuss educational change. Perhaps the greatest single value of the presentation is the stress placed on the actual cost of college education to students. When full costs are computed, the annual costs of a college career are extraordinarily high. Institutional awareness of the full magnitude of those costs should result in educational reforms from several different vantage points. A bachelor's degree program shortened from four years to three years may not result in much institutional savings but would result in substantial savings to students. The relative benefits of an additional year in college should be compared with the cost differential. Perhaps one of the major contributions of the Carnegie Commission and certainly one of the contributions of this report is the demonstration that economic factors can and should be considered without employing a completely business-oriented approach.*

Credit for College: Public Policy for Student Loans

Robert Hartman

For generations college students have borrowed money to finance their higher education, but the volume of borrowing was relatively small until the beginning of the 1950s, when student borrowing increased sharply. Though student borrowing has increased under such programs as the National Defense Student Loan Program, the percentage of students who actually borrow is still relatively small, and amounts borrowed are not large relative to the total cost of higher education. Currently, at the most, perhaps 20 percent of the eligible student population is participating in federally supported loan programs. Some people view the rapid growth of student borrowing as alarming, whereas others view it as encouraging. Those who support expansion of student borrowing see several values. Student loans are a means for providing a general subsidy to encourage the growth of higher education. Student loans can be a flexible means of stimulating enrollments of certain target groups or of stimulating particular types of training. For example, loan programs could be particularly geared to attract low-income students or to increase enrollments in some of the health science fields. Substantial government intervention in the student loan area is a means of compensating for failures of private capital to finance education. Education is a financial risk because capital can not be repossessed in the case of default, and the actual returns either to an individual or to the society are spread over an extraordinarily long term. Discussions of student loans very quickly bring to the fore two polar positions regarding who profits most from higher education and who should pay for it. One holds that the individual benefits the most and should be expected to pay the bulk of the cost as he would for any other economic goods. The other position holds that society profits most and should subsidize almost completely the education of the young.

There are available several models of loan programs which can be used when assessing existing loan programs or assisting in the creation of new ones. One role for loans would be to provide the full cost of instruction. Such a college and university system would be entirely market-oriented. A second model would be a loan program that would cover total student charges (approximately one-third of total instructional cost). Under such a system governmental and private subsidies would continue, but the loan program would be ready to accommodate each student's cost of tuition, fees, room, and board. A third and more traditional model would be loans made in comparison with family ability to pay. The role of the state would be what it presently is, but students could borrow rather than obtain grants, work, or use accumulated savings. The fourth model is exemplified by the currently operative major guarantee and direct loan programs of the federal government, which currently provide about 5 percent of full cost and about 10 percent of student charges for an academic year. The last model, called accessory aid, is a loan program to support students who wanted more than a minimum or basic amount of higher education obtainable and supportable through direct grants to schools. Each of these five models would produce different distributions of cost, with the three more radical programs likely to involve massive changes either in the federal budget or in the private capital market.

Many opponents of increasing the role of student loans are fearful of the accumulation of burdensome large debts by young families; but the burden of debt is affected by interest charged, length of time over which repayment can be made, and postcollege income of graduates. Though there is no general consensus as to how much debt for education a young family can afford, several suggestions have been advanced. One holds that 7.5 percent of disposable income (10 percent of total after-tax income) is tolerable; whether this is true depends obviously on the total debt, the period of time over which it is to be repaid, and whether interest rates are subsidized. There can be some question as to whether in reality students would borrow as much as to require annual repayments of 6 percent or 7 percent of after-tax income for a prolonged period of time. Experience with the National Defense Student Loan Program indicates that loans generally are kept small and that annual repayments are actually miniscule in relation to family incomes of graduates.

Over the past few years the volume of student loans under the guaranteed loan program has grown at a much faster rate than has the volume of loans under the National Defense Student Loan Program. Some have favored this development on the ground that guaranteed loans are less inflationary than National Defense student loans. However, closer analysis shows that the two loan programs would have essentially the same impact on the economy. Nor do the two programs in the long run have any differential effect on the federal budget. In the earlier years of the National Defense Student Loan Program higher contributions were made from the federal budget, but they decreased annually; under the guaranteed loan program the reverse was true.

The guaranteed loan program was enacted in 1965, and though there have been numerous amendments the continuing problem has been that there is an insufficient volume of money to make loans available to all qualified students who desired to borrow. Lenders were not assured of an appropriate yield, and Congress was unwilling to insure the higher yields that the money market demanded. A further restriction was the fact that there was not available an appropriate secondary market for student loans similar for educational purposes to the Federal National Mortgage Association, which serves as a secondary market for government guaranteed mortgages. Several suggested agencies could be developed, as was suggested in the Higher Education Opportunity Act of 1970, which was to provide for a national student loan association to serve as a secondary market fulfilling the warehouse function for loans.

An important question in connection with loan policy is who should and who does benefit from student loans. Thus far, the largest users of guaranteed loan program funds have come from families with incomes above $9000, whereas users of National Defense student loans have come from slightly more modest economic strata. Actually, it is possible that neither the National Defense Student Loan Program nor the guaranteed loan program increased enrollment in higher education substantially because it is possible to infer that substantial numbers of students who did borrow would have attended college anyway. The differential attractiveness of loan programs for students of high and low economic status raises further questions, such as the comparative value to society of a dollar benefit to a lower income student and a dollar benefit to a higher income student. To the strict egalitarian the answer should be obvious that ameliorating the underrepresentation of students from lower income families is the rationale for student aid programs, and that benefits accruing to students from higher income families do not constitute a public benefit. By that criterion, existing loan programs have only been 40 percent to 46 percent effective because of the larger number of upper-income students who have taken advantage of loans. There are, however, some differences between the National Defense Student Loan Program and the guaranteed loan program, with the National Defense pattern aiding poor students and the guaranteed loan program giving wealthier students greater accessibility to capital markets.

There are a number of suggestions for reform designed to facilitate greater utilization of loan funds by low-income students. One is to extend repayment periods so that payment levels annually remain well below the burdensome point. Several specific suggestions have been made, including the creation of a national student loan bank that would allow repayment periods of up to thirty years. The Carnegie Commission bank would relate repayment amounts to actual income earned. Extending repayment periods may have the effect of giving college educated individuals greater access to other goods earlier in their adult lives than is available to non-college people. In effect, lengthening repayment periods under loan programs would provide a subsidized access to greater consumption for young college graduates who have borrowed under that program. In general, there is no good reason to ask society to pay for consumption by college graduates. Perhaps a more equitable program would be a youth loan program to enable the young to start building homes, attending college, or entering business. The student loan bank idea presents some other difficulties such as attracting private capital to be loaned at ever longer periods for repayment, collecting loan obligations, obtaining necessary data for an individual applying for a loan, and making judgments as to whether the loan should indeed be made. Banks are not particularly well suited to initiate student loans; but colleges and universities are not well situated to handle collections. However, if the facilities of the Internal Revenue Service were utilized to collect loans as part of income tax payments, a national loan bank could provide the means to attract new capital into student loans and could make repayment terms more flexible and responsive to income. A national loan bank created by the federal governmennt and endowed with its own funds, possibly raised through bond issues, could also minimize administrative overhead. Still another suggested reform is the creation of an educational opportunity bank that would operate in much the same way that the national student loan bank would operate. It would in effect call for higher repayments for higher incomes and substantially lower repayments for lower incomes. In essence, the scheme allows the rate of subsidization of higher education to be determined ultimately by the willingness of students who expect high incomes to buy insurance against the possibility of lower earnings. A last reform involves elimination of some of the cancellation provisions that have characterized the National Defense Student Loan Program (for example, the cancellation of 10 percent of the loan per year for five years of teaching experience). Evidence indicates that cancellation provisions did not accomplish the desired objective of increasing the number of persons going into teaching. It thus seems wise that other such cancellation addenda ought not to be seriously considered.

Credit for College *is a peculiarly complex and convoluted*

document. The authors seemingly arrive at support for some form of federally supported bank to make student loans and to tie repayment into annual income tax returns. However, the pros and cons of that plan and of other systems are so evenly advanced as to allow even that generalization to be questioned. Probably the weakness in the analysis is that it was not long enough to allow more thorough exemplification of the points raised. With more illustrative materials and with a clearer statement of a favored position the document might have been of considerably more help. In its present form it is not particularly helpful because the various arguments are advanced in such a rudimentary and yet abstract form.

Statistical Portrait of Higher Education

Seymour E. Harris

The most striking aspect of higher education in the United States has been the enormous expansion in enrollment, especially since World War II. From 1940 to 1970, enrollments rose 417 times as compared with the twelvefold increase in population. Expenditures for education have also risen; during the last twenty years they have risen 472 percent, whereas total consumption expenditures have risen 111 percent. Expansion in enrollment is most directly attributable to the increase in numbers of high school graduates. Increases in expenditures reflect the combined effects of enrollment increases and rising costs per student; in other industries expanded productivity results in decreased costs, but inflation, the labor intensive quality of education, and the changed quality of the product have conspired to produce overall increases in expenditures for education. Since World War II, increases in college enrollments have been produced by increases in the college age population and by the steady increase of the percentage of that age group entering college. Many young people have been able to enter college because of the steady increases of family incomes during the post–World War II period, which allowed discretionary expenditures for education, medical care, travel, and the like. Increased family ability to pay for higher education has been aided by increased student aid and student loans as well as by increased support of public higher education. These various resources have been of such magnitude that inadequacy of funds may not have been the major deterrent to people entering higher education.

One argument is that much of public higher education represents a subsidy of the rich by the poor. Eighteen percent of families with students in college in 1966 had incomes of $15,000 or more, yet 46 percent of the college age population in the top 18 percent of families attended low-cost public institutions of higher education. In providing aid to higher education the government may favor the student or the institution. Thus far, students have been the recipients of more aid than have institutions. If aid is channeled to institutions, the net result is to make institutions of higher education more viable, a particularly desirable goal in view of the difficulties private institutions of higher education have recently faced. However, massive assistance to institutions might increase costs of instruction.

The most important factors that determine enrollment in intitutions of higher education are occupation and income of parents, aptitude and scholastic record in high school, and environmental conditions such as the size of town in which the high school attended by the student is located. Generally, graduate students in arts and sciences come from families with lower incomes, lower occupational status, and lower educational achievements than do students in several of the other learned professions. Lack of funds is probably the most important factor preventing individuals from going to graduate school or contributing to early attrition. In early 1961 the majority of college graduates were white, single, native born, and aged 21 or younger, with males accounting for 60 percent of the total. They came from families having higher than average incomes and higher than average educational levels. Student costs have not always varied consistently with the capacity of families to pay. From 1928 to 1940 costs rose relatively more than did family disposable income. From 1940 to 1952 costs lagged behind income, and from 1952 to 1964 costs rose relatively more than did average family disposable income. To compensate for this fluctuation the number and amount of stipends to students have increased steadily, and it is estimated that if greater funds were made available through scholarships, grants, loans, and work-study arrangements enrollment in higher education would increase substantially. But even if more funds were made available, there are problems of distribution of funds. For example, private institutions currently have disproportionate amounts of aid funds that assist them in strengthening their position. The amount of aid available to graduate students has increased, yet a minority of graduate students are still receiving outright scholarships or grants. In the past what grants and loans were available were received disproportionately by young male students without dependents who were attending universities and who were concentrating in one of the sciences or engineering. This imbalance is likely to change over the next several decades because the nonwhite population will increase substantially as a proportion of the total population, and the proportion of nonwhite college attenders will also increase.

Over a century, degree credit enrollments in college have expanded much more rapidly than has the creation of new institutions or the awarding of new degrees. Thus the system has proven quite productive with respect to access to higher education but not necessarily with respect to formal output of higher education. There has also been a fairly steady increase in institutional size. The United States leads the world in providing access to higher education but is much more comparable to other developed institutions with respect to graduates and is decidedly inferior to other developed nations with respect to dropouts.

Numbers and training of faculty members have manifested the same sort of growth characteristic of other parts of higher education. The number of faculty members per institution increased from 10 in 1870 to 279 in 1963. The total labor force increased 35 percent between 1940 and 1963. The number of scientists increased 245 percent. Recent faculty increases have come from the ranks of younger faculty members who are more mobile than older ones, thus encouraging a number of institutional discontinuities. Faculty salaries, which represent a substantial proportion of institutional expenditures, rose during the period from 1950 to 1966 because of substantial shortages, thus allowing laws of supply and demand to operate. Institutions were able to meet these salary increases because income had risen by 107 times from 1909 to 1963–1964. Institutional funds have come from various sources, with private institutions receiving the bulk of voluntary gifts and contributions but with public institutions enjoying larger tax support. Endowment income has increased steadily but is of greater significance in large private universities than in most other institutions. Tuition and fees have increased in both publicly and privately supported institutions but have increased at a much faster rate in the private sector than in the public sector.

Increased costs of higher education are of course determined by increases or changes in various categories of expenditures. Library expenditures represent only about 3 percent of educational outlays, but the costs of books and the costs of acquisition have more than doubled in a ten-year period. The amount of institutional funds devoted to research has steadily increased even though extramural funds have been available for research. Recent decades have also seen substantial increases in the building of physical plants.

As to the future, projections of expenditures by institutions of higher education from 1967–1968 to 1977–1978 indicate increases of 64 percent for public and 57 percent for private institutions.

This reference work contains an enormous amount of statistical information that will be of use in research concerning higher education. Because most of the data are historical the document is not likely to be rendered obsolete, and it gives an overview of higher education up to the early 1970s. The generalizations offered here simply indicate the general tendencies that the full volume elaborates.

VIII

General Reports

The varied works that constitute this section are no more doctrinaire than most of the other Carnegie Commission reports and policy statements. The reports herein indicate that college curricula are being reformed and changed gradually but not in any radical way.

May 1970: The Campus Aftermath of Cambodia and Kent State

Richard E. Peterson, John A. Bilorusky

The protests that broke across the campuses in the United States in May of 1970 represent the most massive expression ever of American student discontent. For hundreds of thousands or even millions of students, faculty, and administrators business as usual during May became unthinkable. The United States invasion of Cambodia and the killing of students at Kent State and Jackson

State Colleges precipitated a wave of discontent. However, those events were insufficient to explain the magnitude of turbulence. The temper on many college and university campuses in April 1970 was tense, ugly, and expectant, with countless examples of student protest and even violence. People on the campuses felt that the president had deceived them with his invasion of Cambodia, and the killing of students at Kent State aroused huge numbers of normally inactive students and gave the upheaval its mass character. Except at predominantly Negro institutions, the shootings at Jackson State did not trigger any significant upswing in active protest nationally. The events of Cambodia, Kent State, and Jackson State in aggregate did, however, trigger a period of perhaps unparalleled strife between the academic community and the national government. Although in the early days following the episodes the national government remained intransigent, the sheer magnitude of campus protest finally forced the White House to realize that it must in some degree improve relations with the campuses. Even more persuasive was the fact that the law-and-order candidates highly critical of campus unrest did not succeed in the elections of November 1970.

Student, faculty, and administrative reaction varied from campus to campus and from region to region. In kind, quantity, and intensity, events had a significant impact on approximately 57 percent of colleges; close to 1350 of the colleges and universities were in some way stirred by the events of late April and early May. On these campuses activities included peaceful demonstrations; development of communications with local residents in adjacent communities; conduct of special meetings, seminars, and projects; letter-writing; political party campaign work; journeying to Washington, D.C., and the state capitals; bringing about shut-downs and strikes; and lastly violence, which took place on approximately 4 percent of all campuses. Apparently the violence that began to accelerate after Cambodia began to decline after the Kent State killings because large numbers of moderate students who shunned extreme tactics had become involved. On a minority of campuses commencement exercises and other end-of-the-year formalities were modified, whereas on a somewhat larger proportion of campuses actual educational activities were modified, curtailed, or eliminated.

In the wake of events in Cambodia, at Kent State, and at Jackson State about 9 percent of the campuses showed renewed concern about other collegiate issues such as governance and decision-making, curriculum and teaching, the relationship of the university and society, the Reserve Officers Training Corps, appropriate methods of protest, and parietal rules. As part of the general uprising, about 18 percent of campus presidents took personal stands against the Vietnam war or the Cambodian invasion: 1 percent of presidents supported the Cambodian decision. A major new development was the fact that 4 percent of the colleges and universities took institutional stands in opposition to the Vietnam war and the Cambodian incident. Implications of these activities in the short run were several, although the intensity of each is difficult to gauge. Some observers believe that academic standards were massively assaulted, but opinions to that effect are countered by opinions that the events actually enhanced academic values. Shortly after the Cambodian incident, observers felt that students could become a major political voice in the following November elections. No such voice materialized.

Whether institutions became scenes of protest depended on the kind of institution and the region of the country. Generally the institutions that had been protest-prone before the Cambodia, Kent State, and Jackson State incidents were also the scenes of more intense reaction to the events of May. Generally independent universities were widely affected as contrasted with public institutions of similar size. Not only were students and faculties active, but presidents of independent universities more often took public stands. Larger institutions were more protest-prone than smaller institutions; this fact has been explained by the impersonality theory or critical mass theory: larger institutions had larger numbers of students politically concerned so that a critical mass for activism was readily available. When institutions were classified according to academic selectivity the more highly selective institutions turned out to be more protest-prone than the less selective institutions. This phenomenon provides partial evidence that brighter students are more inclined to protest than less able students. This observation is corroborated by the high incidence of all kinds of protest activities in forty-nine federal grant universities, which over the past several decades have attracted the most gifted students and scholars. A regional correlate was also identifiable: northeastern and far western institutions experienced substantially more protest than did mountain or southeastern institutions. Since northeastern and far western states manifest other variants of greater liberalism than do other regions, the overall liberalism of an area was probably a factor in the intensity of reaction to the events of May.

Presidential opinion regarding the consequences of the protest activities also varied according to type, size, and location of institutions. Presidents from some of the more afflicted institutions (large size, high selectivity, and national stature) look to a continuation of student protest activities and believe that there will be substantial public backlash. Presidents of other sorts of institutions took a more variegated view.

Several generalizations or hypotheses seem warranted. Many academically gifted students have no firm commitment to academic work, and these students were quite willing to reject academic work for the more exciting activities of protest. American mass student political movements, including the one begun in May 1970, have been unable to sustain themselves in the absence of new issues or provocation. The events of May apparently accelerated some educational reforms already under way. They clearly intensified a growing sense of alienation between the campuses and the federal government; but they also served to intensify an alienation of the public from the universities. Although dissent and protest did not continue long after the Cambodian, Kent State, and Jackson State affairs, there is evidence that the tinder of discontent on campuses remained dry and that another spark could ignite the campuses again. As to the future: "Responsible college leaders in the immediate future will have little choice other than working to keep their institutions intact in the face of internal campus tensions and an unfriendly external environment. A number of changes in the structure and functioning of colleges might be effective in a holding action—until a new era begins" (p. 86). And this new era may rely more and more on youth. "In a time of great cultural change, with youth in the vanguard, American higher education in its conventional form has lost much credibility and legitimacy both on and off the campus. New national understandings of youth and higher education must soon be reached. Both the diversity of youthful interests and the overarching goal of national reconciliation will need to be recognized. Although the search should begin now, now is not the time—because of deep divisions in the land—for promulgating such new national policies" (p. 87).

The report on May 1970 is a useful document, for it presents reasonably good survey data obtained shortly after the events to indicate precisely how various campuses were affected by incidents in Cambodia, at Kent State, and at Jackson State. It is a useful counteragent to the more flamboyant journalistic interpretations of what happened. The exposition of relationships between incidents of protest and type, size, and location of institutions comes as no particular surprise, although it is useful to have precise data to document what informed opinion had suspected. However, when the authors of the report speculate on the long-term significance of the events of May, they depart from their own data and interpret things in a much more personal way. The fact that students turned from academic work to protest activity scarcely supports the opinion that there is no firm commitment to academic work as it is presently carried on. This may very well be true, but to establish such an assertion requires more than a study of the events of that time period. Whether the protest activities furthered educational reform is moot. Father Andrew Greeley in Change Magazine *sees rather that protest movements, including those of May 1970, may in the long run have attenuated reform rather than accelerated it. One can also be somewhat skeptical that campuses continue to be ripe for another explosion. When in the spring of 1972 the federal government intensified its air war against North Vietnam, there were episodes of protest around the country but not of a magnitude comparable to the May 1970 uprising. The protest potential may have run its course for at least several more generations, and what happened in May 1970 may not happen again for an event short of federal use of atomic weapons against an underdeveloped nation.*

International Programs of American Colleges and Universities

Irwin T. Sands, Jennifer C. Ward

During much of the history of American higher education, curricula were exclusively preoccupied with the intellectual traditions of Western civilization. By the end of World War II, this historical parochialism was no longer tenable. The United States and its institutions of higher education found themselves catapulted into an international milieu in which all cultures, both occidental and oriental, impinged directly and immediately on American life. The nation needed specialists in foreign areas, and individuals were becoming world citizens; historic American curricula contributed little to either of these needs. In 1966 Congress passed the International Education Act, which anticipated a much deeper involvement of educational institutions in foreign matters than had been possible. The fact that Congress did not appropriate sufficient funds to make the act operative was a serious blow to institutional aspirations.

A student's understanding of his own civilization is not adequate until he has studied another form of civilization to provide perspective. American higher education provided only the perspective of western civilization. Even as late as the mid-1960s, relatively few institutions offered a rich and varied fare of courses dealing with foreign civilizations, particularly nonwestern ones. The large majority of students could finish their college preparation without any contact with international studies in any form. Changes have been modest as compared with the magnititude of collegiate programs generally.

To rectify this condition, institutions are beginning to modify their curricula to include more international studies. Some disciplines are more easily oriented to international concerns than are others, and though progress is being made, efforts to internationalize American institutions still encounter serious resistance. Faculty training has been excessively narrow, leave policies for faculty have not been adequate, departments have been excessively parochial, and too little attention has been given to modifying career patterns of professors to allow a reasonable exposure to international concerns.

Language and area studies are potential means of adding an international dimension to the education of students, but foreign language instruction in the United States has been insufficient. Greater stress should be placed on foreign language instruction in elementary and secondary schools, and institutional policies should foster esoteric language study. A number of technological advances such as language laboratories could conceivably improve the effectiveness of language instruction, and these improvements could be augmented by relating foreign travel to language instruction. Such language instruction could become particularly meaningful if it were linked with area studies that require students to use foreign languages as a tool rather than view language instruction as just a requirement. Though the number of programs of area studies is still limited, such programs as the National Defense Education Act have encouraged institutions to embrace African studies, Asian studies, Middle Eastern studies, Russian and eastern European studies, Latin American studies, Pacific Basin studies, and even western European studies. Latin American studies have received the most attention. Area studies cannot be viewed as a complete panacea, for there continues to be a question of whether universities should offer courses organized around disciplinary considerations or courses organized with the problem orientation characteristic of area studies. There is also serious question as to whether institutions should place area studies primarily at the undergraduate or at the graduate level, as to what kinds of degrees should be offered in area studies, and as to career opportunities for those who take a degree in an area study rather than in a traditional discipline.

Underlying these institutional vexations is the continuing issue of the relative superiority of area studies or comparative studies as a means of pursuing and organizing knowledge. Those who favor area studies are critical of the superficiality of those who attempt to look comparatively at a number of different cultures, whereas exponents of comparative studies see area studies as fostering another variant of parochialism. Comparative studies allow contributing disciplines to maintain some disciplinary purity and and may be less expensive than various studies centers, which generally require some redundancy of disciplinary specialists. The validity of topical or problem-oriented studies versus comparative studies is also an issue. Topical and problem-oriented studies require one patterning of disciplinary specialists, whereas comparative studies require a different one. There is probably no easy way around this controversy: university administrators would be well advised to follow a pluralistic approach within existing financial constraints and to search for no single panacea.

Of all the international offerings in United States colleges and universities, programs of study abroad are the most numerous and highly publicized. Europe continues to be the most popular area for such programs, although there have been recent advances in interest in other regions. Most students who participate in overseas programs do so during the normal academic year, although such programs are not considered substitutes for other international studies. Although some confusion of purposes of study abroad exists, there is evolution toward generally acceptable goals such as the broadening of students through their total immersion in another culture. Programs are developed with administrative arrangements ranging from single institutional centers abroad to collaborative efforts involving a number of different institutions. Direction of a program may be in the hands of a native of the foreign country or in the hands of an administrator from the institution offering the program. Students who choose to study abroad may not always be the most appropriate ones to profit from such experiences; not only has selection of students been a problem, but orientation of students to an overseas experience has been ineffective as well. Other problems are funding, amount of academic credit given for overseas experience, articulation of the overseas experience with on-campus academic experience, and facilitation of direct contact between the American and foreign students. Students queried about the effectiveness of programs urged an adequate orientation program, courses that focus on the area to be visited, courses that force students to think, programs overseas that force mastery of language, programs that are flexible, programs that stress mingling with people in the foreign country, and program organization that gives students an opportunity to mature and to act like adults.

One valuable variant is the organization of work-study and service programs in foreign situations. Students could continue their professional training as well as gain international insight.

The college environment has always influenced changes in student attitude and behavior. A cosmopolitan environment should allow individuals new perspectives. It can be fostered through emphasizing informal contacts between students and professors, through encouraging organizations of considerable variety, through carefully contrived special events, and through more intelligent use of the mass media, especially foreign films.

The service motif is deeply imbedded in higher education, and it is highly consistent with the American system of values for educational institutions to participate in appropriate off-campus activities. Insights gained by university faculties through foreign experience can be brought to bear upon problems of poor housing, substandard education, racial discrimination, and substandard health care in American communities within reach of the university. Such insights can then lead to more domestic service ventures. However, to translate foreign experiences directly and explicitly into domestic service ventures is difficult. Much care and thought are required to develop the mechanisms and programs by which academic people can translate foreign expertise into a domestic resource. But such efforts are warranted not only because of the possibility of making domestic service better, but because in order for local communities to be enthusiastic about international studies there must be a perceivable payoff.

A relatively unpublicized contribution of the American university is its extensive involvement in special training courses for visitors from overseas as well as for Americans planning to work or study abroad. Professional schools in particular accept foreign nationals for professional training, and the collective experience of the professional schools can indicate guidelines of effective practice. The greatest number of participants return to the same jobs they held before entering an American program, and they frequently find that the program did not give them enough actual practice. A particularly instructive experience for universities was the training of Peace Corps members. That experience indicated that a number of characteristics of the collegiate institution are antithetical to specific training programs.

One of the most dramatic educational innovations of the era was the creation in 1946 of the Fulbright Program, which provided that foreign currencies owed to the United States from the sale of war surplus material be used for the support of educational exchange. That program, reinforced by several other federally adopted programs, has generated a flood of American scholars and students who have had foreign study experience. Though there have been some weaknesses, programs like the Fulbright have been an outstanding success. To those federal programs have been added a number of private programs and university-sponsored programs encouraging Americans to study, lecture, or write abroad and foreign scholars and students to spend time in the United States. The number of foreign students has increased rapidly and seems likely to continue to expand. Several problems have not been successfully solved. Advising both before departure for the United States and after arrival on the campus has been insufficient, as has been the identification of deficiencies in intellectual skills for which remedial help could be provided. Much of the American curriculum has proved somewhat irrelevant for foreign students. And, of course, the problems of finance are always endemic. Institutions have been reluctant to utilize the talents of foreign students to enrich local programs.

Technical assistance on the part of American universities to foreign nations is another major way of facilitating internationalism. There have been some serious failures: an agency may expect one kind of service from a contracting university, but the university may choose to exploit capabilities that lie in a different direction. Technical assistance programs are appropriate, and several criteria must be met: Continuity (that is, will a program be supported long enough), independence of action, and appropriateness to the university mission. Technical assistance projects are likely to be more effective when donor and host institutions discuss and plan together. American universities should also benefit from undertaking technical assistance projects. Such projects can allow universities to exploit their research potential, but many research efforts can jeopardize international relations or contaminate university canons of objectivity. The success of research in foreign areas depends on the receptivity of the host country, the competence of the scholar for the task, and the role to be played by the funding agency.

As a matter of educational policy, it is held that institutions of higher education must assume the responsibility of making Americans more at home in the complexities of the modern world, less afraid of diversity, and more understanding of the problems of other nations. In the light of that overarching policy, boards of trustees should issue policy statements stressing the importance of international programs in their institutions and indicating willingness to adjust policies to express international interest. Central administration should assure high priority for international programs and can underscore concern for the international dimensions of education. Faculty members should become more introspective in their own work, seeking to find international implications for their teaching, research, and service. Faculty members can contribute considerably by fostering and maintaining relationships with scholars in other countries. Students similarly can ensure that they do not cut themselves off from educational and travel experiences that will bring them in contact with other cultures. Foundations should continue their support of travel, study, and research abroad, and legislators should work for more flexible funding arrangements to encourage internationalism in higher education.

This report is peculiar; it is filled with exhortation and justification with which no one could quarrel any more than one could quarrel with the concepts of God, Motherhood, and Country. It also describes a number of programs fostering international understanding that are indicative of a fairly steady trend of greater institutional involvement in international relations. Some of the analyses suggest where programs have failed or succeeded, but criticisms are much less pointed and much less helpful than those in other earlier reports such as From Main Street to The Left Bank, *by Walter Adams and John McGarrity. The document contains many common sense recommendations with which no fault can be found. However, it does not fully confront several perplexing questions such as why the International Education Act was passed and not funded. It does not provide institutions with real help in deciding how to order institutional priorities. For example, saying that institutions should make major efforts at international education does not help an institution decide whether to use its resources to increase its minority group enrollments or to develop new programs of international affairs. The report does not indicate whether importation of foreign students, sending American students abroad, or arranging international experiences for American faculty members are equally effective techniques. The principal weakness of the report is that it does not offer a perspective for comparison, yet for policy makers this perspective is crucial. They cannot reject the virtues of internationalism, yet they must consider other matters that have some claim on time and resources.*

The Rise of the Arts on the American Campus

Jack Morrison

The rise of the arts on the American campus is the result of a long and constant, if not consistent, battle of the natural inclination of human beings to sing, play, draw, paint, sculpt, write, and dance against the forces of puritanism. The vital question is whether higher education and the arts will coexist vulgarly or beautifully, meaningfully or superficially; will the arts be at the center of the university or on the periphery. There is evidence and opinion that art should be central in the life of the university, but there is also considerable evidence that the production of art and the performance of artistic work are still not fully accepted as part of liberal education. In the latter part of the twentieth century, student involvement in artistic activities on campus is clearly on the increase; it may be that the press of numbers will force institutions and faculties to assign a more central role to artistic activities. The student confrontations of the 1960s, with their emphasis on feeling and emotion, may add intensity to those pressures. However, there are still significant problems and barriers such as the separation of art departments from other departments, the lack of systematic planning for incorpation of the arts into the mainstream of the institution, and the lack of correlation between curriculum planning and physical design for facilities for the arts. One of the stronger forces that may produce a situation in which the arts become truly central is a growing scholasticism providing a rationale for such centrality.

The present status of the arts may perhaps be better understood by examining how each of the several arts has entered the collegiate environment. Some interest in drama was present at Harvard at the end of the seventeenth century. Drama appeared as academical exercises or more frequently as extracurricular endeavors. As transportation improved, campuses attracted professional dramatic companies, and gradually institutions began to prepare people for careers in the theater. From the 1930s onward, the professionalization of drama on college campuses has progressed rather rapidly. Dance was never really foreign to American institutions, although some restriction on dancing existed in the society.

Early educators believed that instruction in dance helped produce grace and should be encouraged, but professional concern did not emerge until the twentieth century, when several experimental colleges such as Bennington began to feature professional or semi-professional programs of instruction. Film began to appear in university courses during the 1920s, with the first major in film offered in 1932. Major expansion of institutional concern with films did not occur until after World War II. The 1960s saw a flowering of collegiate interest in film, but even by the end of 1960s most film programs did not exist as separate academic administrative units. Film courses fall into four categories: appreciation or history courses; elementary production; professional production; and scholarly courses dealing with historical, theoretical, or critical aspects of film. As collegiate interest in film expanded, there was a parallel growth of organizations of film educators. Although writing has always been part of instruction in English, only recently has there been a movement to identify university writing programs with the other arts. This rapprochement came about as institutions created programs in creative writing and invited writers in residence to join institutional faculties. Music, long a part of the collegiate scene, has been clearly in evidence on ceremonial occasions; vocal music is a definite part of normal school training. In the nineteenth century conservatories developed rapidly and abundantly, and some of these related themselves to collegiate institutions. By 1915 music as a respected academic discipline had been accepted by colleges and universities across the United States. The sheer rapidity of growth forced the development of accreditation agencies to safeguard standards. The visual arts entered the collegiate scene somewhat later than did other art forms, with the first school created in 1806. Early development consisted of the creation of separate and independent art institutes; rapprochement with collegiate institutions did not occur until the 1930s. Bringing art institutes into alignment with colleges and encouraging colleges to create art departments developed in part from state certification requirements for teachers in the public schools. Now that art departments are well established in colleges and universities, their faculties struggle with the dual and often conflicting responsibility for professional training of talented students and for the general education of students. Museums, though represented somewhat on college campuses, have experienced a moderately slow growth. Architecture as a professional curriculum was first proposed in 1814 but did not become fully established until the Massachusetts Institute of Technology established a professional course in 1865. By the early part of the twentieth century there were accrediting agencies, numerous programs, and full assimilation of architecture into the university structures. From the very beginning, architecture in higher education was faced with integrating the various components of the discipline into a balanced and meaningful program of instruction and professional practice. Of all of the arts in higher education architecture faces perhaps the most critical problems. After World War II, collegiate institutions began to invest in the creation of fine arts centers, and the forces for doing so continue to intensify. Most college and university campuses also have created and pay for various concert series or programs of cultural events.

Some notion of the place of the arts on college campuses may be obtained by examining several interesting though not necessarily representative campuses. At the Washington-Baltimore campus of Antioch College, an attempt is made to use the artistic resources of the Washington-Baltimore area educationally. With their advisors, students work out curricula involving museums, art schools, dance groups, other colleges and universities, theaters, film centers, other campuses, and formal classes on the main campus. There is a struggle between the largely activist social scientists and students in the arts, who perceive artistic work as an agent of change. Bennington College early introduced divisions of dance, drama, music, and visual arts. Seeking to make the arts central to the curriculum, the institution has supported them financially and has provided requisite and appropriate physical space. The College of Fine Arts at the Carnegie Institute of Technology was founded in 1905 as one of the first comprehensive colleges of fine arts in the country. It included all of the arts and stands as a highly successful model for professional undergraduate curricula in the arts. Dartmouth College, possibly because of its remote location, has made the arts integral to campus life both socially and academically. It has created a fine arts center, has extended the definition of the arts to include the crafts, and has linked the administration of the arts center to the administration of the academic program. Much less pretentious is the artistic posture of Duke University, which maintains only two departments, art and music, both located in inadequate physical facilities. Growth is perceivable, and little by little other artistic forms are receiving attention. At Earlham College there is a fine arts office for three departments, but there is no head, chairman, director or dean. These three departments have experienced considerable growth and have maintained good relationships with other academic departments. So significant have their efforts been that a science department renounced funds for its unit until a new arts center was approved. Fisk University has created a division of the arts that is planning a fine arts center, a new interdisciplinary program, programs in the arts for teacher training, and some increasingly professional programs. Harvard University offers work in many of the arts, but the curricular emphasis is on the critical and theoretical; studio work and performance have become extracurricular. Harvard does not judge the creative work of the faculty in the arts equivalent to research in science, social science, or the humanities. The arts on the Indiana University campus began to expand with the support of President Herman Wells. The university maintains strong programs in all of the arts except architecture and film; several fields are provided the largest budgets in the country. At Jackson State College the arts are just beginning, but strong administrative support has begun to appear. At New York University the arts have evolved in irregular patterns as have many of the other interests of that institution. It maintains some highly respected professional programs and exploits the artistic resources of New York City. Although public junior colleges have been somewhat slower than other institutions in embracing the arts, a few have demonstrated considerable interest and can serve as models. Pasadena City College, for example, allocates more teaching personnel, space, and financial resources to artistic work than do some of the largest universities; and leaders report that the courses in the arts are the first to fill up. Indeed, students may be forcing the arts into the center of the curriculum. The college of arts and architecture at Pennsylvania State University is one of the most comprehensive administrative units in the arts. Not only does it administer dance, film, and other art programs, but it administers the Artists Series and the

University Gallery and Art Exhibitions. The dean is directly responsible to the president and feels that because the locale does not provide many artistic resources the university is obligated to do so. The college of fine arts at the University of California at Los Angeles was formed in 1960 out of the college of applied arts. It now has four departments—music, arts, theater arts, and dance. It has consistently received strong administrative support and has been able to make major capital investments in buildings. The college is related to the Committee on Fine Arts Productions, which stimulates artistic efforts on the campus. The University of California at Santa Cruz operates through relatively small cluster colleges. College 5 of this group focuses on the arts and aesthetic education, but there is a major effort to have the arts pervade the entire campus. A new performing arts building was completed in 1971 and serves as a focus for artistic sentiments throughout the institution. The University of Georgia has elected not to try to centralize the administration of the various art departments; possibly as a result, the arts have not penetrated deeply into the rest of the campus. The University of New Mexico has long supported the arts, possibly because through its location the institution was unfettered by the traditional emphasis on critical scholarship as opposed to creative work. The university has a well-organized, comprehensive, and growing program in the arts, with recent developments in theater, dance, and film.

Several recommendations seem reasonable. Each institution should take a stand on its policy of teaching, studying, and performing the arts. Departments concerned with the arts should adopt a two-pronged approach accenting professionalism and general education. Departments, colleges, and schools of the arts should deliberately seek to relate to other disciplines. These departments should plan for optimum size and keep enrollments under control. Institutions should also give more attention to the professional careers of their graduates and should conduct follow-up studies. More trustees with backgrounds in the arts should be appointed. Departments in the arts should constantly assess themselves by current criteria.

This book restates much of current criticism of the role of the arts in higher education. It documents movements, interest, and expansion and illustrates these with case materials. It brings together questionnaire results regarding some institutional activities in the arts and concludes with a series of recommendations, none of which is new nor helpful. The book does not search for the reasons the arts have not been more central, nor does it provide help for a concerned art department chairman, for example, who would like to balance professional or conservatory activities with general education or broad cultural emphases. Many institutions have tried to ensure that students have active studio experience on a limited basis. A detailed analysis of how well some of those programs have fared would strengthen this work as would stronger argument to support active participation in the arts. It is good that the Carnegie Commission has attended to the plight of the arts, but this particular contribution does not significantly advance the solution of the problems.

Curriculum and Context: Essays on College Education

Carol Kaysen, editor

The decades between 1870 and 1910 witnessed the only genuine academic revolution in the United States. Before that time colleges maintained a static educational posture. As a result of their intractability colleges became unpopular and experienced declining enrollments between 1850 and 1880; students gained their primary satisfactions outside the classroom. The revolution that took place in the few years after 1870 not only added the natural sciences and practical subjects to the curriculum but brought about the inauguration of a number of currently standard devices: numbered courses; the unit system for credit; the lecture and seminar modes of instruction; departmental organization of learning; an administrative chain of command involving presidents, deans, and department heads; and the elective system of course selection. Within a very few years all of these reforms were uniformly enacted throughout the country. And the revolution was by no means a simple matter of imitating the German university. Certain ideas originated in Germany, but the new kind of collegiate institution in the United States was brought about by such indigenous factors as increasing affluence, trustee alarm over enrollments, major intellectual change, and the appearance of a secular managerial elite. The first wave of academic reform after the Civil War was dominated by utilitarianism, which gave way slightly around the mid-1870s as knowledge came to be valued for its own sake. The academic ideal of research was instated. By the turn of the century a third ideal had evolved, that of liberal culture or general education. Adherents to this point of view, in sharp opposition to the other two, sought to prepare graduates as well-rounded gentlemen comparable to the elite produced by British institutions. While some of the reforms are traceable to these different intellectual ideals, the important elements of reform were brought about simply by strong administrators seeking to make their institutions more viable. By 1910 the academic revolution was clearly over, and from then until perhaps 1945 American universities were in a state of drift. College education had become an important value in the society but was clearly not the boom enterprise it was to become later. In spite of that apathy there were several distinctive efforts at reform, each associated with one or several individuals. Followers of John Dewey reached their maximum influence during the 1930s through the creation of such experimental colleges as Bennington, Sarah Lawrence, and Stephens College in Missouri. The second group of reformers gathered under the banner of liberal education, an accommodation between the ideal of specialized research and the peculiar needs of undergraduates. Honors programs, small seminars, and independent study arrangements were produced by that group. A third group of reformers, intellectual descendants of the older advocates of liberal culture, were able to give form to their ideas through such institutions as the College of the University of Chicago and St. John's College in Maryland. Most college administrators found themselves uncomfortable with Dewey's instrumentalists or the sombre rationalism of Aristotle. They compromised by maintaining the partially free elective curriculum that had existed since the late nineteenth century. The apathetic period ended with the termination of World War II. The following period ushered in first enormous increases in proportions of high school graduates attending college and then the national shock produced by the Russian launching of Sputnik. Suddenly professors became important, and institutions became pivotal in the society. Nonetheless, curricula during the period of expansion remained primarily within the conventional subject major system. But the shock waves of enrollment expansion and demands for academic rigor were joined by the student protest movement of the late 1960s. Efforts were made to shut down institutions, to make them responsive to critical needs of the society, to force institutions to accommodate new ethnic groups, and to promulgate a new antirationalism. It is too early to tell, but these events may augur a new flowering of curricular change in higher education similar to that which took place in the last quarter of the nineteenth century. This revolution, should it come about, will certainly assail the validity of the course as an important educational impact and characterize formal grades as methods of control not closely related to academic performance. As these two concepts come into question, the concept of unit credits is opened for scrutiny, as are the division of academic years and the number of academic years required for a degree. The new revolution may also seek to displace the nineteenth century lecture system with some new mode of instruction. Nor are academic departments likely to be spared scrutiny, criticism, and quite possibly abolition. It may be that the problem-centered courses and programs will prevail and that attempts will be made to return to the small college environment through the medium of cluster colleges; but it seems clear that new curricular forms will accommodate the contrast between depth and breadth, between elective freedom and prescription, and between absolute abundance and scarcity of course offerings. Of course it could be that curricular reform will not come about in any formal or rational sense but that the real changes will be brought about through such peripheral but significant events as the advent of inexpensive paperback books.

In this potentially revolutionary context professors in the various domains of knowledge report ferment, discussion, and some innovation but little widespread agreement as to what the curricular substance of their fields should be. Some feel that the culture is coming apart and that though the humanities cannot restore the culture, they can contribute through their historic emphases on great texts, studied both for themselves and also to effect continuity with the past. Similarly looking to the past are the social sciences, which historically were philosophical and normative and have now become empirical, specialized, and technical. Though the research gains from those developments have been impressive, they have not contributed to the liberal education of undergraduates. The need then is to restore a humanistic and even normative quality to the social sciences taught to undergraduate students. Courses should seek to speak to the humane concerns of students. Science came late to American higher education and truly reached its own during the post–World War II period. During the 1950s and 1960s there was considerable reform of secondary school science. Now undergraduate science is in need of reform. For both science majors and nonscience majors science should remain true to its traditions of logic, sequence, rigor, and avoidance of the contemporary. It should be presumed that the necessary background in science and mathematics has already been achieved through noncredit remedial courses. Then sequenced programs can be constructed for both science and nonscience students. Although the arts have achieved a role in higher education, they are still regarded as peripheral to the main effort of colleges and universities. There is difference of opinion as to the nature of the arts and whether colleges should stress performance, analysis, or participation. If the arts succumb to demands that they be freely available to all students, they will continue to be regarded as peripheral. However if those in the arts stress rigor, discipline, and sequence the arts can come to be regarded as the academic equals of the sciences and social sciences.

Beyond doubt this volume is an attempt on the part of the Carnegie Commission to fill an earlier void in its work—namely, to face the issues of the substance of the undergraduate curriculum. Unfortunately this volume does not succeed, although it will probably be widely read. The chapter citing the historical context is one of the most incisive analyses of the collegiate curriculum currently available. It reaches the conclusion that a second major revolution in higher education could be in progress. However if the chapters dealing with the various fields are valid profiles of those fields, the revolution is likely to be mild indeed. The authors deal briefly with trends and then seek to express the essence of each discipline. The curricular prescriptions are disciplinary in character and have been made with no awareness of the growing body of knowledge concerning student development. In the past courses have generally been constructed according to disciplinary logic or professorial interests. The guidelines implied in these chapters suggest that those same criteria will obtain (or should obtain) in the future. If they